White Protestantism and the Negro

White Protestantism
and the Negro

DAVID M. REIMERS

New York   OXFORD UNIVERSITY PRESS   1965

To Cordelia

Preface

In 1964 the voice of an aroused conscience of white Protestantism sounded in the ears of congressmen, urging passage of the civil rights bill. Not since the days of Prohibition had the Protestant churches been so active in politics, and not since Reconstruction had they been so involved in a struggle for civil rights. Before the Civil War many churchmen enlisted in the antislavery movement, and during the war and Reconstruction northern Protestants joined the crusade to build an educational system for the freedmen and to protect their civil rights. But in the 1870's this crusade waned, and the Protestant churches capitulated to the system of segregation and discrimination that has characterized American race relations ever since.

The civil rights movement, especially in 1963 and 1964, goaded white Protestantism to new action. Emergency church committees on race relations mushroomed, and many white clergymen threw themselves actively into the civil rights movement. Some were arrested and jailed for their participation in the movement. Newspapers of 1963 and 1964 carried numerous accounts of the increased militancy of churchmen. The historical significance of the churches' role during these years cannot yet be determined. Whether the aroused Protestant conscience will lead to a thoroughly integrated church and society remains to be seen.

This book is not a recounting of these recent events; rather my purpose is to provide the historical perspective for viewing them. I have tried to tell how the churches met the race problem from the beginning of the nineteenth century to the early 1960's, especially within their own organizations. I hope this book will contribute to an understanding of the role of white Protestantism in dealing with America's most nagging social problem.

Two things should be kept in mind. First, I have not dealt with the work of churchmen and church organizations except in relation to the Negro. If, for example, the record of the social gospel movement in regard to the Negro seems poor by contemporary standards, it should be remembered that the advocates of the social gospel were deeply concerned for other oppressed groups, such as labor unions and child laborers. Second, if the Protestant churches seem too often to have compromised and accepted the status quo, the reader should bear in mind that secular institutions behaved much the same. Excepting perhaps during the Reconstruction period, only in recent decades have the assumptions of white supremacy been challenged by large numbers of white Americans, whether Protestant or non-Protestant. The churches might be expected to behave better than secular institutions, however, because they are supposed to be the moral leaders of society.

No treatment of Protestantism in America can be exhaustive. There are simply too many Protestant denominations to include. "White Protestantism" in this book means the major groups: Baptists, Methodists, Presbyterians, Episcopalians, Congregationalists, and, to a lesser extent, Lutherans, Friends, and a variety of interdenominational groups such as the National Council of Churches. The vast majority of Negroes belonging to mixed denominations are members of these churches, but Negroes constitute less than 5 per cent of their membership. About 90 per cent of Negro Protestants are members of all-Negro denominations.

I consulted many libraries and church offices in writing this book. Their staffs were exceptionally helpful. The list of libraries and offices is too long to mention in its entirety here; but I am indebted especially to those of the University of Wisconsin, the State Historical Society of Wisconsin, the University of Chicago, Brooklyn College, Drew University, the New York Public Library, Union Theological Seminary of New York, General Theological Seminary, Garrett Biblical Institute, Princeton Theological Seminary, the Southern Baptist Theological Seminary in Louisville, the Historical Foundation of the Presbyterian Church in the United States, the Board of Missions of the Methodist Church, the Board of Missions of the United Presbyterian Church in the United States of America, the American Missionary Association in New York, the National Council of the Protestant Episcopal Church, and the Department of Racial and Cultural Relations of the National Council of Churches.

Several institutions and many individuals were extremely helpful. The University of Wisconsin provided financial aid for a year's work and the City University of New York provided a typist for part of the manuscript. Among the many church leaders who aided me were Dr. Alfred Kramer and Dr. J. Oscar Lee, both of the National Council of Churches. The late Howard K. Beale of the University of Wisconsin was helpful in the early stages of the work, and Merle Curti of the University of Wisconsin was of great assistance later. Leslie Fishel of the State Historical Society of Wisconsin and Leon Litwack and Sterling Fishman, both of the University of Wisconsin, read part of the manuscript in a different form and made useful suggestions. Norton Mezvinsky of the City College of New York read an early draft and saved me from errors, as did Victoria Lebovics. John Hope Franklin of the University of Chicago read a later draft and offered his helpful counsel. Finally, my wife was invaluable for her editing, typing, and proofreading. I, of course, assume full responsibility for any errors and all interpretations.

New York
June 1965

D. M. R.

Contents

Contents

White Protestantism and the Negro

1

The Kingdom of God and the Kingdom of Cotton

> I never debate the question as to whether man may hold property in man. I never degrade myself by debating the question, "Is slavery a sin?" It is a self-evident truth, which God hath engraven on our very nature. Where I see the holder of a slave, I charge the sin upon him, and I denounce him.
>
> WILLIAM LLOYD GARRISON

"Is slavery a sin?" Garrison may never have debated the question, but many white Protestants did. The debates produced no consensus, however, and white Protestants divided into northern and southern churches. Upon hearing of the Methodist schism over slavery, Henry Clay feared for the Union. Clay's misgivings were justified, for the Protestant divisions were a prologue to war. When the Civil War came, Protestants of the North rallied to the Union and those of the South defended the Confederacy.

The morality of slavery was only one of many issues leading to the Civil War, but for the churches it became the fundamental question. It was not always so. In the colonial era the churches were not deeply concerned with the slavery issue. Some slaveholders were apprehensive about the effects of baptism upon the status of the slaves, but the churches and colonial laws put their minds at ease by saying that freedom did not accompany baptism. Some church leaders urged that the slaves be made Christians; few said Christianity and slavery were incompatible. Small groups like the Mennonites and Moravians disapproved of slav-

3

ery, but of the major denominations only the Quakers developed a significant movement against slavery in the colonial period.

In the eighteenth century the Society of Friends began to criticize slavery frequently and to force their members to cut their ties with it. At first the Quakers attacked the slave trade, but soon they also assailed the holding of slaves. In the 1750's the northern yearly meetings began to exclude members who were connected with slavery. By the 1770's this movement had spread to the South, and Quaker slave-owners began to free their slaves. In some cases they compensated the slaves for their labor in bondage. Having begun with efforts to put their own house in order, the Friends next helped form antislavery societies to stamp out the evil among non-Quakers. The work of John Woolman and other Quakers is a familiar part of the early antislavery movement.[1]

The antislavery movement did not spread to other churches until the Revolutionary War period. Religious critics of slavery multiplied during the first three-quarters of the eighteenth century, but there were still many religious apologists for it. For every John Wesley who was critical there were several George Whitefields who considered slavery a blessing.

Attitudes more critical of slavery became common during and after the Revolution. The Methodists, Quakers, and Baptists led the churches in attacking it. At the 1780 General Conference of the Methodist Episcopal Church the delegates declared that slavery was contrary to the laws of God and required traveling preachers to set their slaves free. At subsequent conferences the Methodists took stronger positions. Other groups attacked slavery, too. The Presbyterians in New York and Pennsylvania did so in the 1780's.[2] Southern churches also joined the chorus. The Virginia Baptists, for example, in 1789 urged their local missions "to extirpate this horrid evil from the land." [3]

Around the turn of the century there was a good deal of antislavery sentiment in the South; in fact, most of the antislavery societies prior to the 1830's were located in the slave states. However, these southern societies were mainly interested in colonization schemes.[4] They had no intention of making the Negro an equal of the white, as some of the northern abolitionists later did.

In the early 1800's the southern churches began to soften their attacks, and by the 1830's southern sentiment was generally pro-slavery. This change in attitude was brought about by a combination of factors. Although slavery was vital to the southern economy before the invention of the cotton gin in 1793, use of the device made cheap labor indispensable; Southerners increasingly geared their economy and social structure to slavery to secure that labor. There was also a considerable element of fear on the part of the southern whites, for during the 1820's and early 1830's there had been a number of slave insurrections. In 1822, the white population of Charleston, South Carolina, was paralyzed by the fear of a slave takeover of the city, even though the insurrection proved to be abortive. The last major insurrection of that type, led by Nat Turner, a slave, resulted in the murder of fifty-seven whites. Such incidents made many southern whites feel that tighter controls were imperative to keep the slaves in check. From 1830 on, the slave codes became more stringent. Also, in the 1830's, the South began to feel strong pressure from northern abolitionists, who not only condemned slavery as a sin, but also denounced the Southerners as unchristian despots and barbarians. These barbs made Southerners defensive about slavery as well as about southern civilization itself. Criticism of slavery gave way to a variety of intricate justifications. One of the most important of these was the religious one.

Led by such divines as Robert L. Dabney and James H. Thornwell, the southern churches not only defended slavery but declared it to be a positive good. Churchmen found passages in the Scriptures to justify the South's peculiar institution. Some Protestants pointed out that the great figures of the Old Testament, such as Job and Abraham, owned slaves and that therefore God sanctioned slaveholding. Southern apologists maintained that Christ and the Apostles did not attack slavery. The Reverend Thornton Stringfellow, a Baptist minister of Virginia, declared, "I affirm then, first, (and no man denies,) that Jesus Christ has not abolished slavery by a prohibitory command; and second, I affirm, he has introduced no new moral principle which can work its destruction, under the gospel dispensation; and that the principle relied on for this purpose, is a fundamental principle of the Mosaic law, under which slavery was instituted by Jehovah himself." [5] The curse on Ham, the supposed ancestor of the Negro, was another major prop of the Biblical defense.

If some southern churchmen did not actually bless slavery, they insisted it was a secular matter, not an ecclesiastical one. To these churchmen, a Christian's duty ended with providing for the physical and religious welfare of his slaves.[6] A few southern religious leaders had their doubts about the ethical position of slavery, but their voices became weaker as the Civil War approached. Southern antislavery sentiment lingered on after the 1830's but became increasingly isolated.[7]

In the North the antislavery movement gained new momentum in the 1830's. How many preachers and laymen were abolitionists would be difficult to say. The number was not large, but certainly slavery morally revolted many Protestants. The work of Gilbert Barnes and others has clearly demonstrated the connection between religion and abolitionism. The radicalism of the Unitarians and Quakers, the perfectionism of the Methodists, and the New School Revivalism provided the energy for a crusade against slavery.[8] The debates at Lane Seminary in Cincinnati in 1834 are the most famous example of the connection between revivalism and the antislavery movement.

When Theodore Weld arrived at Lane Seminary he was the only convinced abolitionist there. His efforts gained other students for the cause of abolition, and eventually the students proposed a debate on slavery. During eighteen nights of debate, Weld and his followers won many converts for abolitionism. The students founded an antislavery society and resolved to improve the condition of Cincinnati's Negroes by opening schools for them. When this action brought a storm of protest, they withdrew from Lane and went to Oberlin, which then became a center of abolitionism. While Weld was preaching abolition in the 1830's, Oberlin sent out graduates dedicated to the cause.[9]

Although Weld and the Oberlin men were the best known of the militant antislavery Protestants, other churchmen, such as Unitarians Theodore Parker and Samuel J. May, joined the movement.[10] The Christian abolitionists were found in all northern denominations, church agencies, and antislavery groups, but they were especially prominent in the American and Foreign Anti-Slavery Society and the American Missionary Association.

The growth of antislavery feeling in the northern churches sharply divided them from southern Protestants. The slavery issue led to a schism in the Methodist Episcopal Church in 1844, when the wife of a southern bishop fell heir to slaves. At the General Conference of that year the church could not agree on the question of slave-owning in the episcopacy; as a result, the Southerners walked out and formed the Methodist Episcopal Church, South.[11]

The Presbyterians split into Old and New Schools in 1837–38; slavery was one of several factors in the schism. The New School became the center of antislavery agitation. The Old School Presbyterians divided after the Civil War broke out, and again the split was partly caused by differences of opinion over the morality of the South's peculiar institution.[12]

Among Baptists the sectional issue came to a head over the refusal of the American Baptist Board of Foreign Missions to appoint slaveholders as missionaries, a decision the Southerners would not accept. Consequently, in 1845, they organized the Southern Baptist Convention. Other Baptist agencies soon divided over slavery and the Baptists split, North versus South.[13]

Antislavery sentiment also took root among the Lutherans. However, the issue was hardly a burning one for them before the Civil War. The Lutherans, who were predominantly immigrants and conservative, usually avoided making stands on most issues of the day. But in 1863 a group of southern Lutherans withdrew from the General Synod.[14]

For various reasons the other major Protestant denominations managed to avoid schisms. Protestant Episcopal churchmen sometimes discussed the slavery issue, but the church never took a position on it. Though relations between northern and southern Episcopalians were severed during the Civil War, they did not suffer a permanent division. As the Congregationalists had few members in the South, they escaped a split.

Some antislavery northern Protestants were not for immediate abolition, even after 1840, when the doctrine became increasingly acceptable in the North. Many simply maintained that ministers should not own slaves. Others thought slaveholding a sin but did not call for an immediate end to it. Many supported the American Colonization Society, especially in its early years.

A few northern churchmen even apologized for slavery, and many emphasized other matters or simply refused to take a stand. Episcopal Bishop John H. Hopkins of New Hampshire stated in a pamphlet that Negroes were better off in slavery than in freedom. In 1836, in Connecticut, the Reverend Leonard Bacon proposed a measure, which was passed by the General Association of Congregational Ministers, restricting the use of Congregational pulpits by abolitionists. The "Connecticut gag-law" was used in other parts of New England, and some of the abolitionists, including those who were clergymen, attacked the churches as bulwarks of caste and slavery.[15] In his recollections of the antislavery conflict, the Reverend Samuel May wrote, "The most serious obstacle to the progress of the anti-slavery cause was the conduct of the clergy and churches in our country." [16] May's stricture was severe, but no major northern church body was willing to adopt abolitionism until the Civil War. The churches reflected northern attitudes, for abolition was not popular in the North in the 1830's. Antislavery sentiment grew after 1840, but even the Republican party accepted abolition only when the Civil War finally forced the issue.

Christian abolitionists, dissatisfied with the mild and compromising attitudes of the churches on the slavery issue, tried to gain control of several of the nondenominational Protestant agencies. [17]

The American Bible, the American Tract, and the American Home Missionary Societies were the three major agencies the Christian abolitionists attempted to take over. Persistent efforts by the antislavery men to persuade the American Bible Society to join the crusade against slavery failed. The managers of the Society maintained that its purpose was to circulate the Bible, not to conduct campaigns to correct civil laws.

Nor were efforts to take over the American Tract Society more successful. This Society published thousands of books and tracts condemning all kinds of sins — except the sin of slaveholding. Led by Arthur Tappan, an officer as well as a leading benefactor of the Society, the abolitionists attempted to add slaveholding to the list. But they were unable to gain control of the important publishing committee, which controlled the agency's publications. Prompted by the abolitionists' criticisms, the Society's 1856 annual meeting established a committee to investigate the slavery dispute. The committee reported that the Society's constitution prohibited it from publishing tracts dealing with the political aspects of slavery; hence, the organization could not support abolition. The 1857 annual meeting approved the report, and at the next annual meeting an effort by the abolitionists to seize control of the organization failed. Frustrated by the repeated defeats, a group of Christian abolitionists from Boston broke with the American Tract Society in 1859 and began to publish antislavery material.

The Christian crusaders' dissatisfaction with the American Home Missionary Society was partly responsible for the formation of the American Missionary Association. In 1846, when the Home Missionary Society tried to avoid taking a stand on slavery, several members, led by Arthur Tappan, founded the Association. The A.M.A. also had roots in the free mission movement and the *Amistad* case. This case involved a group of slaves who had revolted on board ship in September 1839. When they seized control of the vessel they steered it to Long Island. The owners charged them with piracy and murder. The defense, led by Lewis Tappan and John Quincy Adams, won acquittal and freedom for the slaves. The committee defending the slaves became the nucleus of the American Missionary Association. Christian abolitionists and dissenters from the compromising attitude of the Home Missionary Society joined the Association, which became active in the antislavery crusade. Fiercely opposed to caste as well as slavery, the A.M.A. in 1853 condemned Negro pews and other forms of racial discrimination in the churches and decided it would support no segregated churches, Negro or white.[18]

Although many militants shifted their allegiance from the Home Missionary Society to the American Missionary Association, others continued to press the Society to take an antislavery position. In 1856 they succeeded; the executive committee of the Home Missionary Society, faced with a possible loss of funds, agreed that henceforth no churches admitting slaveholders as full members would receive aid from the Society.

Although the Christian abolitionists achieved mixed results from their efforts to get control of the nondenominational agencies, they gradually won over many northern churchmen to the idea that slavery was a sin. Buttressed by the new revivalism, the Christian antislavery men hardened their convictions as war neared. Many carried their zeal into the Civil War, and during the war and the Reconstruction period they attempted to reform the Kingdom of Cotton. Their vision of the Kingdom of God did not let them rest.

While the northern denominations were purging themselves of connections with slavery, they did not rid themselves of the practices of discrimination and segregation. These practices knew no geographical boundaries. The development of segregation within the religious community was well established by the time of the Civil War. It stayed to haunt mid-twentieth-century white Protestantism.

In the colonial era the question of race relations within the religious organizations was not acute because the churches made few efforts to Christianize the Negroes. The Society for the Propagation of the Gospel in Foreign Parts, founded in London in 1701, had as one of its purposes the conversion of slaves. Anglican bishops also urged mission work among the Negroes, and Anglican ministers baptized a few. However, the Church of England converted few slaves during the colonial era. In New England the Puritans exhibited little interest in conversion of the Negroes. The Society of Friends preached the gospel to slaves most actively, but the Friends had little strength in the South, where the slaves were numerous. With the Great Awakening, Baptist and Methodist churches multiplied. At first they, too, showed only a casual interest in the slaves, but gradually they began to preach to Negroes.[19]

In the North, as Negroes were converted, white congregations usually admitted them. Discrimination sometimes developed as the whites forced the Negroes to sit in separate pews; the "African Pew" became part of the Congregational Church in colonial New England. Cemeteries, too, were sometimes segregated.[20]

Not until the end of the colonial era did Negroes become Christian in appreciable numbers. Although the Baptists and Methodists were most successful in gathering new adherents, other groups were also interested in Negro evangelization. The Presbyterians' Assembly of 1801 appointed as a missionary John Chavis, who became the first free Negro ordained by the Presbyterian Church. Chavis was a remarkable man, who is said to have received part of his education at Princeton and who sometimes tutored white children in North Carolina. Although the Presbyterians appointed Chavis to work among people of "his own color," he preached to whites as well.[21]

The increasing numbers of free Negro Christians in the northern states due to the emancipations of the Revolutionary era raised the problem of race relations within the churches. Patterns of segregation appeared, and with the passage of time, racial segregation became the main characteristic of Negro-white relations within Protestantism. Segregation in the churches assumed a variety of forms, often interrelated: all-Negro denominations, all-Negro conferences, all-Negro congregations, and "Negro Pews" in mixed churches.

The founder of the first all-Negro denomination, the African Methodist Episcopal (A.M.E.) Church, was the Reverend Richard Allen, an ex-slave who had purchased his freedom with depreciated Revolutionary War currency. Methodist Bishop Francis Asbury frequently gave this unusual speaker assignments to preach. Allen held special prayer meetings for Negroes and pondered the desirability of establishing a separate Negro church. Both Negroes and whites had dissuaded him from executing this idea, but an incident occurred that reinforced his resolve.

Prior to November 1787, Allen and a group of Negroes had attended the Saint George Methodist Church in Philadelphia, where they sat on the main floor. Because of the white members' objections to the growing popularity of the church among Negroes, church officials decided that henceforth Negroes would be expected to sit in the gallery. Allen and his group took their seats in the front of the gallery, but the officials had designated a place for them in the rear. Allen described the incident that developed:

> We had not been long upon our knees before I heard considerable scuffling and low talking. I raised my head up and saw one of the trustees . . . having hold of the Rev. Absalom Jones, pulling him up off his knees, and saying, "You must get up — you must not kneel here." . . . We all went out of the church in a body, and they were no more plagued with us.[22]

With financial assistance from some prominent whites, including George Washington, Benjamin Rush, and Thomas Jefferson, Allen's Negro followers built their own church. In 1799 Bishop Asbury ordained Allen a deacon; the next year the Methodist General Conference approved the ordination of Negro ministers. Negroes formed other congregations, and in 1816 they officially organized the African Methodist Episcopal Church. A similar but independent development among other Negro Methodists led to the formation of the African Methodist Episcopal Zion Church in 1821.[23]

All-Negro congregations of Baptists gave the Negro Methodists competition. Like Negro Methodists, northern Negro Baptists organized these separate churches because they encountered

racial discrimination in white churches and because they wanted
to control their own affairs. Unlike the Negro Methodists, however, Negro Baptists did not form all-Negro denominations,
although they did organize regional associations in the free states.
In the West the first Negro Baptist associations were the Prov-
idence Baptist Association in Ohio, founded in 1836, and the
Wood River Baptist Association in Illinois, established in 1838.
In 1853 these two groups along with other Negro congregations
organized the Western Colored Baptist Convention. In 1840
Negro Baptist congregations in the Northeast established the
American Baptist Missionary Convention.[24]

Not all free Negroes in the North moved into the new all-
Negro denominations and conventions. Some continued to attend
white churches and others formed their own congregations
within the white denominations. The first all-Negro Episcopal
church in the North was Saint Thomas Protestant Episcopal
Church in Philadelphia, founded by the Reverend Absalom
Jones, who had been an associate of Richard Allen.[25] All-Negro
congregations also developed among Presbyterians, Congregationalists, and Methodists who were still affiliated with the
Methodist Episcopal Church.

The all-Negro congregations in mixed denominations sometimes had equal rights. Several northern church conferences and
presbyteries admitted Negro clergy. Presbyterians not only
granted their Negro congregations equality; they also protested
against discrimination. When two Negro ministers received
warnings to stay away from the 1839 meeting of the Synod of
Pennsylvania, the synod passed a resolution attacking racial prejudice and reaffirming the right of Negro clergy to share in the
meetings.[26]

In other cases, especially among the Methodists and Episcopalians, northern Negroes struggled for a long time to win equality
in church assemblies. In the Protestant Episcopal Church the issue
of Negro representation was broached in the Diocese of New
York in 1819, when Saint Philip's Episcopal Church, a newly

formed Negro congregation, applied for admission to the diocesan convention. The convention admitted the church but denied it the right to vote. Critics of the diocese's action began a long fight for equality for Saint Philip's. In 1846, the diocese finally established a special committee to investigate the issue. The committee reported that it sympathized with the Negroes:

> But this cannot prevent our seeing the fact, that they *are* socially degraded, and are not regarded as proper associates for the class of persons who attend our Convention. We object not to the color of the skin, but we question their possession of those qualities which would render their intercourse with members of a church convention useful, or agreeable, even to themselves. We should make the same objection to persons of the same social class, however pure may be their blood, or however transparent their skin. It is impossible, in the nature of things, that such opposites should commingle with any pleasure or satisfaction to either.[27]

Although they were frustrated at the 1846 convention, the proponents of equality renewed their efforts, and at the 1853 convention the diocese granted Saint Philip's the right to vote.[28]

In the Diocese of Pennsylvania the Negro church founded by the Reverend Absalom Jones had similar difficulties in winning a seat in the convention. The diocese waived the Latin and Greek requirements in ordaining Jones in 1795 but denied representation to his church in the convention. At the 1843 convention, the diocese extended the ruling to other Negro congregations. Efforts to change this discriminatory policy were not successful until the Civil War.[29]

Negro congregations remaining in the Methodist Episcopal Church faced a similar struggle to gain equality. These congregations complained that Negroes preferred the all-Negro Methodist denominations because in the Methodist Episcopal Church they did not have their own annual conferences and often did not have their own preachers.[30] Annual conferences exercised much control over local churches and possessed the right to send delegates to the church's highest legislative body, the General Conference.

At the General Conference of 1848, Negroes requested the organization of Negro annual conferences. The delegates declared it inexpedient to grant the request. Four years later, Negroes from Philadelphia and New Jersey again urged the creation of Negro conferences, and again the church rejected the plea, although it did permit Negro preachers to meet in order to promote Negro religious work.[31] Negro Methodists repeated their proposal at the 1860 General Conference and also asked that they be admitted to membership in the regular annual conferences. The delegates rejected the former request, and the Negroes withdrew the latter before the delegates could consider it.[32] Finally, in 1864, the Methodists allowed Negroes to form mission conferences, and at the next quadrennial conference the church converted these into regular annual conferences.[33] Methodists took these steps partly to meet the repeated pleas from Negro churchmen and partly to accommodate the growing Negro membership in the South.

The General Conference of 1864 also declared that regular annual conferences could receive Negro preachers, but the establishment of separate Negro conferences was the more significant act. Segregated conferences soon became customary.[34]

Although the creation of Negro conferences gave Negro ministers voting rights and participation in General Conferences, some Methodists were uneasy about the church's sanctioning of segregation. The New England Conference criticized the General Conference for its action, and the *Christian Advocate* vigorously denounced segregation in the Methodist Episcopal Church:

> Colored ministers should be invited to membership in our annual conferences, and introduced into our pulpits. Colored families should be welcomed to our churches, not to sit on separate seats assigned to them as a distinct *caste;* but, in free churches, to sit where they please, and in pewed Churches in such seats as they may choose to pay for. No reason can be given against this, but an unreasonable and an unchristian

prejudice, of which a man of sense should be ashamed, and for which a Christian should make haste to repent before God.[35]

Northern Negroes also experienced segregation in mixed congregations. Although white Protestants sometimes treated Negroes equally, on other occasions they did not. Negroes found themselves sitting in a separate "Negro Pew," attending separate Sunday schools, and taking communion after the white members. Frederick Douglass, the Negro abolitionist, once walked out of a Methodist church rather than suffer such humiliating treatment.[36] White Protestants even utilized the "Negro Pew" in death as well as life and segregated Negroes in cemeteries.[37] Thaddeus Stevens was unable to find a white cemetery that would not discriminate. In protest, he arranged for his own burial in a Negro cemetery. These practices, stemming from colonial times, did not disappear in the decades preceding the Civil War. Not even the Society of Friends, a leader in Negro education and in the antislavery movement, escaped charges of racial discrimination. Several Negroes testified that the Quakers forced them to sit in special pews; and at the 1843 World Anti-Slavery Convention, meeting in London, the American Friends were accused of discrimination. Although the Philadelphia *Friend* denied the accusations, there apparently was evidence of their veracity.[38]

As humiliating to Negroes as segregation within the congregation was the refusal of white Protestants to allow Negroes to attend white churches. Some Negroes encountered forceful opposition when they tried to worship in white churches. The Reverend Samuel May, the Unitarian abolitionist, recalled one such incident in Boston:

> In 1835, if I remember correctly, a wealthy and pious colored man bought a pew on the floor of the Park Street Church. It caused great disturbance. Some of his neighbors nailed up the door of his pew; and so many of "the aggrieved brethren" threatened to leave the society, if they could not be relieved of such an offence, that the trustees were obliged to eject the colored purchaser.[39]

The Episcopal Church even discriminated against Negroes at its General Theological Seminary in New York City. In 1836, Bishop Benjamin T. Onderdonk told Isaiah D. DeGrasse, a Negro applicant, that while he would be permitted to attend classes, he would be allowed neither to become a regular student at the seminary nor to live in the dormitory. DeGrasse declined to attend classes under such conditions. The seminary refused to admit a second Negro student, Alexander Crummell, who then secured ordination in the Episcopal Diocese of Massachusetts after attending the Congregationalists' Andover Theological Seminary.[40]

That the northern churches were guilty of segregation and discrimination in the period between the Revolution and the Civil War was no anomaly. Negroes faced segregation, discrimination, violence, and restrictions of their civil rights in most northern states during this era. Some individuals, including churchmen, criticized the North's racial practices and attempted to win justice for Negroes. Certainly religious principles motivated Prudence Crandall and others in their efforts for Negro rights and education. Miss Crandall, a Quaker, opened her school in Canterbury, Connecticut, to Negro students in 1833, but bitter opposition from the community forced her to close it. The Prudence Crandalls were in a minority, however, and the churches reflected the majority view.[41]

In the slave states segregation was closely related to slavery. Before the 1830's some congregations of free Negroes developed and maintained a degree of independence. The Baptists in a few instances admitted these congregations to their regular associations, and on a few other occasions Negroes preached to white or mixed audiences.[42] The intensification of the conflict over slavery hindered the growth of independent Negro congregations. Especially after Nat Turner's insurrection, Southerners became alarmed lest Negro preachers stir up trouble and challenge the slave labor system. Southern states passed laws making it difficult or impossible for free Negro preachers to function. Negro preachers, like all Negroes, encountered obstacles in trying to learn to read even the Bible. In some cases Negroes were not allowed to preach to Negro congregations unless a white supervisor was present.

Even though they tried to make certain that antislavery doctrines could not be spread, southern churches did take an interest in the religious welfare of the slaves in the years before the Civil War. Indeed, southern planters recognized that control of their slaves' religious lives was a means of social control. Led by Episcopal Bishops William Meade and Leonidas Polk (Polk was the owner of a large Louisiana plantation) and Methodist Bishop William Capers of South Carolina, the major church groups urged planters to bring the gospel to Negroes. Some church associations sent missionaries to work among the slaves. Planters and preachers held Sunday school classes for them and, less frequently, insisted upon Christian marriage and baptism. Although all of the southern denominations were active in the work, the Methodists and Baptists were most successful.

The insistence upon white control over the slaves' religious lives led to segregation. The planters and churches built special chapels for the slaves where whites preached. Occasionally the planters allowed Negroes to preach, but under watchful white supervision. If there were no special services or chapels for Negroes, their masters permitted them to attend the regular worship services. In this case they usually sat in segregated galleries or pews and took communion after the white members. Even in the few cases where slaves were not segregated they had no rights in church government. They might have been "members" of the church, but the relation was strictly servant-master. [43]

Thus, well before the Civil War, racial discrimination and segregation were part of Protestant church life in both the North and South. The churches generally agreed that because Negroes had souls they were eligible for salvation, but this did not preclude discrimination and segregation within the religious community.

Although northern and southern white Protestants quarreled little over segregation before the Civil War, their divisions over slavery were acute, and the war and Reconstruction aggravated those divisions. The southern clergy rallied to the cause of the Confederacy. They saw the conflict as a holy war, with God on the side of the South. Southern Presbyterian educator and editor James H. Thornwell was as vigorous in his support of the Confederacy as he had been in the defense of slavery. Bishop Leonidas Polk fought for the Lord as a general in the Confederate Army and was killed on the battlefield. At least one southern churchman complained that his church's music sounded more like military marches than hymns. One historian of the church's role in the conflict has concluded that churchmen were the most important group sustaining the South's morale.[44]

As the southern clergy rallied to the defense of the Confederacy, so the northern clergy rushed to support the Union. To northern churchmen the victory of the Union Army was a sign of God's will. The northern churches' self-righteousness carried over into Reconstruction. Believing that southern society was based on despotism, caste, barbarous slavocracy, and immorality, they saw Reconstruction as an opportunity for a holy crusade to redeem the Southland.[45] The South was in "danger of sinking lower and lower," remarked the Methodist *Christian Advocate*. The journal concluded, "It must reform or go down still deeper into the abyss of self-ruin." [46] Above all, the South was to be taught a new attitude toward the Negro.

During Reconstruction many Northerners felt enthusiasm for the rights and prospects of the freedmen. Motivated partly by the plight of the ex-slaves and partly by the widespread destruction of the South and its need for rehabilitation, many northern churchmen rushed to the domain of the defeated Confederacy to assist the freedmen and redeem the South. They worked within both sectarian and nonsectarian agencies. Although this movement, like the abolitionist crusade, involved only a minority of northern Protestants, it was carried out with the same burning zeal. Not for a century would Protestant churches come close to equaling the enthusiasm and effort for the rights of Negroes that they had demonstrated during the 1860's.

The educational work of the northern churches began even before the end of the war. Missionaries and teachers sometimes
followed on the heels of the victorious northern troops and
established schools for Negroes. Spearheading the work was the
American Missionary Association, which had been engaged in
missionary activities in the slave states before the Civil War. The
Association expanded these activities during the war, particularly
in the field of education. Correspondence between Lewis Tappan,
the A.M.A.'s secretary, and General Benjamin Butler, and later
General John Wool, over the condition of Negro refugees pouring
into Fortress Monroe, Virginia, in 1861, led to the sending of a
missionary there. Upon his arrival the Reverend Lewis C. Lock-
wood opened a Sunday school for Negroes in the home of ex-
President Tyler. Two days later, Mary S. Peake, a free mulatto,
began to conduct classes in the Association's first school.[47] Although the A.M.A. had not originally intended to launch a large-
scale educational effort, thereafter it deliberately increased its
educational endeavors. The Association had begun as an independent and nondenominational organization, but, by the end of
the Civil War, it was the voice of Congregationalism in the
South.

To support their efforts to school the freedmen, the churches
organized agencies and raised funds. The northern Methodists
founded their Freedmen's Aid Society in 1866, and by 1880 it had
collected and distributed nearly a million dollars for Negro education. Baptists, Presbyterians, and to a lesser extent Episcopalians,
Lutherans, and Friends embarked upon similar programs.[48]

The one-room schoolhouse used by the A.M.A. at Fortress
Monroe was fairly typical of the first schools. The schoolhouses
were often flimsy affairs; abandoned buildings or churches were
often the only structures available. Nor were dilapidated buildings the only handicaps faced by the missionaries. To overcome a
shortage of textbooks, the teachers used a variety of makeshifts,
including the Bible, to teach reading. Many white Southerners
opposed the Yankee teachers, and violence was common. The
teachers made up for the poor facilities and the community oppo-

sition by their devotion to the cause. Their commitment was buttressed by the Negroes' great enthusiasm for education. Classes were held either by day or by night, since many Negroes could not attend otherwise.[49]

With the passing of time, the churches closed many of the schools, but from these meager beginnings developed the modern southern Negro colleges. Fisk was an offspring of the American Missionary Association (Congregationalist), Morehouse of the Baptists, and Meharry Medical School of the Methodists. During the period when the southern states were struggling to recover from the war and were hampered by a tradition of sluggishness and hostility toward public education, these schools provided Negroes with an opportunity for an education, however rudimentary.

The energies of the religious teachers and missionaries roaming the South during those years did not spend themselves on education alone. Closely allied to the interest in education were the desires to bring Christianity to the freedmen and to win new adherents to the denomination involved. The Sabbath school was as much a part of the scene as the primary school. The primary schools themselves taught a heavy dose of religion; the teachers used the Bible to teach Christianity along with spelling. Sometimes the schoolroom served as a chapel, and denominational churches grew alongside the schools.[50]

The northern churches had begun missionary work in the South even before the Civil War, and the defeat of the Confederacy opened new doors there. Southern opinion and legal restrictions had hindered this work before the Civil War. Now, although opinion might still be hostile, it was no longer an effective force, and the barriers of law were gone. Indeed, the churches were actively supported by the Union Army and the federal government. The Freedmen's Bureau, for example, gave federal funds to the religious schools, even though they were teaching a sectarian variety of religion.[51]

Of the denominations active in the South, the northern Methodists acquired the largest number of members, and the church had a thriving southern Negro membership by the end of Reconstruction. Northern Presbyterians, Baptists, Congregationalists, and other denominations that had had practically no representation in the South before the war also gained Negro adherents in connection with their missionary and educational work. These churches took as members many of the ex-slaves who had left the southern white churches as well as the previously unchurched Negroes who flocked to their schools.

While northern churches were actively carrying the school and the church to Negroes, southern denominations were doing little. Difference of opinion over what should be done with the freedmen helped maintain antagonism between northern and southern Protestants. Even if southern churchmen had shared their northern brethren's zeal (and a few were interested in Negro education and many more in Negro evangelism), they would have encountered obstacles in working among Negroes. In the first place, the southern churches had been hard hit by the war. Poorer and smaller than their northern counterparts to begin with, they had to rebuild their own edifices and organizations from diminished funds. In addition, many Negroes, desiring to be free of their former masters, had formed their own congregations. These Negroes did not trust whites and wanted to develop their own churches without southern white interference. Here was unpromising ground for evangelism.

As for Negro education, the southern churches were by no means convinced of its worth. Prior to abolition a literate slave was a potentially dangerous one. During Reconstruction, educated Negroes, conscious of their rights now built into the Constitution by the Fourteenth and Fifteenth Amendments, could challenge the established white supremacy of the South. The Negro church, with its educated minister holding Radical Republican views, sometimes furnished political leaders of a type unacceptable to the white South. Some Southerners raised cries of alarm at the products of the northern-operated schools and at the activities of Yankees in the South. Some urged that the southern churches act to protect Negroes from the "tender mercies" of Yankees.[52] The southern Methodists were relieved when the

Colored Methodist Episcopal Church, under their guidance, inserted a clause in the *Discipline* forbidding churches to be used as political forums.[53] Although the hostility toward Negro education began to wane in the 1870's, the southern churches' support for it was meager. Not until a later day did the southern denominations expand their activities in this direction and attempt to educate and evangelize Negroes.

Disagreement over Negro education was not the only cause of continued antagonism between northern and southern Protestants. Northern attacks branding Southerners as traitors and sinners in need of reconstruction irked southern churches. Nor did southern churchmen view favorably the attempts of northern churches to acquire white members in the South. Finally, there was the matter of caste. Most northern churchmen capitulated to segregation in the South, even before the end of Reconstruction. Congregations became segregated. In the 1860's, however, before the northern churches had completely surrendered on the segregation issue, they often attacked their southern brethren for segregating Negroes.

Northern Methodists and Congregationalists in particular resisted a segregated, racist church. The most outspoken critic of the caste system was Methodist Bishop Gilbert Haven of New England. Converted by the Bible and his mother to abolitionism, Bishop Haven was one of those New England Methodists who criticized his church for establishing all-Negro conferences during the war.[54] When Haven became a bishop and carried the banner of northern Methodism south, he took with him a fervor for civil rights. Biship Haven refused, sometimes in the face of much opposition, to draw the color line in southern conferences and congregations. Insisting that segregation was evil, he wrote, "God will ring that bell until He rings out this crime of caste." Haven even advocated interracial social contact and intermarriage.[55] It made little difference to the South that he denounced the North for segregation, too. Such activities and utterances were strong medicine for Southerners and eventually even for northern Methodists.

Bishop Haven's voice became more and more lonely, however.

During Reconstruction and the remainder of the nineteenth century, northern and southern Protestants often disagreed over the
status of the Negro in American society. But they were moving
closer together in both practice and preaching. By the time of
World War I, agreement was nearly complete; at least conflicts
of the kind that occurred in the 1860's no longer existed.

2

Southern Protestants "Solve" the Race Problem

> No, Mr. Durel, it [the race problem] isn't dead, it's
> merely 'possuming. I say it wi' no vaunting, but wi'
> drread. Ye may crrack its bones and get never a
> whimper, yet 'tis but 'possuming. Lorrd! Ye can't
> *neglect* it to death; the neglect of all America can't
> kill it. It's in the womb o' the future and bigger than
> Asia, Africa, and America combined. Ye'll do well to
> be friendly wi' its friends and trreat it kindly while it's
> young and trractable.   GEORGE W. CABLE
> *Lovers of Louisiana*

In *The Strange Career of Jim Crow*, C. Vann Woodward
pointed out that the South did not fully capitulate to racism until
the 1890's. Woodward also noted, however, that some institutions
were segregated by the end of Reconstruction and that white
Southerners believed in Negro inferiority before the Civil War.
These two facts cannot be overemphasized, for the South was
well prepared to accept "scientific" racism and the Jim Crow
laws and Negro disfranchisement of the 1890's. The Protestant
church, a major southern social institution, was among the first
groups to segregate after the Civil War and to accept racism as
the basis of race relations. Protestantism helped pave the way for
the capitulation to racism at the turn of the century.

When the southern churches confronted the race problem following the war, they did so amid various cultural and social
forces that influenced the outcome of that confrontation. The
concepts of scientific racism and Negro inferiority were, of
course, current before the Civil War, and the South did not dis-

card them after the cessation of hostilities. Social Darwinism
added to the body of pseudo-scientific thought affecting the discussion of race relations.[1] This doctrine assumed that there was a
struggle or competition among races, in which the superior ones
triumphed. To white Americans this meant that Caucasians, or,
to be more precise, peoples of northern European background,
dominated society because they were superior. It was easy to
conclude that inferior peoples should be segregated and ruled by
the superior races. Thus, Social Darwinism buttressed prejudices
and gave a scientific justification to the growing system of discrimination and segregation.

The political turmoil in the South also impressed southern
white Protestants. Many white Southerners feared Negro domination. Use of the Klan and violence to push Negroes out of government and verbal attacks on Negroes in politics were familiar
parts of the post-Civil War southern scene. Other groups besides
the churches urged segregation and disfranchisement.

While these various domestic stresses were driving the nation
toward acceptance of segregation, America was turning her attention overseas. In the 1880's and 1890's the United States began
to emerge as a world power, and with her victory in the Spanish-
American War she became absorbed with the problems of em-
pire. From the churches, too, came urgings toward imperialism to
satisfy the missionary impulse of Christianity. The duty of the
church was to carry the gospel to all parts of the globe; there was
a world to win for Christ. American Protestants had been active
in foreign missionary work before the Civil War, but they
greatly increased their interest and activities in the second half of
the nineteenth century. The Methodists, for example, increased
their expenditures for missionary work fivefold between 1860
and the turn of the century.

Racism had a strong influence on the foreign missionary impulse. The churches considered the peoples of Asia and Africa to
be heathens living in darkness. The Christian's duty was not only
to bring them Christianity but also to bring them the white man's

civilization. "The preaching of Christianity not only makes the pagan a participant in the blessings of salvation through Christ," declared the Episcopal *Churchman*, "but it also renders him a civilized being. Civilization follows in the wake of the cross. The statesmen and soldiers who have visited the hut of the missionary in Africa and India have seen grouped around it the homes of men and women reclaimed not only from religious darkness, but from social savagery." [2]

Here were implications for the race problem in the United States. Clearly, some churchmen asked, did we not have a white man's burden at home with millions of Negroes in the South "an Africa at our doors?" [3] If the Negroes of the "Dark Continent" needed the gospel and uplift, did not those in America fall into the same category? Southern churchmen asked how the North could defend the Negro in the South and his right to political participation when it was insisting upon white control over inferior peoples abroad. Said the Methodist *Christian Advocate* of Nashville in 1899, "We cannot just see why white men have a right to govern 8,000,000 people in Luzon and the adjacent islands at the point of a bayonet, and yet have no right to set up an educational test for the purpose of preventing an American Commonwealth from falling into the hands of negroes who are only three or four generations removed from the jungles of Africa." [4]

The most important factor influencing the churches' attitudes was the heritage of slavery. The churches had accepted slavery and Negro inferiority in ante-bellum days; they easily accepted segregation and Negro inferiority after the war. Though they realized that slavery was gone, southern Protestants exhibited little desire to accept Negroes as equals. Segregation and second-class status simply replaced slavery. Negroes had attended mixed congregations before the Civil War; during the early part of Reconstruction southern Protestants occasionally urged the continuation of this practice. But white churchmen did not intend to grant Negroes equality within the churches. As the whites had controlled under slavery, so they were to control under freedom.

If Negroes would not accept this arrangement, then separation must come; indeed, separation soon came to seem desirable in both religious and secular institutions.

A few southern religious spokesmen took extremist views. Around the turn of the century the American Book and Bible House published Charles Carroll's *The Negro A Beast*, a classic example of Negrophobia. This vicious book, complete with inflammatory pictures, argued from the Scriptures that the Negro was not the descendant of Ham and was not a man at all, but a soulless beast. Carroll said the Christian had no duty to the Negro; Negroes were to be repressed and degraded.[5] Although published by a religious publishing house, Carroll's amazing diatribe was not subscribed to by any responsible religious leaders. Alarmed by the wide circulation of the book in the South, Texas Baptists passed a resolution calling upon "our ministers, teachers, and membership everywhere to expose and denounce the insulting and outrageous book, now circulating in the South, which professes loudly to prove from the Bible that the Negro is not human, but a beast without a soul." [6]

The most strongly worded derogatory statement by a major church leader about the Negro was by Bishop William M. Brown of the Protestant Episcopal Church. In *The Crucial Race Question*, published in 1907, Bishop Brown presented a gloomy picture of Negroes. The northern-born Bishop of Arkansas declared that Negroes were making no progress. According to this white-supremacy polemic, they were degenerating into an almost hopeless position. He advocated a rigid separation of the races.[7] However, his church rejected his proposals and his analysis of the race problem. The bishop's views on various social questions tended to be extreme; in the 1920's the Episcopal Church defrocked him for his pro-communist sympathies.

Most southern church leaders in the last third of the nineteenth century were not so hard on the Negro as Bishop Brown, nor did they insist upon rigid segregation. But their views were not radically different from his. The consensus on race relations emerging among Protestant leaders in those years favored a segregated

society, second-class citizenship for the Negro, a subordinate position for Negroes in the economy, and the doctrine of white supremacy. Protestants were not the only group accepting racism
in the late nineteenth century; few whites, religious or secular,
protested against the credo by the turn of the century.

Denomination mattered little, for support for the racist creed
ran the gamut from urban Episcopalians to country Baptists.
Episcopalians did resist segregation more than the other groups,
but for the most part accepted it. While the churches used God
to justify segregation, they possessed no elaborate theology on
the subject. The churches agreed that the Negro was the descendant of Ham, that he did have a soul, and that the Bible
preached brotherhood, but these did not add up to racial mixing.
The Creator had made the races different; hence, they should be
segregated. As one southern Presbyterian declared, "The color
line is distinctly drawn by Jehovah Himself. . . . [It would be]
a sin and crime to undertake to obliterate it." [8]

Southern white Protestants marshalled other arguments for
segregation. Not only was racial mixing a violation of God's law,
but it was also a violation of the law of nature. A Georgia Episcopal priest said, "There is by nature a barrier raised which pro-
hibits its [the Negro race] blending with the white races on terms
of social equality." [9] "Social equality" meant mixing in the
churches, for the church was a social institution. In white
churchmen's minds one reason social mixing violated the law of
nature was that it led to intermarriage, the great taboo. Said the
Reverend W. M. Leftwich, "The race problem will never be settled upon the basis of social equality. Equality is impossible without amalgamation, and amalgamation is too revolting to be entertained for a moment." [10]

If the law of God or the law of nature were not enough, the
churches could appeal to race "instinct," which supposedly made
clear the distinction between justifiable separation and prejudice.
The editor of the southern Baptist *Western Recorder* summarized
this view of segregation when he wrote, "While race prejudice and
race hatred are wrong, race instinct is right. There can never be

social equality of the races. . . . Let race instinct be recognized, but let it be kept within its bounds, and let it not degenerate into race prejudice and race hatred." [11]

As a further justification for segregation, church leaders pointed out that Negroes had taken the initiative in the 1860's in establishing their own churches; and they maintained Negroes preferred this arrangement. "Naturally enough the negroes prefer to have their separate local churches, and for these to be presided over by ministers of their own race. They prefer also to have their own organizations for education, missionary and other benevolent work," remarked a southern Baptist committee in 1888. Yet the Negroes had had little choice, for they would have had to sit in Negro pews and suffer second-class status in the white churches. They were not welcome, at least not as equals, regardless of whether or not they preferred their own churches. This Baptist committee concluded on a revealing note (italics mine): "It is not likely that this condition of things [segregated churches] will be changed, nor is it *desirable* that it should be." [12]

Within the southern churches segregation was nearly complete by the end of Reconstruction. During the decade after 1865 Negroes, asserting their new freedom and independence, left the white churches' slave galleries to form their own congregations. Only here and there did Negroes remain in the churches of their former masters. With the passage of time their numbers thinned, and only a few Negroes attended white churches by the turn of the century. Ray Stannard Baker described the situation in 1908:

> Now a Negro is never (or very rarely) seen in a white man's church. Once since I have been in the South, I saw a very old Negro woman, some much-loved mammy, perhaps — sitting down in front near the pulpit, but that is the only exception to the rule that has come to my attention. Negroes are not wanted in white churches.[13]

The Negro Methodist and Baptist denominations, especially the Baptists, made spectacular gains due to the exodus from white churches and the postwar freedom to proselytize openly in the South. Negro Baptists organized state associations, culminating in the formation of the National Baptist Convention in 1895. The African Methodist Episcopal Church, the African Methodist Episcopal Zion Church, and several new Negro denominations grew rapidly. So great was the expansion of the all-Negro churches that by 1890 they claimed nine out of ten Negro Protestants.

The mass exodus from white churches naturally contributed to the growth of segregated church life in the South. The Southern Baptist Convention became practically an all-white church by the 1870's, as Negro Baptists left the churches of their former masters. Immediately after the war, some southern white Baptists suggested that Negroes be encouraged to remain in white churches, but there was no suggestion that the freedmen be allowed to participate as equals.[14] As Negroes would not sit in Negro pews, the alternative was segregated congregations, a condition that southern white Baptists easily accepted. Because white Baptist conventions would not accept Negro churches as equals and because Negroes would not accept inferior status, the separate Negro congregations were not admitted to white conventions. Negro and white Baptists exchanged fraternal delegates to each other's conventions, but otherwise there was little contact between them. In keeping with the white Baptists' belief in segregation, Negro fraternal messengers sat at the rear of the assembly.[15]

The Methodist Mobile Conference in 1865 called upon its churches to open their doors to Negroes. Yet the white Methodists certainly entertained no desire to admit Negroes on a basis of equality. This feeling, in addition to the desire of Negroes to assert their independence in their own churches and church organizations, led to the formation in 1866 of the Colored Methodist Episcopal Church.[16] In the same year, one church editor rationalized the separation: "We stand before the world with a church constitution that accords to blacks and whites equal church privileges, while by a happy and prudent separation, it pays due respect to those mysterious antipathies which seem to be the indications of Heaven with regard to the two races." [17]

Southern white Methodists co-operated with the colored Methodists in some projects, but the policy and philosophy of segregation was a *sine qua non* for such co-operation. Noting the difference in racial policy between northern and southern Methodists, a southern Methodist committee reported in 1874, "They have mixed Conferences, mixed congregations, and mixed schools. We do not ask them to adopt our plan. We could not adopt theirs." Time only confirmed the "wisdom" of this policy. The southern bishops declared in 1898, "Experience corroborates and confirms the wisdom of our Church in its established ecclesiastical relation to the colored people, which has relieved both them and us from needless jealousies and irritating and damaging complications." [18] So determined were southern white Methodists to maintain a separate denomination for Negroes that it became a matter of contention between northern and southern Methodists when discussions on reunion began around 1910.

Most Negroes left the southern Presbyterian Church after the Civil War, but a few remained and established their own congregations. This raised two questions: should the church encourage Negroes to remain, and what rights were the Negro members to have? At first the white Presbyterians urged Negroes to stay in the church. The General Assembly of 1866 declared that it was "highly inexpedient that there should be an ecclesiastical separation of the white and colored races." [19] The problem of Negro rights caused the Presbyterians to take a second look at this decision. When those urging ecclesiastical equality suggested that Negroes be given a voice in church government, the opponents of this policy marshalled their forces. While the Synod of Virginia pondered the issue of equality, the Reverend Robert L. Dabney, a vigorous proponent of white supremacy and a power in the church, rose to attack. Negroes were made to follow and not to lead, declared Dabney; and he continued, "I would make no black man a member of a white Session, or Presbytery, or Synod, or Assembly; nor would I give them any share in the government of our own church, nor any representation in it." [20] In the 1870's several presbyteries presented overtures to the General Assembly calling for the creation of a separate Negro denomination. The General Assembly of 1874 established a policy of setting up Negro presbyteries and synods whenever possible, looking to the eventual establishment of a Negro Presbyterian denomination.[21] So few were the Negro congregations, however, that implementation of this policy proceeded slowly.

In 1882 the church, though not without conflict, sustained the right of Negro ministers to sit and vote at presbytery meetings. The Presbytery of Memphis had denied a Negro minister the right to vote. Overruled in an appeal to its synod, the presbytery carried the case to the General Assembly. The Assembly ruled that the Reverend Samuel Park, the minister in question, had the right to vote because he was a duly ordained minister of the presbytery.[22] This decision strengthened the movement for an independent Negro church among those who opposed Negro participation in white church affairs. It was held, furthermore, that a separate Negro church would encourage Negro development and that since fears of a mixed church would perish, whites would render financial assistance to a Negro denomination.[23]

To those who were concerned because they feared that separation violated Christian ethics, some white churchmen pointed to Negroes who requested a separate church. Moreover, God Himself drew the color line. One Virginia churchman declared, "No Christian ought to allow his conscience to be disturbed by the thought that he violates the unity of the Church by insisting on an independent organization for the colored race. The distinctions of race are drawn by God Himself, for reasons not known to us, but worthy of His wisdom. His reasons for fixing them are better than any reasons man can have for breaking them down, and any design or policy which leads, however remotely, to destroy them, is both foolish and wicked." [24]

With the organization of a separate Afro-American Presbyterian Church in 1898 the "long cherished plans of the Assembly" matured. The independent church failed to grow, however, and

eventually disintegrated. Southern Presbyterians officially abolished it in 1916 and brought the Negro churches back into the
southern Presbyterian Church, organized into separate presbyteries and a separate synod.[25]

Protestant Episcopalians also encountered the problem of segregation. Almost all local congregations, as in other denominations, were segregated by the 1870's. In 1873 the issue of segregation reached the diocesan level when a Negro congregation
applied for admission to the Diocese of South Carolina. The application prompted a lively debate that wracked the diocese for
over fifteen years.[26] South Carolina was not the only diocese to
face the issue, and a general discussion concerning Negro membership quickly spread to other southern dioceses. Although
some churchmen saw no danger in mixed dioceses with equal
rights for Negroes, others feared a Negro invasion of southern
dioceses and declared that dangerous social questions would arise.
In 1883 a group of southern white church leaders gathered at
Sewanee, Tennessee, to ponder the problem. From the Sewanee
Conference emerged a proposal to allow dioceses to establish separate missionary districts for Negroes, which would be under the
supervision of the regular dioceses. Bishop Richard Wilmer of
Alabama, who was a dissenter at the Sewanee Conference, branded
the Sewanee plan "class legislation." [27] A conference of Negro
churchmen, the Conference of Church Workers Among Colored
People, meeting in New York protested to the church's General
Convention. The General Convention of 1883, in reviewing the
Sewanee plan and the Negroes' protest, upheld the Negroes'
appeal and rejected the "drawing of lines of classification and distinction between the followers of our common Lord." [28]

The dispute over Negro representation dragged on, however,
and several southern dioceses either refused to admit Negro
churches or limited their rights of participation. In 1889, the
General Convention declined to consider this matter, thus leaving
discrimination to the discretion of the local dioceses.[29] Northern
and southern delegates could agree in this decision because northern Episcopalians, like most Northerners, were losing interest in

the southern race problem. Few northern churchmen protested when southern dioceses discriminated against Negroes. Reflecting the growing North-South *rapprochement* on the race issue, the *Churchman* of New York declared of the Diocese of South Carolina's exclusion policy, "The wisdom of their action must after all be decided by their own knowledge." [30]

But not all southern churchmen acquiesced to a policy of segregation or shared the fears of Negro participation in church government. The dioceses of West Texas and Florida, both on the fringes of the Deep South, not only allowed Negro participation on a basis of equal rights in their conventions but also, in the 1880's, elected the first Negro delegates to the General Convention's House of Deputies.[31] Such elections were exceptional; they were not repeated for decades. Even in those dioceses where Negroes possessed equal voting rights, they did not participate fully in diocesan affairs. Bishop Robert Strange of the Diocese of East Carolina described the situation in his district:

> In East Carolina the negroes have, as yet, all the formal rights of the white man; but this formal position is hardly more satisfactory [than no rights]. In the first place, they take no real part in the deliberations of the Council. The clergy go as their duty; but the laity hardly ever attend; they sit on back seats, have little or nothing to say and they get little or no good out of the work of the Council. . . . I *know* that if the work among negroes grows in East Carolina, the diocese will exclude all of them from its Council; the growth of the Church among the negroes thus assuring their ecclesiastical disfranchisement.[32]

Episcopalians organized Negro convocations in the South, but these conventions were denied the important rights of electing their own bishops, making their own rules, and sending delegates to the General Convention. These restrictions were in keeping with the separate and unequal pattern.[33]

The belief in and practice of segregation carried over into church schools. School segregation was never an issue for the churches. Schools were social institutions; the implications were obvious. "Mixed education is the beginning, social intercourse and amalgamation is [sic] to be the end," said the *Southern Presbyterian*. Professor Kinloch Nelson of the Episcopal theological seminary in Virginia was equally candid: "In the first place I am not ashamed to say that I have no more wish to have the colored children in the schools with my children than to intrude my children into the schools for their children." [34] Some of the attacks on school integration foreshadowed those of the 1950's. The Baptist *Religious Herald* of Richmond asserted in 1874:

> The aversion of the people of the South to mixed schools . . . is an instinct, divinely implanted, for the wise and beneficent purpose of keeping separate races which are, by nature, widely different in color, social qualities and moral tendencies. God has made the difference, and human government should not ignore it. . . . If necessary, let the public schools be abolished.[35]

The churches did not often comment when the southern states passed a rash of Jim Crow laws after 1890. When they did comment, it was with approval. They sometimes maintained that the laws did not discriminate against Negroes. The *Christian Advocate* of Nashville declared:

> The negro leaders in the South and their injudicious friends up North who are making such an ado over "Jim Crow laws" quite overlook the fact that such laws do not discriminate against the blacks. They assign to the use of negroes certain seats in trolley cars, equally desirable with others, and certain sections of the railway cars, usually the same cars in which the whites ride. In these places under the law they have rights. Without such a law those rights would often be challenged.[36]

The theme of white supremacy, inherited from slavery, ran through the discussions of segregation. Churchmen agreed that Negroes were inferior to whites and vigorously asserted this belief. Although a few Negroes like Booker T. Washington might prove to be outstanding leaders, in the churches' eyes such exceptions only proved the rule.

Some churchmen maintained that the inferiority of the Negro was due to his background — the heritage of Africa and slavery — and that eventually, in some far-off day, he would reach the white man's level of civilization. Yet most saw the Negro's supposed inferiority as innate and permanent. In 1868 the *Southern Presbyterian Review* set the tone for the remainder of the century when it declared that nothing could be done to solve the race problem "while the patent fact of the essential inferiority of the black race is denied, or even ignored." [37] Negro inferiority was obvious to another writer, James W. Hinton of Georgia, who wrote fifteen years later, "It would seem to be superfluous to point to the inferiority of the Negro, viewed as to mental and moral capactity. If history, if philosophy, if observation teach anything, they have put this claim of equality to rest, except with those disordered minds that revel only in abstractions." [38] Thus, the churches never lost their ante-bellum belief in Negro inferiority; and those discussing the race problem agreed that whether inferiority was permanent or a temporary phase, for the present Negroes were a "child race." The Social Darwinism of the late nineteenth century merely gave new grounds for believing in white supremacy.

With the questions of segregation and white supremacy "settled," southern Protestants could turn to other aspects of the race question. A position to replace slave status had to be found for the Negro if the South were to achieve racial harmony. Some individuals, such as Bishop Henry Turner of the African Methodist Episcopal Church, urged that Negroes leave for Africa. But few white Protestant leaders accepted this view. The Negro's home was in the South and he would remain a part of southern life. The churches generally frowned upon mass deportation, whether to the North or to Africa. [39]

In the eyes of the churches, the "racial inferiority" of Negroes by definition doomed them to second-class citizenship. If Negroes were inferior, how could they be expected to participate in the political process, to hold office or even vote? The argument against Negro participation in the legislative, executive, and judicial functions of society was similar to that against Negro participation in church government. The churches had uneasily watched Negro political participation during Reconstruction, and looking back they concluded that Reconstruction with its Negro ballot had been a mistake. In 1890, when Mississippi passed a disfranchisement provision, one southern churchman declared, "Giving the franchise to the negroes immediately on their emancipation was committing the estate to the child yet in his teens." [40] Since most church leaders could see little progress of Negroes since Reconstruction, they could easily support the disfranchisement movement in the South. "The Negro is not fit to rule, still less to rule white men," went the refrain.[41] Indeed, churchmen saw disfranchisement as a positive good, for not only did it remove the ballot from untutored hands, but it also removed the Negro from politics and agitation. Now unscrupulous politicians could not appeal to the Negro voter with ideas dangerous to the social order of the white South. Declared the *Alabama Baptist* in 1891, "The Southern whites and Southern blacks are getting along admirably, and always will, if blatant politicians keep hands off." [42]

Removed from political life, the Negro's "place" in the South was to be subordinate to the white; Negroes were a "people destined to work at manual labor, in the main." [43] Negroes had always worked in the fields and fulfilled the household tasks as slaves; why not continue these funtions in the post-bellum South, churchmen asked. "They cannot as a rule be legislators, nor even lawyers or doctors or teachers, except among their own people. The plainer service is, and must be, their lot for the time being," declared one religious educator.[44] To southern white churchmen, such a position of occupational subordination fitted the Negro's nature, and they thought that the Negro himself exhibited a willingness to accept the subordination forced upon him. The southern Baptists' Home Mission Board told the 1891 Southern Baptist Convention, "Nothing is plainer to anyone who knows this race than its perfect willingness to accept a subordinate place, provided there be a confidence that in that position of subordination it will receive justice and kindness. That is the condition it prefers above all others, and this is the condition in which it obtains the highest development of every attribute of manhood. Whenever it shall understandingly and cheerfully accept this condition, the race problem is settled forever." [45] The churches called for Uncle Toms — Negroes who knew their subordinate "place" and willingly accepted it. Militant Negroes demanding their constitutional rights were "agitators." The generation of the 1880's and 1890's regretted the days of Reconstruction when Yankees stirred up Negroes and Negro pulpits became political platforms. The kindly bonds between master and slave had been broken during Reconstruction as Negroes entered politics and freedom; southern churchmen longed for the humble Negro again.

Well into the 1890's many southern religious leaders still defended slavery and praised the religious instruction received by the slaves under the institution. Negroes had come from Africa as "barbarians" or "savages," ran the argument, and under slavery they had been introduced to Christianity and the white man's civilization. It seemed as though the Negro had learned only good habits during slavery and bad ones during freedom; freedom had turned liberty into license. The *Southern Methodist Review* summarized this view in 1887:

> But a new generation of negroes is already on the stage of action. They know nothing of the benefits and blessings of their fathers' estate in the time of slavery, and they hear many things which the lovers of strife and discord convey to them in a thousand forms of evil. To the extent that this younger generation is unacquainted with the past history of their race, will they be open to the cunning agitators' appeals and misrepresentations.[46]

It is not surprising that the churches defended slavery long after the Civil War. The southern Protestants' view of race relations changed little after 1865; segregation and Negro subordination merely replaced slavery under the philosophy of white supremacy. The religious community defended both the ante-bellum and post-bellum systems. Perhaps some southern Protestants were still rationalizing their own defense of slavery before the war. They believed that slavery was a benevolent institution even though God, using the Union Army as His weapon, had chosen to end it; slavery had served its, and God's, useful purpose.

The churches claimed a special duty to fit the Negro for his subordinate place in the South and to correct his defects. To the churches the Negro was not only innately inferior, but also un-educated, poor, and untutored in the ways of freedom. Church leaders were concerned, too, about Negro work habits and Ne-gro crime. The Negro, ran the argument, was in need of self-discipline, character building, and training in the habits enshrined by the Protestant ethic. Protestants admitted there was a race problem. The problem was, however, not segregation, discrimi-nation, or denial of democracy and Christian ethics; it lay in the Negro himself and his defects. If the Negro were uplifted through Christianity the race problem would be solved.

The church had a mission to convert the world, Negroes in-cluded. When southern white Protestants spoke of "carrying the gospel to the Negro," they were not talking of the social gospel or the gospel of brotherhood, but the gospel of piety and Chris-tian obedience. White churchmen were to teach the Negro a Christian's duty to obey, to become moral in personal conduct, and to become a useful worker. Then crime among Negroes would diminish. Their homes would be clean and stabilized by Christian marriage. Drunkenness would vanish. Frugality and the gospel of work would enter their lives. To fail to uplift the Negro might be a disaster to the South. The southern Baptist Committee on Missions to the Colored People said in 1890, "Their ignorance, superstitions, and immoralities tell upon us. . . . We must Christianize and educate them in self-defense, and all the higher motives of religion should impel us to cultivate this home field." [47] Many of the freedmen professed to be Chris-tians, but their preachers were poorly qualified and uneducated;

hence, it was the blind leading the blind. Their religion was too emotional, too primitive. Better ministers and better instruction in the Bible hopefully would correct this situation.[48]

This "pure gospel" would not only save the Negro's soul; coupled with segregation and second-class citizenship, it would also be the solution to the race problem as defined by southern white Protestants. Properly Christianized Negroes would not be agitators and would cheerfully accept their place. Thus, the right kind of religion would serve as an instrument of social control. The *Southern Presbyterian* summed it up:

> Would it [genuine piety] not regulate the dangerous influences of political power? Would it not restrain lawless freedom? Would it not promote industry and thrift? Would it not keep secular education from becoming an instrument of increased mischief? Would it not introduce into all social distinctions and their apparent opposites in the way of leveling principles, an element of true conservatism and genuine order? The negro may need some change in his political status, a better system of labor, or a different method of education. But he needs most emphatically the *influence of pure gospel truth;* its regulating, restraining, purifying, elevating power. . . . He has natural defects, and perhaps some physical disadvantages, as well as intellectual; but his chief disability is moral. He needs higher, purer, and stronger principle. Without that no other improvement would suffice. With it, all his present weaknesses would be diminished.[49]

Related to evangelism in the program of Christian uplift was education, particularly when under church auspices. Christian education was valid for all men, according to the churches, but for Negroes it was especially important in view of their socially disorganized state following slavery. They needed the restraint and proper values that Christian education and the gospel would bring. Church education for the Negro meant character building and the training of ministers, although white churchmen preferred industrial to academic education.

The leading southern religious spokesman for Negro education was Bishop Atticus G. Haygood of the Methodist Episcopal Church, South. Haygood was born in 1839 in Watkinsville, Georgia. Raised in a strict religious home, he went to Emory College and following his graduation entered the ministry. Sympathetic to the Confederacy, he served, like many ministers, as a chaplain in the Confederate Army during the Civil War. At the end of the war he resumed his activities in the southern Methodist Church and for a time served as secretary of the church's Sunday school publications. Strongly interested in education, he accepted the presidency of Emory College in 1875. While editor of the *Wesleyan Christian Advocate* in the late 1870's, he began to expound his views on Negro education and the race problem. Haygood expanded these in his book, *Our Brother in Black*, published in 1881. Though it was not a radical document, some Southerners attacked it; and Haygood, normally a popular preacher, was not invited for some months to fill a southern pulpit.[50] He spent the remainder of his life speaking and writing about the need for Negro education, serving for several years as general agent for the John Slater Fund, one of several groups supporting Negro education in the South.

Although Haygood's views were ahead of those of his fellow churchmen and were criticized at times, his church as a whole did not repudiate him. The General Conference chose him bishop in 1882, but he turned down the position. Elected again in 1890, he accepted and served until his death in 1896.

While accepting many of the beliefs of southern white churchmen regarding the Negro, Haygood set forth his own program to solve the race problem. He desired segregation in church and school and thought that Negroes generally should be limited to industrial education, though he did not totally exclude higher education for them. He did not, as some of his fellow churchmen did, dwell on the Negro's supposed innate inferiority. Though he thought giving the ballot to the Negro was a mistake, he urged that Negroes be educated so that they could be intelligent voters and citizens. He was a strong advocate of public primary education for Negroes and urged the churches to do more for secondary and higher education for them. Consequently, he was quicker than most to praise the work of northern missionaries during Reconstruction. He saw with approval that proper education might be a conservative force, and he stressed that Negroes needed opportunities to develop their abilities. Basically he was arguing for separate but truly equal treatment of Negroes and was urging his fellow Christians to use their missionary spirit, good will, and dominant position to aid, not degrade, their brother in black. He felt that the solution of the race problem would require much time, but he wanted the South, with northern financial help, to move ahead rather than stand still. Moreover, he did not hesitate to criticize the white South, particularly on the subject of lynching.[51]

During Reconstruction the southern churches had been suspicious of Yankee-controlled education. This hostility had waned considerably by the 1880's. One reason for the changing southern Protestant attitude was the changing northern attitude, which increasingly accepted the southern view of the race problem. The official journal of the southern Methodist Church in 1880 noted with relief that the "visionaries, the shallow enthusiasts" were leaving the northern Methodists' Freedmen's Aid Society.[52] Yet Yankee education could still send chills down the spines of some Southerners. After hearing a Negro speaker praise John Brown at the 1886 commencement of the northern Methodist Church's Clark University in Atlanta, the commissioner of education of the southern Methodist Church compared him to speakers from the southern church's Paine Institute in Georgia. "Such an utterance would never find expression from a pupil in Paine Institute," declared the commissioner; and he pointed out that Paine's graduates said things that would please any southern white audience.[53]

Moreover, indifference to Negro education was widespread. In 1895, on the death of the Reverend C. A. Stillman, who had led the southern Presbyterian Church in establishing a school for Negroes, the Presbyterian Executive Committee on Colored Evangelization noted, "There was much hard feeling toward the negro growing out of reconstruction. In the church at large, there was indifference and hostility to the work, and it was not regarded with special favor by his [Stillman's] own congregation." [54]

Some southern ministers' attitudes toward Negro education went beyond indifference; they actively opposed it. Samuel Porter Jones, perhaps the leading southern evangelist of the late nineteenth century, maintained that the best Negroes he knew had never attended school, and he did not believe Negroes had a right to enter the public schools. Such a view was in keeping with his general position on the race problem, for he was an ardent segregationist and racist. Jones, who was a member of the North Georgia Methodist Conference, once declared he had no sympathy with those who were "blubbering over the death of the miscegenationist, Fred Douglass, a nigger with a white wife." [55] Jones's attitude was typical of the strain of anti-intellectualism running through revivalism in the late nineteenth and early twentieth centuries. This anti-intellectualism was skeptical of the value of higher education in general and especially unfriendly to Negro education.

In spite of hostility and apathy toward Negro education and in spite of fears of Yankee influence in Negro schools, by the turn of the century southern churchmen were more receptive to Negro education. Bishop Haygood's philosophy no longer seemed radical, excepting his belief in the Negro's right to vote. The churches gradually moved into the Negro field, but their efforts were meager.

Immediately following the end of the Civil War, southern Methodists had called for aid to Negro schools, but not until the 1870's did the church begin to establish institutes to train Negro preachers. From these beginnings there emerged two Negro schools, Paine and Lane Institutes. Southern Presbyterians founded Stillman Institute for Negroes in 1878, though the school was constantly starved for funds. Southern Episcopalians supported Negro education through the American Church Institute for Negroes; however, this was not a large-scale effort. The southern Baptists were content to leave most of the responsibility for Negro education to the northern Baptists. They did run a few institutes for Negro preachers, but did not begin educational work for Negroes until 1913, when they opened discussions with Negro Baptists about the possibility of helping to support a Negro Baptist seminary. The race problem in general interested the southern Baptists less than other southern churches. Their rural, fundamentalist nature was probably one explanation for their lack of enthusiasm for any education, white or Negro. Moreover, they were convinced that the duty of the church was to save souls and not to dabble in political questions, though this attitude did not stop the church from dabbling in temperance reform. The Southern Baptist Convention summed up its position in 1905 when it declared, "It is no affair of this Convention to solve the so-called negro problem." [56]

Following the Civil War the southern churches established committees for Negro work and called for a continuation of their ante-bellum concern for Negro conversion, but the membership did not give much support to these committees and calls. In part the lack of support stemmed from the weak financial condition of the southern churches at the end of the Civil War. However, as the churches improved their financial status, they did not spend much for Negro evangelism. In part, too, the lack of a strong program was due to the Negroes' reluctance to work with southern whites. Furthermore, many southern white Protestants were simply indifferent to the program.

In the southern Episcopal Church the problem of Negro rights in the dioceses hindered Negro evangelization. A successful Negro proselytism would have complicated the problem by creating a large Negro membership requiring accommodation in the church. Lamenting the meagerness of work among the Negroes, one North Carolina Episcopal clergyman noted that the church gave more for evangelism among American Indians than among Negroes.[57] Southern Presbyterians faced the same question of Negro rights within the church. The Committee on Colored Evangelization noted that the limited success of its program was due to "apathy" in the church.[58] Even with the establishment of a separate Negro Presbyterian denomination the work of evangelism did not substantially increase. The evangelic southern Baptists aided a few Negro home missionaries, and for a time co-operated with northern Baptists in Negro work, but these activities had low priority in the church. Southern Methodists did more than the other southern churches. Working in co-operation with the Colored Methodist Episcopal Church, the Methodists steadily increased their appropriations for Negro evangelization.

There were, of course, individual churchmen who gave money to Negro schools and sometimes taught in them. Still others taught in Negro Sunday schools and occasionally preached to Negro congregations. The number of persons engaged in such activities was small, however, and on the whole the white churches put forth but a feeble effort to meet the religious needs of Negroes.

Accepting and advocating segregation and white supremacy in the South, most churchmen could see no injustice in the southern system of race relations. If anything, southern Protestant leaders were in the vanguard of those urging white supremacy and racial segregation. The one injustice that the churches did recognize was mob violence. The church press and church leaders universally condemned lynching, particularly after 1890. The Episcopal *Southern Churchman*, lamenting the increase in lynching, wrote, "Of late years some of the Southern States have gotten into a most unsavory condition, the very scorn of civilization and the sorrow of Christendom." [59] Such a comment was typical; churchmen depicted mob violence as "barbarous," "brutal," and an attack upon civilization and Christianity themselves. Mob violence was not condoned by the better elements of the South, the churches declared.[60]

At times the attacks on lynching were apologetic and pointed out that the North had lynchings, too, and should not condemn the South alone.[61] As for the cause and remedy, often the denouncers of lynching accepted the myth that most lynchings were prompted by the attacks of "Negro brutes" upon white women. Remarked one Louisiana clergyman, "White men don't commit such diabolical outrages. . . . Which would be worse, to have pure, good white women violated, outraged, crushed, blighted and ruined for life by the beastly negro man, or have one innocent negro man executed through mistake? . . . Mob executions are deplorable, but negro brutes' violating white women is infinitely worse." [62] That some churchmen apologized for lynching was not totally surprising, for the churches had sometimes defended the Klan and denied the existence of violence toward Negroes during the turbulent days of Reconstruction.[63]

Some felt that the remedy for lynching was quick enforcement of the law against Negro criminals. The Baptist *Western Recorder* recommended special courts, resembling military courts-martial, in rape cases.[64] Others suggested that white women be shielded from public testimony about the "unmentionable" crime that prompted lynchings. Still others urged enforcement of the law against whites who were guilty of mob violence.[65]

From the chorus favoring segregation and racial inferiority there were only a few voices of dissent that went beyond the moderate position of Bishop Haygood. At an 1882 session of the Church Congress of the Protestant Episcopal Church, the Reverend W. W. Williams of Baltimore protested against speakers who characterized Negroes "as a race devoid of almost every principle of humanity." [66] During the debates over Negro participation in southern dioceses of the Episcopal Church, Bishop Richard Wilmer of Alabama dissented from the southern bishops' proposals for segregation, told his listeners not to worry about the social relations of the races, and asked, "Why draw a color line and have a rainbow church?" [67] The Reverend O. Sievers-Barten of the Diocese of Southern Virginia echoed this theme when he criticized his own diocese for drawing the color line. Declaring the move to be an injustice to Negroes, he asked, "Is not our own indifference, our prejudice, our separation from them and their affairs, a sin to be accounted for?" [68] Some southern dioceses refused to draw the color line and exclude Negroes from diocesan affairs.

The leading critic of the South's system of race relations was George Washington Cable. Known for his contributions to American literature, Cable was also an active Protestant layman. A man who kept the Sabbath, regularly attended church, and wrote for Sunday school publications, he was in part motivated by religious humanitarianism when he spoke out against the South's race relations. Cable taught Sunday school at the Prytania Street Presbyterian Church in New Orleans and became a deacon in the church. He shifted into the Congregational Church when he moved to the North. In the 1880's Cable's pen and voice were active in exposing the fallacies in southern arguments. "The Freedmen's Case in Equity," "The Silent South," "The Negro Question," and other essays cried out against segregation and discrimination. In 1889, he felt compelled to speak out against segregation in his own church. So telling and prophetic were his arguments, based on logic, democratic principles, and Christian precepts, that they make pertinent reading three-quarters of a century later.[69]

Cable was a lone voice in the 1880's, however, and he was an unwelcome figure in many parts of the South. Churchmen sometimes branded him a traitor to the South and denounced his views. One minister wrote,

> George W. Cable and others may tell us many unpalatable truths about our treatment of the negro, but these truths do not help to the solution of the race problem. Mr. Cable is a renegade Southron living in the North, and feeding Northern fanaticism and in turn being fed by Northern flattery and money, which are evidently more to him than the principles underlying the race problem. . . . They [Cable and the like] hinder, but do not help us. . . . [They] are enemies of the negro, and not the friends of the South. They do not help the settlement of the race problem.[70]

With the removal of the Negro from politics and the widespread practice and acceptance of segregation by the 1900's, the churches felt less compelled to assert white supremacy; it was simply assumed. Methodist Bishop Charles Galloway summed up this acceptance in 1904, when he addressed the Conference for Education in the South:

> In the South there will never be any social mingling of the races. Whether it be prejudice or pride of race, there is a middle wall of partition which will not be broken down. . . . They will worship in separate churches and be educated in separate schools. This is desired alike by both races, and is for the good of each. . . . The political power of this section will remain in present hands. Here, as elsewhere, intelligence and wealth will and should control the administration of government affairs.[71]

Some churchmen noted that with northern influence gone it was once again possible for Negroes to work with their "best friends," the white Southerners.

By the time of World War I the southern churches had come to believe that the relations between the races were settled, with the Negro occupying a subordinate and segregated place, and that the southern solution was wisest and best for both races. Religious leaders more frequently criticized the inequities of the southern legal system and lynching and urged equal protection before the law for Negroes. The race problem — meaning the Negro's character — was not solved because the Negro still needed Christian uplift. "He must have moderation and self-control, to restrain the evil impulses and proclivities of the fleshly nature," declared the Reverend Arthur J. Barton, a Baptist minister, in 1913. Yet the same speaker noted the "lack of justice in the courts," and the "fiendishness of the [lynching] mob" that still plagued the South.[72] Furthermore, religious leaders noted that the products of Negro schools, especially church schools, were not dangerous but were useful citizens; hence Negro education was desirable. A Baptist leader declared, "These [Negro] leaders have never been arrogant, never presumptuous, never turbulent or self-assertive against the white race, but always patient, always respective, and their influence on their own race has been a potent good beyond measure." [73]

Shortly before World War I, the rumblings of concern for social justice for Negroes became more frequent in the South. A few ministers, churchwomen, and Y.M.-Y.W.C.A. groups began to take a fresh look at the social conditions of Negroes and to criticize some southern practices. Though these groups were only beginning their work around 1910, they contributed substantially to the interracial movement of the 1920's.

The expressions of concern for the Negro were in part a manifestation of some white Protestants' uneasy consciences about southern race relations. These expressions came at the end of a long period in which white churchmen had fully accepted racism. In the years after the Civil War the churches were in the vanguard of those urging second-class status as a replacement of slavery for Negroes. The churches themselves were among the first southern institutions to segregate. Following the war southern Protestants gave divine sanction to the Negro's new status. In their eyes the Protestant God was a racist God; few saw any incompatibility between white supremacy and Christianity. Many white church leaders urged decent treatment for the Negro and education for him, but they did little to ensure that their urgings would be fulfilled. The philosophy of Christian uplift as the solution to the race problem fell neatly into the white supremacy pattern, for Christian uplift implied that the Negro was the problem, not the white man and his treatment of the Negro. Not until the middle of the twentieth century was this conception of the solution seriously challenged by the white Protestant South.

3

The North Compromises

In fact, the more I see of conditions North and South,
the more I see that human nature north of Mason
and Dixon's line is not different from human nature
south of the line.　　　RAY STANNARD BAKER
Following the Color Line

After much discussion and amid some anguish, northern white
Protestants in the last quarter of the nineteenth century over-
came their earlier commitment to Negro rights. They came close
to accepting the South's "solution" to the race problem. The
northern churches compromised at various times. Some expanded
segregation in the church and school even before the end of Reconstruction; others waited longer, but they, too, succumbed.
The attacks on racial injustice, which in the 1860's had assumed
the proportions of a crusade to redeem the South, gave way to
new attitudes by the 1880's and 1890's. Education, the vehicle for
Negro mobility and equal participation in American society, began to change its emphasis by 1880; industrial education and
manual training, fitting the Negro for a subordinate role in society, became the policy of the northern-run church schools in the
South. In the 1860's the churches often pictured the freedman as
a heroic figure who was the equal of the white man, given equal
opportunity. Gradually this picture gave way to unflattering
stereotypes, and northern Protestants began to adopt practices
and attitudes not much different from those of their southern
brethren. By the time of World War I the area of disagreement
had narrowed considerably.

The secular developments and patterns of social thought of
those years affected northern as well as southern Protestants. So-

cial Darwinism, racism, and overseas expansion, including foreign missionary work, were among these influences. Other factors, too, were relevant for northern churchmen: the growing desire for national unity and reconciliation, the declining interest of the North in the race problem, and expanding interest in other social problems.

Northern industrialists wanted a stable South for investments and markets; hence, the arguments of Henry Grady had great appeal. Grady, editor of the *Atlanta Constitution*, told the North that the best way to achieve stability in the South, build a New South, and develop national harmony was to let the white South handle race relations on its own terms. Northern politicians sometimes wanted southern white support; hence, they were willing to let the southern whites deal with the Negro unhindered by northern interference. Although the road to reunion was often rocky and the "bloody shirt" was still waved, the North and the South were increasingly in agreement on the race problem. Northerners made compromises even before the celebrated one that brought Hayes to the White House in 1877. By the 1890's the Negro had ceased to be an issue in national politics; there were no election bills, force bills, or educational acts introduced after 1891.

The churches shared the mood of reconciliation. Before the war several denominations had split, partly over the slavery issue. Now factions in both the northern and southern churches desired reunion to form national churches. For a successful church union movement, compromises were necessary; in particular, northern and southern Protestants needed to agree on the status of the Negro within the church. By the turn of the century a growing number of northern Protestants were willing to sacrifice Negro rights to achieve church unity. This was apparent in the northern Presbyterian Church's union with the Cumberland Presbyterians in the first decade of the twentieth century and in the active negotiations over Methodist unity that began in 1910.[1]

The Progressive movement clearly demonstrated the North's

declining interest in the race problem and its preoccupation with other social problems. Some Progressives were racists and readily accepted segregation. A few defended the civil rights of Negroes, but most were not concerned with them. In the South, Progressivism was for whites only. Theodore Roosevelt, who occasionally spoke out for Negroes' rights, threw his lot in with the "lilywhite" delegations from the South at the Bull Moose Convention of 1912. Under Woodrow Wilson's administration, in the heyday of the reform movement, an executive order segregated Negro government employees in the use of certain facilities.[2]

The religious phase of reformism, the social gospel movement, shared Progressivism's concerns and neglects. When the churches turned their attention to problems of industrialization and urbanization, they turned away from concern for the Negro. There is little evidence that the social gospelers had much contact with the National Association for the Advancement of Colored People or the Negro protest movements.[3] Some social gospel leaders, such as Josiah Strong, were outright believers in Anglo-Saxon supremacy. In *Our Country*, Strong declared,

> It seems to me that God, with infinite wisdom and skill, is training the Anglo-Saxon race for an hour sure to come in the world's future. . . . The representative, let us hope, of the largest liberty, the purest Christianity, the highest civilization — having developed peculiarly aggressive traits, calculated to impress its institutions upon mankind, will spread itself over the earth.[4]

More often, the leading figures of the social gospel movement neglected the Negro's plight and concentrated their reforming energies on other pressing social problems. William Dwight Porter Bliss's *Encyclopedia of Social Reforms* devoted only a couple of pages to the race question. The *Encyclopedia* had no solution for the race problem except to urge that friends of humanity create a more friendly attitude toward the Negro.[5] Walter Rauschenbusch, dean of the social gospel movement, writing for a southern Methodist audience, said that, although no

solution to the race problem would be final unless it satisfied the
Christian conscience of the nation, the North could not solve the
problem for the South. So tough was the problem, admitted
Rauschenbusch, that he rarely mentioned it.[6] Washington Gladden, active in labor relations while pastor of the First Congregational Church in Columbus, Ohio, took a greater interest than
Rauschenbusch in the race problem and insisted that Negroes be
granted the right to higher education as well as industrial education. Yet Gladden accepted the turn-of-the-century view of Reconstruction as folly and apparently accepted segregation.[7] Lyman
Abbott went so far as to endorse the southern white approach to
race relations.[8]

When the social gospel movement reached an unofficial culmi-
nation in the founding of the Federal Council of the Churches of
Christ in America in 1908, the plight of the Negro was scarcely
considered. At the 1905 New York meeting leading to the founding of the Federal Council, only one of the many white speakers,
Bishop Charles Galloway of the southern Methodist Church, addressed himself to the race problem. Galloway was a firm believer
in Negro disfranchisement and racial segregation. Although he
denounced lynching, he emphasized that the church's main duty
in solving the race problem consisted of making Negroes Christians and giving them a Christian education.[9] At the 1908 meeting
in Philadelphia officially establishing the Federal Council, the
delegates totally ignored the race question. While the official
creed of the Council, which several major Protestant denominations adopted, covered certain social problems in detail, it
touched upon the race question only in a vague generalization.
We stand, declared the Council, "For equal rights and complete
justice for all men in all stations of life." [10] The Federal Council
ignored the Negro, except for missionary and educational work,
during the first decade of its existence.

If the proponents of the social gospel neglected the race problem, so did the great revivalists of the late nineteenth and early
twentieth centuries. Before the Civil War the evangelic tradition
was closely associated with the antislavery movement and social

reform. The later revivalists tended to shy away from reform movements and to identify themselves with social conservatism. The social thought of southern revivalists, such as Warren A. Candler, bishop of the southern Methodist Church, and Samuel Porter Jones, was colored by white supremacist attitudes. In the North, Dwight L. Moody, the famed Chicago evangelist, did not protest against the white man's treatment of the American Negro. When Moody held revival meetings in the South he did so on a segregated basis. On one occasion Negroes boycotted Moody's Chattanooga meetings in protest against the segregated arrangement. Years later, when Billy Sunday went south, he followed in Moody's footsteps and held segregated meetings.[11]

A final factor influencing the northern churches in dealing with the southern Negro was northern Protestantism's desire for expansion into the South among whites as well as Negroes. Not only did this bring into the churches new white members with southern attitudes, but it also created a problem in the relations of the Negro and white members in the South. Ultimately the churches had to choose between nonsegregation without white membership and segregation with white membership in the South; they chose segregation.

The most important aspect of the race problem directly confronting northern churchmen following the Civil War was racial segregation within the churches themselves. Segregation was a sensitive issue, for the churches had become keenly interested in the relations between Negroes and whites during the 1860's, and many churchmen had declared segregation a violation of the will of God. In the end, however, northern Protestants submitted to segregation, though they generally did not declare it was ordained by God or dictated by the law of nature. More often, churchmen argued for segregation on the ground of expediency or the supposed preference of Negroes for their own church organizations. Although Negroes sometimes denied a preference for segregation, white churchmen overrode their protests and chose separation. The churches had inherited segregation from pre-Civil War days; now they extended it, particularly into the sec-

ondary levels of church government — the geographical conferences and conventions.

The Methodists were the first to expand segregation. Their
surrender was especially important because over half the Negroes
belonging to mixed denominations were members of the Methodist Episcopal Church. The Methodists made some efforts to avoid
drawing the color line, but they gradually capitulated to a policy
of segregation in their annual conferences in the South and most
areas of the North. In the 1860's the northern Methodists had
provided for several all-Negro conferences at the request of their
Negro members. Whether to extend this arrangement to blanket
the South, where the church had organized mixed conferences
during Reconstruction, became an immediate issue as the church
expanded into the South. The desire for southern white membership was the deciding factor.

Although many of the Methodist preachers in the South were
originally from the North, the white congregations opposed
mixed conferences. Not even the forceful tactics of a Bishop Gilbert Haven checked the opposition. Haven insisted that southern
annual conferences under him be mixed and attempted to enforce
this policy by ordaining ministers in alphabetical order and by
administering the sacraments to whites and Negroes together.
Speaking of communion at one conference, he wrote, "I gave
them [the Negro presiding elders] the elements before taking
them myself, so that none should say I was not willing to do as I
would have others do." [12]

In spite of the efforts of Bishop Haven, white ministers and
laymen and some Negroes began to agitate for separate annual
conferences. Shortly before the 1868 General Conference, Negroes from the Kentucky Annual Conference, with white approval,
called upon the General Conference to establish a separate Negro
conference in that state. Concerned about segregation, the *Christian Advocate* declared,

> There is so much of a social character in the relations of
> members of the same local church, and of pastors and people,
> that it may be necessary to still indulge the social prejudice of

color in respect to these relations. But that consideration cannot apply to Christian ministers of the same Church. We
should pity the minister of the Gospel who should find it at
all difficult to sit down in the house of God with any other
ministers as his equals, without respect to race or color.

However, the General Conference of 1868 approved the Kentucky division.[13]

The next General Conference, that of 1872, debated the matter
of segregated conferences again. When the delegates discovered a
division among Negroes, they took no action. Amid much discussion the issue came to a head at the 1876 sessions. The General
Conference of that year passed a resolution declaring, "That
whenever it shall be requested by a majority of the white members, and also a majority of the colored members of any Annual
Conference that it be divided, that it is the opinion of this General Conference that such divisions should be made." [14] With this
green light, the Methodist conference system became segregated.
Although some Negroes protested, in the end they had no choice
but to submit. By 1895 all the conferences of the South were segregated. The Reverend Wilbur P. Thirkield, who devoted his life
to Negro education, said of the segregated conferences, "It is a
matter of history that in nearly every instance they [the Ne-
groes] were forced to a separation. The white man put in the
wedge and applied the maul. To preserve their manliness and self-
respect our colored preachers were sometimes fairly forced to
vote for separation." [15] The Methodists also used segregated conferences in the North, except for a few Negro churches, and
separation became the rule above as well as below the Mason-
Dixon Line.

Northern Baptists, not having a southern white membership,
managed to avoid segregation in the South. But they did not avoid
the race problem in the activities of some of their agencies. Discrimination practiced by the American Baptist Publication Society
and by the American Baptist Home Missionary Society strained
relations between Negro and white Baptists and gave impetus to a

movement among Negroes to form the all-Negro National Baptist Convention, Inc., in 1895. Thus, the northern white Baptists were partly responsible for furthering racial division within Protestantism.

Some Negro Baptists, who wanted freedom from white control, had already begun to question the motives of the American Baptist Home Missionary Society when the Society in the 1880's excluded them from participation in its management.[16] Then the American Baptist Publication Society withdrew an invitation to several Negroes to contribute articles to its publications. Dr. Benjamin Griffith, the Society's director, had withdrawn the invitations because Southerners were threatening to discontinue use of the Society's publications unless the invitations were canceled. Southern Baptists were especially irked because the proposed Negro writers had severely criticized the southern treatment of the Negro. One Virginia Baptist warned the Society against publishing articles by Negro writers who had "outraged the people of the South in language that should be condemned in any court of common decency." [17] The incident precipitated the organization of the National Baptist Convention, Inc., which then established its own publishing house.

The longest dispute over racial segregation occurred within the Congregational churches. Largely because of the opposition of the American Missionary Association, Congregationalists hesitated to draw a color line in the South. During Reconstruction some of the churches founded and financed by the Association included both Negro and white members. This was in accordance with the A.M.A.'s principle, "Slavery, caste, all distinctions in the church on the ground of color, race, nationality, or status are sinful and anti-Christian." In 1884 the A.M.A. refused to aid some white North Carolina churches that rejected the integration policy.[18]

Yet such a militant stand precluded the advance of Congregationalism among whites in the South, and Congregationalists, like other northern Protestants, had their eyes on southern white expansion. In the early 1880's the church's American Home Missionary Association (A.H.M.A.) moved into the South. Immediately a conflict developed between the A.M.A. and the A.H.M.A., particularly in Georgia. Members of the A.M.A. charged that the A.H.M.A. was fostering segregation by organizing all-white congregations in the same areas in which the A.M.A. already had churches.

The most vocal critic of the policy of dual congregations was the Reverend Horace Bumstead. Born in Boston, Bumstead was a graduate of Yale. During the Civil War he had commanded a contingent of Negro troops. After the war he graduated from Andover Seminary and taught at the A.M.A.'s Atlanta University. Eventually he became president of Atlanta, and in this capacity he was a strong proponent of Negro rights and opponent of segregation in churches and schools. When the possibility of segregation loomed, Bumstead asked, "Are Northern Congregationalists prepared to have this experience [of segregated churches] repeated throughout the South? Do they wish their missionary funds to erect a 'colored' church on one corner of the street, and a 'white' church on the opposite corner? Are they ready for the virtual establishment of a color line in our missionary operations?" [19] In the long run, the answer to Bumstead's questions was "yes."

In 1883 the two agencies reached an agreement stating that the South would be primarily the A.M.A.'s territory and that each agency would consult the other before moving into its area. In any case neither group would draw the color line in its congregations. The agreement never worked satisfactorily. The A.M.A. itself was willing to assist all-white churches in the South. The executive committee remarked in 1889,

> We have no principles which would prevent our aiding two churches in the same town — one with a membership of white, the other of colored people. We have done it. In our church work, we simply maintain that a Christian church should

stand ready to fellowship any one whom Christ fellowships,
that it should turn away no one because of his color or because he, his father or his mother was a slave. We maintain
there is no Christian reason why there should be either State
or local organizations of churches which will not fellowship
churches whose memberships differ in race.[20]

As whites would not join "Negro" churches and as Negroes
would not join "white" churches or were not welcome there, this
meant in effect that there were two sets of churches, though
theoretically all churches were open to both races.[21] Thus Congregationalists accepted segregated local churches; the battle
next shifted to the state and local conferences in the South.

Soon there were enough white churches claiming recognition
as Congregational churches that they could form associations for
church administration. The inevitable occurred: separate Negro
and white associations appeared in Georgia and Alabama. In
1889, when the all-white Georgia United Conference asked for
recognition at the National Council of the Congregational
Churches, the conflict was dragged into the church's highest
body, for the Congregationalists already had a Negro Georgia
Congregational Association covering the same area. A debate
flared. The tradition of local autonomy in the church complicated the issue. Some churchmen thought the issue could be compromised, especially in view of the tradition of local autonomy;
others took a different view and condemned any solution that
brought the color line into religion. George W. Cable, the inde-
fatigable critic of segregation and the South's racial practices, defended the latter view:

> But in the present case the Church is not put at issue with
> government at all, but only with certain usages and sentiments
> of private society, where in all questions of right and wrong it
> is the Church's radical duty to be the teacher, not the pupil;
> to pronounce, and not to yield or compromise. Neither have
> we here a case in which the conscience of the Congregational
> Church is not educated. For fifty years it has held that the

spirit of caste is unequivocally wicked, and a step backward
is a step fifty years back.[22]

In spite of protests by Cable and others, the National Council
agreed to accept delegates from both white and Negro churches,
on the ground that Georgia churches shared the Congregationalist belief in the "equality of all brethren in Christ," and "in the
expectation that they will use the uttermost of their endeavors at
home to realize and manifest the fact [of equality] in the promo-
tion of organic union among all Congregational churches of that
commonwealth." [23] A similar situation arose when two groups
from Alabama asked for recognition in the 1890's. The National
Council in this case refused to recognize either association and
advised the claimants to unite in one body.[24]

Whether in Georgia, Alabama, or elsewhere in the South, the
efforts for unity failed, however, and the Congregationalists
began to accept segregated conferences.[25] By the time of World
War I, the church had a system of dualism in the South. Declared the Commission on Missions in 1917, "We have churches
composed of Negroes and churches composed of white people
with their separate state organizations and schools of every
grade from kindergarten to college for both races." The Commission went on to point out that, though this situation was
not ideal, it was the way to better race relations. Said the Commission:

> It may be said at this point that Congregationalists have
> accepted the customs and judgment of the South concerning
> the separation of the races in church life, as in other depart-
> ments of community relationship. This is not mere deference
> to the sentiment of the region under discussion, but represents
> the deliberate view of our southern Congregational leaders of
> both races. In reaching this view they do not for a moment
> maintain that the matter of race relationships is in satisfactory
> shape either North or South. We are still at a depressing
> distance from the goal of brotherly feeling and brotherly
> helpfulness. But as things stand, such feeling and helpfulness

will be far more rapidly promoted through separation into race groups, than by an attempt to mingle the two, which is certain to prove inoperative and disastrous.[26]

Local church segregation was the basis for segregation in the conferences. Separate congregations existed everywhere, even in those northern areas where conferences were mixed. Here and there a Negro belonged to a local white church, but such cases were the exception, not the rule.[27] Nor did white congregations ever appoint Negroes as their ministers. No denomination had an official policy of segregation; some were officially on record against it. The Methodist Episcopal Church, for example, in 1884 passed a resolution stating that no one should be excluded from places of "public worship in any and every edifice of the denomination." But church resolutions are often meaningless in the face of social realities.[28] Four General Conferences later, in 1900, when a Negro delegate suggested that the General Conference declare itself in favor of establishing colored churches in northern cities for newly arriving Negroes, one member objected, "It strikes me, Mr. Chairman, that it would be very unwise for this General Conference to place itself on record as being in favor of this iniquitous discrimination between the races. It appears to me that these matters must be left to the good sense and judgment of the presiding elders and conferences in these cities and towns." [29] The matter was left to the "good sense and judgment" of local church officials, and segregation continued in the northern Methodist Church and in all of Protestantism.

When Negroes began to migrate to the North in great numbers just before World War I the churches responded by setting up special divisions for Negro work to organize Negro congregations in northern cities. Whites generally abandoned their churches in the face of a Negro influx into the neighborhood.

To segregated congregations and segregated southern conferences, the churches added segregated schools in the South and even some in the North.[30] In this case northern Protestants faced a dilemma. The schools established in the South during and after the Civil War quickly became Negro schools, though in some instances a few whites attended them. While these schools were intended primarily for Negroes, they did not exclude whites. Yet white students, for the most part, would not attend, even though educational facilities were lacking in the South. As a Presbyterian committee put it, "The door [of churches and schools] is freely open to all, and white and black enter it on the same conditions. If the whites are not represented in the church or school membership to any considerable extent, it is not because the freedmen allow prejudice of race to debar them." [31] Hence arose the dilemma. If the churches established other schools for whites they would be giving in to segregated education, a capitulation that some churchmen wanted to avoid. Yet if they did not establish separate schools for whites they would be neglecting to provide schools that were badly needed in view of the South's backward system of education.

The churches decided upon separate schools, though often both races technically could attend. The problem presented more difficulties for the Methodist Episcopal Church than for any other; the other denominations concentrated their efforts on the freedmen and established few schools for whites in the South. The Methodists had a substantial white following in the South and felt that something should be done to provide educational facilities for them. In 1880 the General Conference authorized the establishment of schools for southern whites "as can be done without embarrassment to the schools among the Freedmen." [32] This opened the door for segregation, but the church did not enunciate an official policy of segregated schools at that General Conference. It waited until 1884. Although the church then declared that no one should be denied admission to a church or school on account of race, it agreed to grant aid and recognition to the growing number of white Methodist schools. In deciding to assist white schools, the delegates proclaimed, "That the question of separate or mixed schools we consider one of expediency, which is to be left to the choice and administration of those on the ground and more immediately concerned." [33] The resolution gave tacit consent to local segregation. Several years later, the Board of Managers of the Freedmen's Aid Society did overrule the trustees of the University of Chattanooga when the trustees tried to exclude Negro students. The trustees claimed to be acting in accord with the 1884 resolution, but the Board said otherwise. The open policy was temporary, however; soon the church operated only segregated schools in the South.[34]

The most militant stand taken by a religious agency on the school issue was that of the American Missionary Association. The A.M.A. always maintained that its schools were open to all, even though it gradually set up separate schools for Negroes and whites. The Association insisted upon a "no caste" policy before it would furnish a teacher for a white school in Beaufort, North Carolina, in 1867.[35] Yet in the 1870's the leadership of the A.M.A. was moving toward acceptance of segregated education in the South.[36]

In the 1880's the Association began to work among mountain whites, especially in Tennessee and Kentucky. The A.M.A. insisted upon a no-exclusion policy, although only a few Negroes might be involved. When it opened a school in Williamsburg, Kentucky, the Association said that it would admit Negroes in spite of the fact that the school was instituted primarily to serve the predominantly white local population. Even when many whites left upon the entry of Negroes the Association refused to alter its policy. Eventually most of the white students returned.[37] In the long run, the A.M.A.'s schools in the mountain region became schools for whites only, because so few Negroes lived there.

Due to the fact that several of its schools for Negroes had a few white students, the A.M.A. ran afoul of southern legislatures. In 1887, a Georgia committee investigating the Association's Atlanta University discovered to its horror that several white students were in attendance. These were the children of some of the white faculty members who practiced what they preached. To remedy the situation, the Georgia lower house quickly passed the Glenn bill, which prohibited mixed private schools. Vociferous protests from the A.M.A. elicited a compromise.[38] The bill as finally passed by both houses allowed mixed private schools but cut them off from state aid. The Association stood firm, and President Horace Bumstead of Atlanta University managed to solicit extra funds to make up for the loss of the state's subsidy.[39]

The Association's militancy also brought it into conflict with the state of Florida several years later. In this case Florida prohibited the teaching of Negro and white children in the same building. This law would have ended white attendance at the predominantly Negro Orange Park Normal and Industrial School. When several teachers were arrested the A.M.A. challenged the law, and the courts declared it unconstitutional. The General Conference of the Methodist Episcopal Church supported the A.M.A. in this action. Although the northern Methodists had no mixed schools in Florida, they branded the law "repugnant to the genius of our Christian civilization." [40]

Berea College, another school founded by the Association, was not so successful in resisting the state legislature. The Reverend John Fee, an abolitionist, had founded a school in Berea, Kentucky, before the Civil War, but community hostility had forced him to leave and a mob burned the school. After the war, Fee and the A.M.A. returned and founded Berea College. Berea was unique in that it was a truly interracial college in the South, perhaps the only one by 1900. In 1866, when the first Negroes entered, half the white students left; however, they soon returned.[41] In 1904 the state legislature passed a law prohibiting mixed private schools. When the law was tested, it went to the United States Supreme Court. In 1908 the Court upheld the legislature, thus ending Negro attendance at Berea College.

Interracial schools were exceptional, however; in the long run the churches had to face the realities of southern life. Whether they took militant stands, as some of the A.M.A.'s schools did, or gave in more easily, the northern churches eventually adopted a pattern of segregation in the schools they supported in the South. The operation of segregated schools was recognition of the growing segregation of southern society in the latter part of the nineteenth century.

Northern Protestants also demonstrated their racial attitudes and practices in the struggle of Negroes to achieve high office in the churches. This struggle was important in the two denominations with an episcopal arrangement, the Methodist Episcopal and the Protestant Episcopal Churches. In both denominations Negroes sought the post of bishop, a position of power, influence, and prestige. Especially when the churches adopted segregation in their administration, many churchmen, Negro and white alike, thought that the only effective way to advance Negro church work was to have Negro bishops for Negro churches. In the last analysis, the growth of segregation made it possible for Negroes to obtain their own bishops.

The struggle for Negro bishops was basically similar in the two denominations, even though it was more complicated in the Episcopal Church. It began during the latter part of the nineteenth century and was settled in both churches at about the same time, 1916–20. Paternalism, prejudice, fears of racial mixing, and fears of constitutionally drawing the color line were all present in both denominations. Ultimately the churches found a solution that avoided writing segregation directly into their laws but allowed the tacit and unofficial practice to prevail.

In the Protestant Episcopal Church, the issue of Negro leadership was closely linked to the limited participation allowed Negroes in some southern dioceses. As Negroes organized their own congregations, Negro churchmen began to agitate for the elevation of a Negro to the bishopric to supervise Negro churches. Under existing church law individual dioceses elected bishops to supervise church work in their regions, which meant that a Negro bishop would have jurisdiction over both Negro and white churches. In those southern dioceses that excluded or limited Negro participation the election of a Negro bishop was impossible, but not even the most liberal northern diocese was willing to elect a Negro bishop under such conditions.

At the 1874 General Convention, the Diocese of Texas broached the subject of Negro supervision when it asked the convention to appoint a suffragan bishop for supervision of the freedmen. In another proposal Bishop William Whittingham of Maryland suggested the creation of special missionary districts and bishops for different races. The House of Bishops appointed a committee to report to the next General Convention on episcopal supervision for the freedmen.[42] At the 1877 General Convention, the committee reported that it was "inexpedient to take any action in regard to providing Bishops exclusively for persons of different races and tongues." [43] The General Convention followed this recommendation and took no action on the request for bishops for Negro work. In 1883 a memorial from the Diocese of Indiana urged that Negro bishops for supervision of Negro work be chosen, but no action resulted. [44]

As Negro leaders witnessed their own disfranchisement in southern dioceses and realized the impossibility of electing a Negro bishop, they dropped their opposition to the segregation of dioceses in the South. It was a strategic retreat. They had opposed the Sewanee plan providing separate and unequal status. If they now favored the creation of separate Negro dioceses or missionary districts, they insisted that these districts have equal rights with regular missionary districts.[45]

The Conference of Church Workers Among Colored People, which had been organized to protest the Sewanee plan, proposed at the 1904 General Convention that Negro missionary districts be established. The General Conventions of 1904 and 1907 discussed the plan, and in 1907 the General Convention rejected the Negroes' request on the ground that it meant separation along racial lines.[46] In place of the missionary district plan, several churchmen recommended the resurrection of the office of suffragan bishop.[47] The suffragan, an assistant bishop without the right of succession, would sit in the House of Bishops but would not be able to vote. Individual dioceses were to choose their own suffragans. Churchmen understood that the office of suffragan was being re-established in part to permit the election of Negro bishops. Furthermore, if a diocese elected a Negro suffragan, churchmen assumed that he would supervise only Negro work. Support for the suffragan plan also came from the West and the heavily populated Northeast; both areas wanted suffragans to help supervise expanding church work. These suffragans were to be white. Thus a coalition formed because the new position could fill two different needs. The General Convention of 1907 hammered out the suffragan proposal, which then became church law.[48]

Many Negro leaders opposed the suffragan plan. The Conference of Church Workers Among Colored People consistently favored the racial missionary district plan.[49] The Reverend George Bragg, Negro editor of a church journal, labeled the suffragan bishop "a suffering bishop." [50] The Negroes objected on several grounds. First, they maintained that the suffragan plan would not end the disfranchisement of Negroes by some southern dioceses; whereas separate but equal districts for Negroes would enable them to send delegates to the General Convention. They asserted that as long as segregation was an accepted and integral part of the church, it was better to have equal rights than no rights.[51] Second, the suffragan would lack the vote in the House of Bishops, which meant that a Negro bishop would be a second-class bishop. On the other hand, a bishop from a racial missionary district would be a voting member of the House of Bishops. Third, the local dioceses would elect the suffragan, which meant he would be chosen essentially by whites and would be supervised by the regular white bishop. In the South, where the suffragan plan was most likely to be employed for Negroes, nothing would guarantee his being able to vote in the regular diocesan conventions. In other words, the suffragan plan when used for Negroes would have the hallmark of paternalism, not equality.[52] The church instituted it nevertheless.

Several attempts between 1910 and 1913 to elect a Negro suffragan in the Diocese of South Carolina failed. Bishop William Guerry of that diocese requested the election of a Negro bishop, but his diocese after a bitter debate refused to heed his urging. The bishop assured his flock that there was no danger in a Negro suffragan: "If the Suffragan Bishop should become unruly or rebellious we could secure his resignation to the House of Bishops, as provided for by Canon, and retire him to a parish." He pointed out that the Negro suffragan would "have no seat or vote in this Council, and would not attend its sessions unless you invited him to do so." [53] His plea was in vain. One white priest, who wanted no part of either a suffragan or missionary district Negro bishop, termed the suffragan plan a "nefarious scheme against the social order of the South"; and he continued, "Ask your wife, or any good woman that you know, and she will tell you promptly enough that no Negro on earth is fit to be a Bishop in the Church of God. . . . The bestial nature, the ape . . . the satyr, that lurks in all men, is, relatively, larger and stronger and more dominating in the Negro, than in the white man." [54]

As no diocese elected a Negro suffragan, the question was brought up again at the General Convention of 1913. By this time the church was divided on the issue and unusual alliances had formed. Some southern bishops, especially those in the dioceses where Negroes were disfranchised, desired the suffragan plan in order to keep Negroes under white supervision.[55] Certain northern liberals also rallied to the suffragan plan because they feared that the missionary district scheme would write segregation into the church's canons. Bishop Arthur Hall of Vermont declared that he opposed the missionary district plan "because we feel that this would separate rather than unite races or peoples who ought to be made one in the body of Christ." [56] Other northern churchmen, wanting to help Negroes as much as possible within the existing framework of racial segregation, agreed with the Negroes in favoring missionary districts. Some Southerners sympathized with the Negroes' complaints; they supported a consistent policy of segregation, hence the "separate but equal" missionary district plan. Finally, some churchmen pointed out that Negro exclusion in southern dioceses would spread if Negro church work expanded.[57] The debate among white bishops, clergy, and laymen was not over segregation versus integration but over what form segregation should take. If Negroes were to have a bishop, he would deal with Negro work only, whether as a suffragan or missionary district bishop.

The House of Deputies and the House of Bishops did not agree at the General Convention of 1913; instead, they appointed a committee to report to the next General Convention. This committee reported to the 1916 sessions in favor of the missionary district plan. The majority pointed out that Negroes already had their own priests and congregations; hence, the proposed change would be consistent with church policy and "consistent with our unfailing methods of practical administration in the Church." [58] The minority report, reflecting both opposition to racial division and paternalism, objected to the missionary district plan on the ground that the church's mission was not "to minister to race pride or to foster race ambition, and deliberately write into her organic law a principle of division which tends to obscure the larger truth that 'God hath made of one blood all nations of men' and that 'in Christ Jesus there is neither Jew, nor Greek, bond, nor free.'" The minority also noted that the adoption of the missionary episcopate plan would preclude the suffragan plan; and if the church ruled out the suffragan plan, the minority added paternalistically, "The Negro himself would be the greatest loser by this policy of separation. He would lose what he now so sorely needs, the white man's kindly interest, advice and cooperation." Both reports were introduced and discussed, and the minority report prevailed. [59]

Between 1916 and the next General Convention, two Negro suffragan bishops were elected. In December 1917 the Diocese of Arkansas elected the Reverend Thomas Demby, and in May 1918 the Diocese of North Carolina elected the Reverend Henry B. Delany. Although the church created the office of suffragan bishop in part to solve the Negro bishop problem, this solution never proved satisfactory. Episcopalians elected only two Negro suffragans exclusively for Negro churches, and the church used the office primarily for the supervision of both Negro and white church work by white suffragan bishops. Southern whites had never been united on the issue, and Negro churchmen had generally opposed the suffragan plan. Negroes did support it once the church made clear its intention to use the suffragan rather than the missionary episcopate. However, as Negro church work lagged in the South and as the issue of disfranchisement in southern dioceses remained, agitation began anew in the 1920's and 1930's for the racial district plan. But the representatives killed it again at the 1940 General Convention, and after that time there was no attempt to create racial districts in the Protestant Episcopal Church.[60]

Because of the successful evangelism of the northern Methodists among southern Negroes, the Methodist Church quickly began to feel pressure for the election of Negro bishops. By 1900 Negroes comprised over one-tenth of the Methodist Episcopal Church's total membership. The church had first organized all-Negro annual conferences in the 1860's, and the 1876 General Conference sanctioned segregation in annual conferences. Yet white bishops presided over these Negro conferences. Negroes began to urge that Negroes be elevated to the bishopric to preside over their own conferences, and they were numerous enough in the church to state their case and participate in the debates.

A memorial to the 1872 General Conference requested Negro bishops. The committee on the episcopacy replied by saying that race and color were not barriers to the episcopacy and that only fitness for the office should be the criterion. However, the conference did not elect a Negro bishop. A similar request to the next General Conference produced a similar statement but again no Negro bishop was elected.[61]

The question of fitness was a real problem, for the standards for the Negro ministry were lower than those for whites. Because Negroes were rarely allowed an education by slaveholders and because the discriminatory educational practices of both the North and South after the Civil War limited their opportunities, Negro ministers were often poorly educated. During Reconstruction, white Northerners often filled Negro pulpits. But as the growth of Negro congregations was rapid and as Negroes were now free, Negro preachers, feeling the call, began to staff the Negro churches. With the establishment of Negro schools, such as Gammon Theological Seminary in Atlanta, standards improved among the Negro clergy, and Negroes produced leaders. The northern Methodists appointed Negroes to the various church boards, though their functions were limited to Negro church work. Hence the argument of fitness began to have less weight.

Negroes renewed their request at the 1880 General Conference, which turned the resolution over to the committee on the episcopacy. A large majority of the committee recommended the election of a Negro bishop; but the delegates, after a brief debate, decided to postpone the issue.[62]

For the next two decades Negroes introduced requests for Negro bishops at every General Conference. The church responded by passing resolutions saying neither race nor color was a bar to the bishopric. The delegates to the General Conference of 1896 went a step further:

> In the election of Bishops there should be no discrimination on account of race or color, but men should be chosen because of their worth and fitness for this position. In presence of this statement, often reiterated by various bodies of our Church, we believe the time has come when the General Conference may safely and wisely choose a Bishop from among our seventeen hundred ministers of African descent.[63]

Yet the time had not come when a Negro minister could muster the two-thirds majority needed for election.

By the turn of the century the church was subjected to various pressures. Clearly Negroes wanted bishops and clearly there were qualified Negroes. Behind these facts there loomed the whole issue of segregation and Christian ethics. According to the church's constitution, a bishop elected by the General Conference was eligible to preside over any annual conference, white or black. The lines of segregation within the church had become rigid since Reconstruction, and there was strong sentiment in the white annual conferences against Negro bishops' presiding over them. The church had reached a point where, as a New England

Methodist journal put it, "There is no likelihood that in our generation a negro bishop will ever be allowed to preside over a white conference. It is possible that a Conference of white preachers might, for once, request such an assignment for the sake of the principle involved, but we do not believe there are three Conferences in the denomination which would under any circumstances or pressure make such an administration by their own choice a possibility." [64]

There were ways to circumvent this problem. The church could choose a Negro bishop and allow the Board of Bishops to assign him to Negro conferences. This would have followed the unwritten law of segregation. Or the church could have amended its constitution explicitly to limit Negro bishops to Negro conferences. This choice, however, pricked the consciences of some white Methodists and ran into Negro opposition as well. The church toyed with both schemes and ultimately allowed the unwritten law of segregation to prevail.

Negro leaders at the 1900 General Conference again introduced a petition calling for a Negro bishop. To alleviate the whites' fears of Negroes' presiding over white conferences, the petition declared it would leave assignment "to the wise and godly judgment of the Board of Bishops to so assign him, as they do all others, to the people of the church among whom he may be of largest service and with whom he would be most acceptable." [65] When the delegates produced the usual pious resolution against discrimination in selecting bishops but still did not elect a Negro bishop, a switch in tactics was called for.

The 1904 General Conference passed an amendment to the constitution providing for the election of "Bishops of African descent," who had limited rights and who were limited to Negro conferences.[66] The amendment touched off a debate in the annual conferences, of which two-thirds had to give their consent before it could become valid. The amendment failed to win the required majority largely because of the opposition of Negro conferences. Negroes attacked it because Jim Crow bishops would not be admitted to the Board of Bishops and would not be

allowed to preside over the General Conference.[67] One Negro
summed up some of the opposition when he wrote, "The Southern States enacted the separate coach law, which is an abridgment
of a God-given right. Now what will the General Conference do
if this awful measure obtains? They will practically create in the
church of our choice an annex, and compel us to live in it as
Christians or members of the race or language church, which is
un-Methodist." [68] The 1908 General Conference, like its prede-
cessors, failed to elect a Negro bishop.[69]

After 1908, Negro opinion shifted; by 1912 most Negro leaders
were willing to accept a compromise written into church law,
though some still resisted the prospect of a legally restricted
bishop. Years of frustration had forced Negro Methodists to attempt a strategic retreat not unlike that attempted by Negro
Episcopalians. The General Conference of 1912, which again
failed to produce a Negro bishop, added momentum to this retreat
when a special committee reported that it was "not feasible" to
elect a regular Negro bishop and limit him by indirection to
Negro conferences.[70]

Shortly after the 1912 sessions, the *Southwestern Christian Advocate*, the Negro journal, began a movement for a compromise
amendment providing for Negro bishops.[71] An official gathering of two hundred Negro Methodist leaders held in Nashville,
Tennessee, in October 1914, unanimously endorsed the amendment.[72] Backed by this action, the Negro Mississippi Conference
proposed an amendment to the church's constitution to provide
for the election of Negro bishops for Negro conferences, but it
failed to win the needed two-thirds majority even though Negroes overwhelmingly supported it.

In spite of the failure to elect a bishop or amend the constitution, there was reason for optimism among Negro Methodists as
the 1920 General Conference approached. White leaders generally agreed that the election of a Negro bishop was desirable and
that a solution could be found that would keep a policy of segregation out of the constitution and still maintain it in fact. During
the opening days of the 1920 General Conference, William Lucas,

a Negro layman, called for a committee to investigate the need for Negro bishops. Attempting to avoid the involved amendment process and recalling the failure of past efforts to secure a Negro bishop through a constitutional change, Lucas declared, "We ask no statutory enactment. We do not ask you to disrupt the constitution. We simply ask that through the common sense of the Board of Bishops you make provision now for men of our own race to look after us in the future." [73] Taking their cue from this approach, and reversing the Conference's 1912 position, the members of the committee on episcopacy recommended the election of two Negro bishops, but on a separate ballot. The committee's chairman assured the delegates that the "unwritten law" of segregation would dictate proper assignment of the Negro bishops.[74] Following approval of the committee's report, the delegates elected Robert E. Jones and Matthew W. Clair the first two Negro bishops in the Methodist Episcopal Church.

Although the Methodists had chosen segregation, their solution was more satisfactory than that of the Episcopalians. To be sure, the Methodists confined the Negro bishops to Negro conferences, but Negro conferences had representation in the General Conference with equal rights, a situation unlike that of the Protestant Episcopal Church. And Negro Methodist bishops were full bishops and not limited, while Negro Episcopal suffragans did not have the right to vote in the House of Bishops. Another milestone was passed in 1928, when Bishop Robert E. Jones became the first Negro to preside over a session of the General Conference of the Methodist Church.[75]

Thus, from the congregational level to the office of bishop, northern Protestants had given in to racial segregation. Churchmen had instituted segregation before the Civil War, and they gradually extended it in the decades that followed. Protest there was, but the protest diminished, until, by the time of World War I, the churches had come to accept segregation as the normal pattern of race relations in their institutional life.

Although the northern churches were increasingly giving in to segregation in their own practices, sometimes over their Negro members' protests, this did not keep them from attacking racial injustice in the South and, on occasion, in the North. Interest in the race problem was waning in the 1870's and 1880's, but it was still strong.

Lynching and mob violence drew the strongest attacks from the northern denominations. Northern churchmen had condemned violence when Negroes were assaulted and Negro schools and churches burned during Reconstruction, and they continued their protests in the years that followed.[76] Not only did the church press and church leaders denounce lynching, but periodically the national conventions passed resolutions on the subject. The Methodist bishops requested that the 1904 General Conference condemn lynching, and the delegates passed a resolution calling for equal protection of Negroes' rights.[77] Northern Presbyterians and Congregationalists also denounced lynching and mob violence.[78]

The strictures of northern churches sometimes pointed to the forcible denial of the franchise to the freedmen and the policies of repression that were common in the 1880's and 1890's. Spokesmen from the various church agencies working with Negroes were particularly severe. Declared the *Baptist Home Mission Monthly* in 1889, "Unless they [incidents of violence] are stopped by the authorities in the several States themselves, the United States government ought, in order to protect its fair name, to demonstrate its power to protect its citizens, and, if necessary, declare martial law again." [79]

Such attacks did not endear the northern churches to the South. The southern churches were defensive about northern criticisms concerning the race problem and resented the Northerners' self-righteousness. They sometimes pointed out that discrimination existed in the North and that the northern churches were vulnerable on the segregation issue.[80] In northern eyes, the Civil War had vindicated the North, and northern churchmen were not reluctant to proclaim this demonstration of God's will. "The South must do right toward the Negro or perish," stated the Reverend J. C. Hartzell, later bishop of the northern Methodist Church, in 1879.[81] With the passage of time, however, northern attacks gradually weakened and became less frequent.

In the last quarter of the nineteenth century northern churchmen found it easy to criticize violence, fraudulent legal practices, and political repression in the South, but attacks upon segregation by Northerners were less frequent. Undoubtedly the reluctance of the northern churches to attack segregation was due to the fact that their own institutions were becoming segregated; hence, they were vulnerable. Then, too, the rash of Jim Crow laws came during the 1890's and 1900's, when northern churchmen had lost their militancy of the 1860's.

Nevertheless, on occasion, some northern Protestants attacked Jim Crow laws and practices. The Congregationalists' National Council in 1913, for example, passed a resolution criticizing President Wilson's orders segregating Negro employees in Washington, D.C. The resolution read in part:

> Therefore this Council views with profound concern the tendency to extend the principle of segregation in discrimination against the negro race. We regard this form of race humiliation as violating the spirit of the Constitution and opposed to the teachings of Jesus Christ. The Council, therefore, makes earnest and respectful appeal to President Wilson to use his authority to prevent any such humiliation of employees under the National Government.[82]

When one examines northern Protestantism's views on the race problem, one can see the difference from southern attitudes in the decades following Reconstruction. But one can also perceive the change in the northern position so much in evidence by the turn of the century.

Looking at the Negro following Reconstruction, few northern churchmen said he was the equal of the white man. Poverty, illiteracy, social disorganization, and emotional forms of religious observance were evident. Though enthusiasm for defending the freedmen and their capacity to learn waned after Reconstruction, the prevailing northern view held that the condition of the

Negro was temporary and could be explained by the African heritage and the evils of slavery. And did not the South still hold the Negro down? northern Protestants asked. Some believed in innate inferiority, a view that gained more acceptance in time, but most disposed of the question by stressing the Negro's background. In an 1890 editorial, which condemned Reconstruction as a period of a "political profligacy, a financial corruption, an ignorant demagogism, for which no parallel can be found in American history," which accepted segregation, and which urged the virtual disfranchisement of southern Negroes, the editor of the *Baptist Quarterly Review* still said that it was "unchristian and unscientific" to assert there was "permanent inferiority of any race." [83]

Even if the Negro were innately inferior, this was all the more reason for the white man to take up his duty. Said the Episcopal *Churchman*, "The colored people are and will be incalculably inferior in culture, in organization, and administrative power, and in all the inherited accumulations of a complicated civilization, to white people among whom they live." But the journal insisted that this meant the whites had a duty "of giving to the negroes all the benefits of the wider knowledge and experience of 'the superior race.' " [84]

Northern spokesmen were quick to point to the decline of illiteracy among Negroes and the increasing amount of property owned by them. With increased education and property holding, Negroes would take their place in American society, said the northern churches. To solve the race problem, the churches reasoned, the Negro must improve himself, but opportunities for improvement must be granted. Though the churches hedged on segregation and eventually accepted a "separate but equal" doctrine, they insisted that Negroes must have equal opportunities and rights. As the *Christian Advocate* put it in 1889, "As far as the colored man is concerned, that duty [of whites] is plain. Afford him every opportunity of improvement, and every right of a citizen, and the difficulties which seem so alarming will disappear of themselves." [85]

Even before the turn of the century, however, the educational and religious needs of the Negro — meaning Christian uplift — were receiving the greater emphasis; political participation, justice, and equal rights and opportunities for Negroes were being shuffled to the background. This meant that to northern Protestants "the race problem" was coming to mean the Negro and his faults, a definition similar to that given by many southern churchmen. Northern churches were in part accepting the southern arguments, in part re-evaluating their estimate of the Negro's potential, and in part losing interest in the problem. Though Northerners still protested against racial injustice, they did so less frequently and less vociferously by 1900. The denial of the franchise seemed an outrage in the 1860's and 1870's, and even sometimes in the 1880's; yet by the turn of the century this attitude was changing. Some churchmen held that the Negro should eschew politics and that educational and property qualifications for voting would be incentives for Negroes. In 1899, the *Congregationalist*, which had vigorously attacked the suppression of Negro voting in the 1870's, commented, "He [the Negro] will be wise if he holds in abeyance for the present his claims to political office and even his claim to citizenship. The disposition of the people of the United States is manifestly to limit suffrage to those who have some knowledge of the requirements of government and some sense of responsibility for it. The Negro who possesses his share of these qualifications will get formal recognition as a citizen on the same level with the white man, and if in some localities he does not get it actually, he may reasonably expect it in time." [86]

The Reverend Lyman Abbott was typical of those whose attitude toward the race problem shifted during the last quarter of the nineteenth century. Abbott spent his life involved in social reforms, including activities for the freedmen during Reconstruction. He had served as head of the American Union Commission, an agency devoted to education for southern Negroes. He had opposed segregation in schools and had favored equal rights for Negroes during the hectic days of Reconstruction. But

by 1900 Abbott had changed his mind. The American Union
Commission had opposed segregation in education, but Abbott
later wrote, "I no longer think it is inherently right that no one
should be excluded from a school because of his color. . . . [Jus-
tice] does not demand that they [equal educational advantages]
should be afforded under the same roof." Abbott also reached the
conclusion that the ballot for Negroes was a mistake. Accepting
the southern disfranchisement provisions at face value, he remarked, "Any man can vote, white or black, if he can read the
English language, owns three hundred dollars worth of property,
and pays his poll tax." [87] His belief that the white man's duty was
paternalistic made Abbott's retreat easier. As he put it, "My mes-
sage has always been the same; by so much as the white man is
the superior of the black man, by so much it is the duty of the
white man to minister to the welfare of the black man." [88] It was
the "white man's burden" at home.

   Along with the re-evaluation of the race problem and the Negro's potential came the shift in emphasis in the freedmen's aid
societies toward industrial or manual training, which was particularly noticeable in the 1870's. In part the change was due to the
fact that many of the Christian abolitionists who had gone south
in the 1860's were leaving or retiring from the societies. These
early crusaders had often joined hands with the Radical Republicans, had vigorously supported the Reconstruction Acts, and had
assailed the South's historic treatment of the Negro. The newer
staffs did not share the militancy of the original crusaders. Yet
even the old-timers began to lose interest in the plight of the
southern Negro. Perhaps it was psychologically impossible for
Northerners to maintain a crusade for a prolonged period. Then,
too, the depression of the 1870's hurt the aid societies, and stories
of corruption in southern Reconstruction governments influenced the thinking of many Northerners. In any event, the
freedmen's aid societies, which had been the backbone of Protestant militancy in the 1860's, began to accommodate themselves to
the New South and what it entailed for Negroes.[89]

The northern churches emphasized the manual training aspects of the schools along with their religious orientation. Speaking of Saint Paul's Institute, the Episcopal Church's "Tuskegee," the *Churchman* said, "The object of training at St. Paul's is to give the highest Christian education, coupled with a useful trade, in order that its graduates may go out and teach both the dignity of working with the hands and how to make good citizens and useful members of society. To do this, it makes Christian and moral training the basis, and upon this foundation builds the superstructure." [90] Manual training would give the Negro an appreciation of the Protestant ethic — hard work, thrift, and property ownership. The *Congregationalist* declared, "What the great mass of them [the Negroes] need is decent family life with orderly government of their children, industrious habits, skill to make themselves useful in departments of labor open to them, and ambition to save the money they can earn and to use it wisely. Their problems for the present are social, industrial and moral rather than political." [91] Once the Negro learned the virtue of toiling with his hands and accepted the gospel the race problem would be near solution. The churches were coming to picture Negroes as shiftless, lazy, immoral, a race in need of Christian uplift which the superior white man could give. Said the Baptist *Examiner* in 1906, "Which is better — that he should remain an ignorant, vicious animal, or be taught to be a self-respecting, cleanly, intelligent, helpful member of society?" [92]

There were church leaders after the 1890's who still championed higher education for Negroes, explained the Negro's "backwardness" as resulting from discrimination, sharply criticized the degradation of Negroes by white supremacists, and attacked segregation and discrimination in the South. The Methodist *Zion's Herald*, published in Boston, had been an abolitionist organ before the Civil War and had upheld the spirit of Bishop Gilbert Haven after it. At one time the journal suggested that southern representation in Congress be reduced in retaliation for Negro disfranchisement. In 1902, noting the plight of the Negro and the change in northern attitudes, the editor lamented, "It is only within the last few years that the conscience of the North, once so sensitive to the welfare of the Negro, has become so calloused as to slumber in indifference."[93] Less frequently, the church press or church leaders looked at the North or at the churches themselves and were appalled. The Methodist *Northwestern Christian Advocate*, which was published in Chicago, asserted in 1913:

> Separate sections in our cities, separate churches, and in some instances separate schools for separate nationalities or races, exist at the behest of race prejudice, and in turn foster and intensify that feeling. . . . If one cannot kneel down between a Chinaman and a Negro and pray the Lord's Prayer he cannot really pray it anywhere. . . . Exclusion of persons from occupations . . . from public institutions, from hotels and railway trains, from schools and Churches, because of difference of race is quite against the spirit of the New Testament and against all such distinctions the Christian citizen should cast his influence and his vote.[94]

Except for the remnants of the tradition of protest against racial injustice, the northern churches had come to share the northern mood concerning the race problem. Booker T. Washington expressed this mood, for he was the spokesman for compromise. The northern churches took the Washington solution and gave it a religious slant.[95] This meant accepting the Negro's second-class citizenship, both economically and politically. Northern and southern Protestants were not far apart on this subject by 1914. The northern denominations did considerably more than their southern brethren by way of evangelism and education for the Negro, but the northern churches' schools were also preparing Negroes for second-class citizenship by the time of World War I.[96] Although the northern churches were reluctant to justify segregation as compatible with Christian ethics, in their own practices they had given in to it. There was little contact between Negro and white Protestants except in northern state or regional conferences and at national conferences. This kind of contact was infrequent, and it was limited to the church leadership. Eleven o'clock on Sunday morning was probably the most segregated hour in America. Thus, in church practice northern Protestants had also moved closer to southern ways.

4

The Churches Edge Forward

The increasingly intolerable burden which discrimination is placing upon Negroes in the United States can
no longer be regarded with indifference by the white
church, nor can pronouncements discharge the responsibility.   TREVOR BOWEN
Divine White Right

On a warm July day in 1919, a Negro youth swam across an
imaginary line separating the Negro from the white swimming
areas of a Chicago beach. Whites yelled at him and some threw
rocks. Hit or not, the boy drowned, and the incident touched off
a race riot that rocked Chicago for nearly a week. When the state
militia finally restored order, 38 were dead and 537 injured. The
Chicago outburst introduced what one historian has called "the
greatest period of interracial strife the nation had ever witnessed." Another riot erupted in the nation's capital in August.
Even before the Chicago riot, racial tension had flared into violence at the end of World War I. Negro soldiers returning home
were even lynched in uniform.[1] The racial disturbances of those
years were a prelude to the 1920's, a decade noted for its racism
and the revival of the Ku Klux Klan.

The racial outbursts and rumors of more violence to come
helped to launch the interracial movement of the 1920's and
1930's, which affected both the North and South. The beginnings
of the movement go back to shortly before World War I, when a
few white groups and individuals became interested in the race
problem in the South and began to talk with Negroes. Several
foundations, the Y.M.C.A., the Y.W.C.A., and the Southern Sociological Congress promoted discussions of the race problem

between Negro and white leaders. Although nearly all ministerial associations in the South were segregated, here and there individual white clergymen met with Negro clergymen.

These pioneers were trying to bridge the gulf that existed between the races in the South. Sometimes the initial step consisted merely of Negroes and whites meeting to discuss the race problem. On other occasions Negroes addressed white groups. These modest steps were out of the ordinary, for few white groups consulted Negroes in those years. Katherine Lumpkin wrote of her experience at a Y.W.C.A. gathering, when a leader proposed that a Negro woman speak to the group on Christianity and the race problem:

> We were like a little company of Eves, who, not from being tempted — surely, we did not long to eat the fruit which up to now had been called forbidden — but by sheer force of unsought circumstances found ourselves called upon to pluck from the Tree of Life the apple that would open our eyes to see what was good and evil. But here confusion reigned. We had been taught it was wrong to eat this apple. Yet as it was put before us we felt guilty not to. Most certainly we were afraid to do it. Did we have the glimmering notion that if we did, something that hitherto had always seemed decorous and decent might, if our eyes were opened to see its naked reality, seem quite otherwise? [2]

Books and articles attempted to present to various white groups a sympathetic picture of the Negro's plight. Dr. Willis Weatherford, a student of Negro life in America and Africa, wrote about the social and economic conditions of southern Negroes for Y.M.C.A. study groups. The early leaders in race relations were concerned because whites tended to think of Negroes in unflattering stereotypes.[3]

Shortly after the war, a group of white Southerners who had worked with the Negro community during the war began meeting to discuss the race problem and methods of handling returning Negro servicemen. The lynchings and threats of racial outbursts that permeated the postwar atmosphere made the need for action urgent. The meetings held in early 1919 led to the formation of the Commission on Interracial Cooperation.[4]

Although the Commission did not spring from organized Protestantism and although the churches defended the prevalent views on the race issue, individual churchmen played an important role in the founding of the Commission and in its activities. John Eagan, a Georgia industrialist and prominent layman in the southern Presbyterian Church, served as president of the Commission. Plato Tracy Durham, another leader in the movement, was a Methodist educator and theologian. From the southern Baptists came the Reverend M. Ashby Jones of Atlanta. One of the Negro leaders was Robert E. Jones, the first Negro bishop of the Methodist Episcopal Church. The publicity director for the Commission from the early 1920's until it went out of existence in 1944 was Robert Eleazer, prominent Methodist layman and onetime editor of the journal of the Board of Missions of the southern Methodist Church. Will Alexander, an ordained southern Methodist minister, was responsible for the work of the Commission more than any other single individual.[5]

Born on a farm in Polk County, Missouri, in 1884, Will Alexander grew up in a community that had no Negroes. A few preachers, he later recalled, occasionally told "coon" anecdotes and he read the "Uncle Remus" stories of Joel Chandler Harris in the *Atlanta Constitution;* but Alexander had no firsthand experience with the race problem during his childhood. He studied at Scarritt-Morrisville College and then entered Vanderbilt University to prepare for the ministry. At Vanderbilt, Alexander took some sociology courses and occasionally attended a concert at Fisk University, but he recalled that he rarely, if ever, heard the race problem discussed among his fellow Southerners at Vanderbilt.

Although he was somewhat skeptical about his "calling" to be a preacher, Alexander entered the ministry in 1911. His first real contact with The Problem of the South occurred when, as minister of a small church in Nashville, he helped to organize unemployment relief for Negro and white workers. It was in Nashville in the spring of 1915 that Alexander began to wonder why his Christian responsibility should be for whites only. When he saw a white man beating a small Negro child, he felt a sense of outrage and tried unsuccessfully to take the man to court.

Promoted to a church at Murfreesboro, Tennessee, Alexander became involved with the juvenile court and Negro children. As there was no state institution for Negro children, the sheriff, when he arrested a Negro child, brought him to Alexander's house. Alexander then placed the child in a home in the Negro community. So many children were being brought to Alexander's home that the situation at Murfreesboro was getting out of hand.

During the years just before World War I, Alexander also began to read the social gospel literature and to reflect more seriously on the social implications of the gospel. When the war came he accepted an offer from John R. Mott to work with the Y.M.C.A. and army camps. Once again his work brought him into contact with the Negro community. Hopes that better race relations would prevail after the war were shattered when racial tension and rumors of potential violence plagued the South at the end of the war. A group of those who had been connected with Alexander during the war met in Atlanta in January 1919 to discuss the race problem; from this meeting emerged the Commission on Interracial Cooperation.

The interracial movement of the 1920's and 1930's, in which the Commission played a vital role, was essentially an attempt to provide a better social climate for American Negroes, especially in the South. The movement was often paternalistic and its goals were limited. It aimed at eradicating lynching, securing improved public facilities for Negroes within a segregated society, and portraying Negroes in a favorable rather than a derogatory light. So taboo was the subject of segregation that the Commission never attacked it. Once when Alexander was speaking at an interdenominational youth conference at Birmingham, he was asked whether he believed in repeal of Jim Crow laws. Alex-

ander's reply that he believed any unjust law should be repealed
brought violent protests and wild charges against him.[6]

The contacts between the churches and the interracial movement went beyond individual participation. The southern Presbyterian Church in 1921 endorsed the work of the Commission
and encouraged church members to work with it and its local
committees. The southern Methodists expressed similar senti-
ments at their 1922 General Conference, and other major Protestant denominations also endorsed the Commission. In addition,
various church boards and agencies gave it financial support.[7]

The most enterprising race relations work within the southern
churches was carried on by women. These women, especially
Presbyterians and Methodists, exhibited courage in facing the
race problem and were sometimes willing to ignore southern
taboos. They may have only scratched the surface of the problem, but they made important beginnings and were a good deal
ahead of — even in contrast to — the rest of the church. The
southern Methodist women were trying to increase contacts with
Negroes and improve their living conditions during the same years
when many laymen, ministers, and several bishops were stirring up
fears of "race mixing" and a "nigger church" in the controversy
over the unification of Methodism.

In 1920, the southern Methodist Woman's Missionary Council
invited Will Alexander to speak at its annual meeting in Kansas
City, Missouri. As a result of "Dr. Will's" prodding, the women
established a Commission on Race Relations under the leadership
of Miss Estelle Haskins and Mrs. Luke Johnson. These two
women attended the July 1920 meeting of the National Association of Colored Women's Clubs at Tuskegee, Alabama. So
unusual was a request by whites to discuss race relations that
when the white women approached the Negro clubwomen, the
Negroes thought there was a servant shortage! [8] As a result of
this meeting, and with the co-operation of the Commission on Interracial Cooperation, white clubwomen and churchwomen held
a conference at Memphis, Tennessee, in October 1920, to which
four Negro women were invited.[9]

At the Memphis meeting, the four Negro women, sitting in the front of the hall, told the white women about living conditions among Negroes and made an eloquent plea for justice. The meeting was a revelation to many of the churchwomen, whose only contact with Negroes was through their hired help. Many of them for the first time actually heard Negroes speaking frankly about the condition of southern Negroes. From the Memphis meeting emerged a broad manifesto for racial justice and the establishment of a continuing committee of women. The continuing committee became the Woman's Department of the Commission on Interracial Cooperation. State interracial women's committees appeared throughout the South, and churchwomen were often the backbone of these committees.[10]

When southern women formed the Association of Southern Women for the Prevention of Lynching in November 1930, under the leadership of Mrs. Jesse Daniel Ames, churchwomen participated again. They persuaded local sheriffs to take action to prevent lynching and solicited pledges to fight it. Sometimes they went into the field to help stop lynchings. Certainly their activities deserved some credit for the decline of lynching in those years.[11]

Not only did the southern Methodist women devote their energies to the founding and work of the Woman's Department of the Commission on Interracial Cooperation, but they also had their own race relations program. The Woman's Missionary Council of the southern Methodist Church had been interested in Negro welfare before World War I. In 1911, under the leadership of Miss Belle Bennett and Miss Mary DeBardeleben, the church's first deaconess to work with Negroes, the women established the first Bethlehem Center, a settlement house for Negro children, in Augusta, Georgia. The second Bethlehem Center, at Nashville, was established several years later, when a Negro woman called Mother Sawyer came to Miss Haskins, a teacher at the Methodist Training School, and described the condition of Negro children in the community. Upon hearing the Negro woman's plea, Miss Haskins agreed to help. She walked through the Negro section of town and selected the site for the Nashville Bethlehem Center. Teachers and students at the Training School provided the funds, including their Christmas money, to make possible the center's founding.[12]

During the 1920's and 1930's, southern Methodist women established other Bethlehem Centers, campaigned in local communities against lynching, and argued for better public facilities for Negroes. The Commission on Race Relations of the Woman's Missionary Council was busy throughout this period, and the Methodist women also established local interracial committees. By 1925, the women reported that a total of 571 interracial committees were active, that 11 clinics and 3 libraries were being run for Negroes, and that 2 kindergartens were caring for Negro children. The activities of the Methodist women extended to making surveys of the Negro community, agitating for improved health facilities for Negroes, and distributing and studying literature concerning race relations. The Methodist women also developed their contacts with the women of the Colored Methodist Episcopal Church. So active were the southern women that Mrs. Luke Johnson journeyed to the North to tell the northern Methodist Woman's Home Missionary Society what the southern women were doing and what needed to be done.[13]

The Woman's Auxiliary of the southern Presbyterian Church also participated in race relations work. In 1916, under the direction of Mrs. W. C. Winsborough, the "patron saint" of the Woman's Auxiliary, a conference was held at Tuscaloosa, Alabama, for Negro women. Encouraged by the results, the women expanded their activities and the state women's groups (synodicals) held similar conferences each year. By 1930, thirteen conferences were being held annually for Negro women. The white women partly financed these conferences, and interracial faculties taught Negro women how to improve their living conditions.[14]

The southern Presbyterian women, like the southern Methodist women, co-operated with the Commission on Interracial Cooperation. By 1927, nearly all of the synodical presidents reported that they were representatives on the state interracial committees. Several served as chairwomen of the women's divisions of the state committees. The head of the Woman's Auxiliary, the forceful Mrs. Winsborough, was a member of the Woman's Department of the Commission on Interracial Cooperation in Atlanta. Southern Presbyterian women also worked for better community conditions for Negroes, helped finance educational work for Negroes at the church's Stillman Institute, and helped organize church activities among Negro Presbyterian women.[15]

The activities of the southern Presbyterian women in race relations were in direct conflict with those of the church generally. The southern Presbyterian Church was a conservative church, both in matters of theology and in social Christianity. One wing of the church vociferously agitated for the denomination to withdraw from the Federal Council of Churches because of the Council's liberalism on social issues. In 1931 this group succeeded. While the women pioneered in race relations work, the church's General Assembly, an all-male conclave, as late as 1935 explicitly refused to recognize the Federal Council's Race Relations Sunday program, which was a modest undertaking, to say the least.[16]

Several factors explain the leadership of southern women in race relations during this period. The crusade for women's rights reached a milestone in 1920 with the ratification of the Nineteenth Amendment. In the 1920's women asserted their independence, and they participated more and more actively in all aspects of American life. Women were generally more active than men in church work, and in their study groups they had an opportunity to study particular social problems. This was especially true of the Methodist women, who had a well-developed study program. Of course in the early days the churchwomen only scratched the surface of the race problem in their study groups, but this was an important beginning. Over the years the women have continually deepened their studies of the problem. The nature of the race problem also influenced women, for many southern women and children actually witnessed brutal lynchings. Women had closer contacts with Negro women as servants in their homes. Finally, there is undoubtedly an element of truth in the saying that churchmen allow churchwomen to be their consciences.

While churchwomen's groups and individual churchmen were active in the South, northern churchmen were becoming involved in the interracial movement, though it was not so extensive in the North as in the South. The major church group dealing with race relations in the North was the Commission on Race Relations of the Federal Council of Churches. The Federal Council had had a Committee on Negro Churches since its founding in 1908. During World War I this committee merged with the newly formed Committee on the Welfare of Negro Troops.

The migration of southern Negroes to the North during the war demonstrated to some northern Protestants that the race problem was a national rather than sectional one. The outbreak of racial violence in the North in 1919 emphasized this. In the fall of 1919 a conference of Federal Council leaders issued a call for racial justice in America. Further meetings and discussions led to the formation of the Commission on Race Relations in July 1921.[17] The southern interracial movement influenced the Commission; Southerners such as Will Alexander and John Eagan assisted in formulating its early program. The first two secretaries of the Commission were Will Alexander and Dr. George Haynes, a Congregationalist who was the first Negro to serve in an executive position of the Federal Council of Churches. Dr. Haynes, the first Negro Ph.D. in sociology from Columbia University and one of the founders of the Urban League, thus launched an active career that lasted over twenty-five years.

Protestant churchmen and women, especially those connected with the race relations work of their own churches, co-operated with the Federal Council's Commission on Race Relations. Congregationalist leaders such as Dr. Haynes, Fred Brownlee of the American Missionary Association, and Dr. Allan Knight Chalmers, later defender of the Scottsboro boys, participated in its activities. From the Methodist Episcopal Church came men like Bishop Wilbur Thirkield, long-time educator in the church's

Negro schools and bishop presiding over Negro conferences. Miss Belle Bennett, Mrs. Luke Johnson, and Mrs. W. C. Winsborough, the crusading women from the South, were active in the women's work. As the denominations themselves generally ignored race relations, aside from missionary and educational work, the Commission provided denominational leaders with an opportunity to explore new approaches to the field. Many churchmen and women gained experience through the Commission which they later utilized in their own denominations.

Hampered by lack of funds, both in the 1920's and in the Depression of the 1930's, the Commission ran a limited program. Its aims were to educate the public about the race problem and to encourage Negro-white co-operation. The Commission embarked upon an active campaign against lynching and distributed literature condemning it. Co-operating with other agencies in the field of race relations, the Commission sponsored a national interracial conference in Cincinnati in 1925 and another in Washington, D.C., in 1928. It also urged the Federal Council of Churches to adopt resolutions on various aspects of the race problem, especially lynching and mob violence. In the late 1920's the Commission began the Harmon Award program, which annually cited outstanding individual Negroes and whites for service in the field of race relations. In the 1930's the Commission concerned itself with the plight of Negro tenant farmers in Arkansas and Alabama. It also sponsored Race Relations Sunday, which was observed annually on the Sunday nearest Lincoln's birthday. On that Sunday, Negro and white ministers exchanged pulpits. The Commission distributed literature in connection with this event.[18]

Following the establishment of the Commission, several northern communities set up race relations committees. Churchmen and local church federations participated in the formation of these committees, which often maintained loose ties with the Federal Council's Commission on Race Relations. Churchwomen in the mid-1920's organized a Woman's Committee of the Commission. This committee co-operated with the Commission but also had its own race relations program. The leader in the women's work was

Miss Katherine Gardner, a professional church worker of the northern Presbyterian Church's Board of National Missions.

Northern churchwomen, like their southern counterparts, moved forward in the field of race relations between the two world wars. Members of the northern Methodist Woman's Home Missionary Society supported the church's Negro educational work and homes for Negro working girls (Friendship Houses) in northern states before World War I, and the women expanded this work in the next two decades. Moreover, in 1923, the women organized a committee to co-operate with other church agencies in the field of race relations, notably the Woman's Committee of the Federal Council's Commission on Race Relations. Women such as Mrs. May L. Woodruff, Miss Muriel Day, and Mrs. Wilbur Thirkield, wife of Bishop Thirkield, provided leadership in the interracial work. Although the northern Methodist women were not so active in the interracial movement as their southern counterparts, they contributed more money to Negro education and welfare and opened several new Friendship Houses as well as welfare agencies for Negroes.[19]

Except for churchwomen, the denominations as such did little in the 1920's and 1930's to come to grips with the race problem and to change traditional attitudes and practices. The one denomination that developed its own race relations committee was the Congregational Church. The 1921 session of the National Council of Congregational Churches urged local churches to establish interracial committees, and it set up a committee to assist in this effort.[20] This committee co-operated with the Federal Council's Commission on Race Relations. It also distributed literature on race relations, worked with the Congregational Women's Home Missionary Federation, and sponsored seminars and meetings dealing with the race problem.[21]

In the late 1930's, at their national conferences, Congregationalists and northern Presbyterians began to hold special interracial meetings and seminars on race relations. A number of national conferences, especially in northern churches, established temporary race relations committees and passed resolutions dealing with the race problem. In the 1930's the social action groups of the churches also looked at the race problem, but they were more concerned with economic problems and were hampered by a lack of funds.

That a movement to improve race relations made any headway at all during the 1920's is perhaps surprising, for it was an era of bigotry and racism. The events of the decade were paradoxical in many ways. (In an age of wild speculation, for example, frugal Calvin Coolidge occupied the White House.) Even though social reform was losing its appeal, the interracial movement took root. This is not so surprising when one recalls that the social gospel movement virtually ignored the race problem. An interest in better race relations did not depend upon the type of reform of the Progressive era. Often those churchmen active in the interracial movement had been outside the turn-of-the-century social gospel movement.

Then, too, the very fact that the aims of the interracial movement were so modest enabled it to find some acceptance in religious quarters. The settlement of the Negro's "place" gave a degree of freedom to reformers, provided they did not challenge the basic settlement. Accepting segregation, the movement could work for the "equal" part of the "separate but equal" doctrine. Still, some churchmen were disturbed by the implications of the movement and most were indifferent to it.

The importance of the interracial movement should not be exaggerated. In certain respects it reversed the decline of interest in the race problem so noticeable in the decades preceding World War I. It certainly stood in contrast to the bigotry of the 1920's. It did involve many churchmen and women and church agencies, and it did prod the churches to look at the race problem in a new light. But the basic approach of Protestantism to a solution to the race problem still consisted of evangelism and Negro education. This "solution," with its paternalism and acceptance of segregation, remained intact until World War II.

When the churches looked at their social concerns, race relations had a low priority. The Federal Council of Churches did organize a Commission on Race Relations, but the Commission at first had to find its own money. In the years immediately following World War I, the churches exhibited more concern about the great fund-raising drives of that era. In the 1920's Protestants sometimes worried about flagrant violations of the Fourteenth and Fifteenth Amendments, but they gave much more attention to infringements of the Eighteenth. James Cannon, Jr., the powerful bishop of the southern Methodist Church, typified this attitude. While the bishop thundered for enforcement of Prohibition and energetically campaigned against the "wet" Al Smith, he said nothing about the right of American Negroes to vote. In the 1930's the main social concerns of Protestantism revolved around the Depression and the war in Europe, not the Negro.[22]

To be sure, the churches did issue many social pronouncements dealing with race relations and many individual church leaders spoke out on this issue. But one should be cautious in assigning much significance to such pronouncements. First, they did not bind individual congregations and church members; hence, they were not necessarily translated into action. Second, the resolutions coming from national bodies were usually formulated by the liberal clergy and laymen who tended at times to dominate such gatherings. Such statements did not necessarily represent the thinking of the rank and file. Finally, the pronouncements were often more significant for what they did not say than for what they said.

Lynching and mob violence drew the greatest attention from the churches. Major Protestant denominations in the 1920's and 1930's condemned lynching in strong terms. Although the northern denominations denounced it more frequently, southern groups also attacked it. The southern Methodist bishops in 1922 called lynching the "crime of crimes, which is not only a complete subversion of law but a stroke at the very life of law itself," and the General Conference of 1930, meeting at Dallas, Texas, assailed a lynching at nearby Sherman. On the other hand, Arthur Raper in his study of lynching noted that when lynchings took place, some of the clergy in or near the community involved, especially of the smaller congregations, either said nothing or condoned the violence.[23]

Moreover, when Protestants advocated a particular method to curb lynching, they tended to fall into line with regional mores. The northern churches favored federal antilynching legislation. The Congregationalists officially endorsed federal legislation in 1919 and again in 1923 and 1934, as did the major journal of the church, the *Congregationalist*. After many years of prompting from Negro delegates, and from the bishops in 1920, the northern Methodists at the 1920 General Conference urged federal action to stamp out lynching. Methodist leaders also spoke in behalf of the Dyer antilynching bill of the 1920's. Other northern church conferences and spokesmen endorsed the Dyer bill and the Costigan-Wagner antilynching bill of the 1930's.[24]

Those churches which had a large number of southern white members did not approve of federal antilynching bills. The two largest southern Protestant denominations, the southern Baptists and the southern Methodists, hoped that states and individuals would eradicate lynching; they did not support federal legislation to this end.[25] Nor did the southern Presbyterian General Assembly feel that an endorsement of federal action was called for. The Episcopalians pondered the Dyer bill at their 1922 General Convention. Although they opposed mob violence, the delegates did not consider themselves competent to decide questions regarding the constitutionality of the bill and did not support it. In 1934 the General Convention again condemned lynching, but the House of Deputies refused to back a federal antilynching bill.[26] Some southern churchmen and women, however, did favor federal action. The southern Methodist women, for example, endorsed congressional action to end lynching.[27]

Related to racism and lynching was the rise and decline of the Ku Klux Klan in the 1920's. Several historians have recently pointed out that there is little evidence to link the Klan directly with the Protestant churches, though some ministers joined it. One of the most recent writers on this subject has stressed that Protestant churches publicly and officially criticized the Klan.

Individual church leaders, the church press, and official pronouncements did attack it.[28] Yet the church's denunciations of
the Klansmen should be accepted with certain qualifications and
some explanation.

The Congregationalists and Episcopalians officially blasted the
Klan, and their press assailed it.[29] These two denominations
probably spoke more harshly against the Klan than did others,
but their theological approach and social-economic base differed
from the Klan's. Congregationalists and Episcopalians were usually middle class and were not inclined toward the evangelic style
of the Klansmen. The strength of the Congregational Church,
moreover, lay in regions where the Klan lacked members and influence.

The northern Baptists in their national convention of 1927,
after the heyday of the Klan, approved an attack on the Klan by
their Committee on Interracial Relations. Earlier, the *Baptist* had
assailed the Klan; it declared in 1921, "In the name of liberty, humanity, justice, Christianity and the principles of Americanism,
we must denounce this order as criminal and dangerous. No com-
munist conspiracy could be more so." [30] The northern Methodist
press and church leaders took the Klansmen to task, and the bishops denounced them at the 1924 General Conference. A resolution was introduced at that General Conference to place the
church on record against the K.K.K., but it was not reported out
of committee. The delegates did pass a more general, watered-
down criticism of the Klan. Two Methodist annual conferences
in the Midwest, where both the church and the Klan were
strong, passed resolutions against the K.K.K. and then quickly
toned them down. Ohio Methodists watered down their resolution because many of the "best laymen" were joining the Klan.[31]
Although the northern Presbyterian press and church leaders
criticized the Klan, the General Assembly said nothing.[32] Another northern denomination, the United Lutheran Church, remained silent on the subject.

In the South, the southern Presbyterians' General Assembly
remained silent on the issue of the Klan, and the fundamentalist

Presbyterian of the South, violently opposed to the Federal Council of Churches, criticized the Council for attacking the Klansmen and cautiously endorsed them. Said the journal, "So far as we have been able to learn, the leaders of the Klan are honorable men. They claim that the organization has only beneficent aims, looking toward the advancement of Americanism among the people." [33] The southern Baptists' Commission on Social Service condemned violence by masked men, but the church's convention made no pronouncement on the subject. The southern Baptist press sometimes avoided the issue and even occasionally endorsed the Klan.[34]

Perhaps the best example of Protestants' dodging the issue occurred at the 1922 General Conference of the southern Methodist Church, when Will Alexander tried to get the Methodists to go on record against the Klan. Alexander had been fighting a running battle with the Klansmen. On one occasion the Klan had tried to frame Alexander in order to discredit him but the attempt failed.

Alexander claimed that he had written a report for the Commission on Temperance and Social Service, attacking the Klan and ministers who joined it, which was to be given at the 1922 General Conference. According to his account, so many Methodists were affiliated with the hooded men that the church squelched the report. Alexander asserted that this discouraging experience prompted him to sever his official ties as a minister of the southern Methodist Church.[35] Whether many Methodists were joining the Klan, as Alexander maintained, is unknown. The General Conference did not discuss his report and the church made no pronouncement on the Klan at that or any other General Conference. Although the bishops singled out lynching in the episcopal address to the 1922 General Conference, they made no reference to the Klansmen. The Commission on Social Service, however, later attacked the Klan for a demonstration staged at Tuskegee Institute.[36]

Apart from their attacks on lynching and occasional denunciations of the Klan, the churches passed resolutions on various as-

pects of the race problem, and some church leaders and church
journals spoke out for racial justice. Criticisms of the American
system of Negro-white relations were stronger in the North than
in the South. Sometimes the churches called for equal rights before the law and for enforcement of the Fourteenth and Fifteenth Amendments. The Federal Council of Churches, for
example, made periodic pleas for the protection of Negroes'
rights.[37] During the Depression years, the churches occasionally
acknowledged that Negroes were the last hired and the first fired.

The southern churches were less eager to pass resolutions
concerning race relations; when they did so, the pronouncements
were usually vague and avoided pointed references. Southern
churchmen often denied the existence of injustice toward the
Negro and accepted the white southern view that race relations
in the South left little or nothing to be desired. Though this view
was perhaps more prevalent among southern Baptists than other
groups, almost all southern Protestants accepted the southern
practice of race relations.[38] A general survey by the Commission
on Interracial Cooperation of the situation in the South in 1922–
23 yielded a report stating, "The majority of the church people,
ministers and laymen, have only a slight conviction as to the implications of Christianity in this field. . . . We have not found
that ministers are better informed in this question than other
leaders and often [they are] not so well informed." [39] Nor had
this situation changed by 1941.

Yet even northern Protestants fell short of a full understanding
of the implications of segregation and racial discrimination. In
1940, the *Churchman* of New York noted, "There is too much
reliable evidence that Jim Crowism still colors our American democracy. In our churches, in our choirs, in our schools, in our
church hospitals, in our offices Negroes are still fighting for the
measure of justice which our Constitution guarantees to *all* citizens of our country." [40] Such utterances by the churches about
Jim Crow were rare. And sometimes in the 1920's organizations
that pointed to the denial of the American creed in practice, such
as the National Association for the Advancement of Colored People, were branded as dangerous, if they were mentioned at all.[41]

Protestants did exhibit a growing awareness of the Christian implications of the race problem, as evidenced by the interracial movement and the growing number of resolutions that touched upon racial justice, but a serious challenge to the racial situation had to wait until the 1940's. Perhaps the shortcomings of Protestantism may best be seen in the churches' failure to deal with segregation and discrimination in their own organizations. The trend toward segregation in church practices, which had been growing since Reconstruction, continued unabated during the 1920's and 1930's. Nowhere was this more clearly illustrated than in the Blackshear incident of the fall of 1929.

At the Sunday morning service on September 15, 1929, at Saint Matthew's Episcopal Church in Brooklyn, the southern-born and southern-educated rector, the Reverend William Blackshear, read a section from the church bulletin before he began the sermon. Looking over the congregation, which included a few Negroes, the rector declared, "The Episcopal Church provides churches for Negroes. Several of these churches are within easy reach of this locality. They are in need of the loyal support of all true Negro churchmen; therefore, the rector of this parish discourages the attendance or membership in this church of the members of that race." [42] A few Negroes had been attending the church for some time, but the growing Negro population of the Bedford-Stuyvesant neighborhood and the increasing number of Negro worshippers at Saint Matthew's prompted Blackshear's remarks.

This was certainly not the first time Negroes had been told that their presence was not desired in "white" churches, but Blackshear's method of printing the request in the church bulletin and reading it to the congregation created a sensation. The following Sunday 11 Negroes attended the service and police detectives stood by to prevent any demonstrations. The rector did not mention Negroes in his sermon, but he defended his action on the ground that although Christ preached "love for all, there were times when even Christ refused the company of certain people." Blackshear also insisted that he was a "friend of the negro" and believed that he had the "right to maintain the integrity of my church as a white church." He added that his policy was identical with that of the denomination, as the Episcopal Church established separate churches for Negroes. The vestry announced that it was "in harmony" with his policy.[43]

The leading Episcopal journal in the Midwest, the *Living Church*, thought that the rector had been wrong in this particular instance and that in certain cases Negroes should be admitted to white churches, but defended segregation in the churches, which was "done for the mutual comfort and well being of both [races]." [44] The *Churchman*, published in New York, denied that the Episcopal Church had ever had a practice of discrimination at the altar and, though disagreeing with Blackshear, thought that his critics were going too far in labeling him a "Jim Crow Christian." [45]

There were criticisms of Blackshear's action. The most severe stricture came from James Weldon Johnson, secretary of the N.A.A.C.P. Johnson called upon the vestry to demand Blackshear's resignation and protested to Bishop Ernest Stires of the Diocese of Long Island. The bishop explained to the N.A.A.C.P. that, although he disagreed publicly with Blackshear's action, he was powerless to remove the rector because under church policy this authority resided with the local vestrymen, who had already supported their minister.[46] Some of the clergy also protested Blackshear's conduct, but with the backing of his vestrymen, he won his point, at least in his parish.

Recognizing the widespread segregation within the Protestant churches, an interdenominational group calling itself the Conference of Younger Churchmen declared that one Brooklyn rector should not be singled out for criticism for having "done openly [what] many of us have tended to do subtly, though perhaps unconsciously." The forty-two younger churchmen, including some of the outstanding young Protestant leaders in the country, concluded by saying:

> If the Church seriously intends to make her congregations spiritual fellowships, she must look squarely at this by no means easy question of rendering it homelike to folk of

various races. We therefore think it behooves us and our fellow churchmen to re-examine the nature of the religion we claim to be universal, to study the situation in our neighborhoods, and to endeavor to create brotherhood worthy of the name of Jesus.[47]

The Blackshear incident proved embarrassing to some northern Protestants; similar incidents involved southern churchmen. In 1932, Dr. William J. McGlothlin, president of the Southern Baptist Convention, refused to attend a dinner in Rochester, New York, because a Negro clergyman was present. McGlothlin said that as "the representative of four million Southern Baptists" he felt it would be unwise to violate a southern taboo.[48]

Here and there Protestants did make some effort toward desegregation. In the Episcopal Church in 1931 the Diocese of Virginia removed its restrictions upon Negro clergy, though not upon laymen, at diocesan conventions. Four years later the Diocese of Southern Virginia followed suit.[49] Northern Presbyterians dissolved one of their all-Negro presbyteries, the Lincoln Presbytery in Kentucky, and integrated its churches into the regular geographical presbyteries. It should be noted that this presbytery was the only all-Negro one located in a predominantly white synod and that it was a small presbytery in a border state region.[50]

Northern Presbyterians also granted Negroes more participation at the top levels of church administration in the 1930's. The 1932 General Assembly increased by one member the size of the Board of National Missions and elected the Reverend Joseph W. Holley, the first Negro on a national church board of the northern Presbyterians. In 1933 Dr. Henry L. McCrorey, president of Johnson C. Smith University, became the first Negro elected to the Board of Christian Education. When John Gaston, the white secretary of the Unit of Work for Colored People, retired in 1938, he was replaced by a Negro, Albert B. McCoy, who thus became the first Negro to serve in a top administrative post in the church. Several of the predominantly white presbyteries of the North elected Negro moderators.[51]

The area in which the churches made the greatest effort to deal with their internal race problem in the 1920's, and especially in the 1930's and later, was that of segregation and discrimination at the national church conventions. This was a long-standing problem that came to a head in the 1930's and 1940's.

The Congregationalists had had a general policy for years of securing unsegregated hotel facilities for their Negro delegates, but their success was limited. At the 1927 meeting the delegates explicitly favored holding meetings in hotels and clubs where there was no discrimination.[52] This resolution did not solve the problem, for many hotels broke their agreements with the church committees when the delegates arrived. Such was the case at the 1931 gathering in Seattle, Washington. The problem could not be solved until the church took a firmer stand and instructed its committees to see that the policy was carried out. When the delegates to the 1931 sessions learned of the discrimination, they committed themselves to meet only in cities where reasonable assurance of nondiscrimination in hotels could be obtained, and they instructed the church committees responsible for arrangements to make preparations in advance to ensure nonsegregation. After that General Council meeting, the church was generally able to secure such facilities.[53]

Like the Congregationalists, the northern Methodists had a long-standing, vague policy against discrimination, which was sometimes ignored in the selection of meeting sites.[54] At the 1932 meetings several Atlantic City oceanside hotels refused to accept Negroes. Led by the Reverend Ernest Tittle, long-time crusader for racial justice and minister of a large church in Evanston, Illinois, several delegates moved to commit the General Conference to meet only in cities where equal treatment was possible. The General Conference passed the Tittle resolution even though some delegates said it was impossible to find such a city, others worried about the effect of this policy on unification with southern Methodists, and some bishops were privately critical of the resolution. The committee responsible for the next General Conference implemented the resolution, and at the 1936 meeting, held in Columbus, Ohio, there apparently was no discrimination.[55]

The resolution applied only to the General Conference, but the Methodist bishops had already decided upon such a policy before the 1932 sessions and the Methodist women adopted a similar one after 1932. In 1926, a Washington, D.C., hotel excluded the two Negro bishops and their wives from a social gathering of the bishops. When the white bishops learned of the reason for the Negroes' absence, they unanimously resolved not to accept invitations to future social gatherings of the board unless all the bishops and their wives were welcome. Bishop Francis McConnell, a leading proponent of the social gospel, remarked that if the bishops could not secure desegregated facilities, then they did not need banquets. In 1930, the bishops refused to use a Boston hotel's dining room that would not serve their Negro members.[56]

When discrimination occurred at a luncheon of the sesquicentennial celebration of American Methodism in Baltimore in 1934, a group of white leaders from the Woman's Foreign Missionary Society refused to attend and declared their accord with the 1932 General Conference resolution.[57] In 1941, the newly formed Woman's Division of Christian Service, the major women's organization in the united Methodist Church, committed itself to the nonsegregated policy and refused to hold a meeting in St. Louis when it was unable to secure nonsegregated hotel facilities for Negro delegates there.[58]

The northern Methodists' policy had to be renewed when they united with the southern Methodists in 1939. At the 1944 General Conference of the united church, Negroes encountered discrimination in Kansas City hotels. Bishop G. Bromley Oxnam and the church officially apologized, and the Conference set up a dining area at the rear of the auditorium where Tittle and a few other whites joined the Negroes in a special effort to demonstrate that the tables were not segregated. The delegates passed a weak resolution committing the church to meet "only in places where adequate and suitable entertainment can be provided for all." Subse-

quent General Conferences more specifically committed the
General Conference meeting to nonsegregation and nondiscrimination.[59]

While Congregationalists and Methodists were taking the lead
in securing nondiscriminatory facilities for national church gatherings, and while the Commission on Race Relations of the Federal Council of Churches was exerting its influence less publicly,
other denominations moved more slowly.

Discrimination at the 1928 General Assembly of the northern
Presbyterian Church at Tulsa, Oklahoma, prompted a vigorous
Negro protest. The Assembly replied by saying it hoped that in
the future "both groups may share in its entertainment" in the
South, but it did not promise to forgo southern meetings.[60]
When the 1932 General Assembly of the northern Presbyterian
Church accepted an invitation to hold its next annual meeting in
Texas, a Negro commissioner, who was an African mission-
ary, protested:

> He [the Negro] feels that to go to a town or city where the
> colored commissioners will be forced to be Jim Crowed and
> humiliated is not only to insult the colored commissioners and
> the people they represent, but that it is an insult to Jesus
> Christ and to God Almighty, for did not the Master say: "In
> so much as ye do this to the least of these my brethren, ye do
> it unto me"?

The church ignored his protest and planned the meeting for
Texas.[61] The 1933 General Assembly was later switched to the
Midwest, but this was done in the interest of economy forced by
the Depression, and not because of the discrimination issue. Although Presbyterians periodically proposed that the church follow the example of the Methodists and Congregationalists, it did
not adopt a policy like theirs until the 1940's.[62] On the other
hand, Presbyterian women took a forceful position concerning
nonsegregated facilities. With a nudge from the Negro women,
the 1938 national meeting of organizations of Presbyterian
women sought and secured a change in the policy of the inn at

Buck Hill Falls, Pennsylvania, and Negroes were allowed to stay there.[63]

Northern Baptists at their 1935 national convention passed a resolution urging that "Baptist conferences and conventions be held in cities where accommodations may be available to all delegates without racial discrimination." Yet at the same convention the delegates agreed to meet the next year in St. Louis, a Jim Crow city. The Baptists didn't make an unequivocal commitment to nondiscriminatory national meetings until 1949.[64]

Protestant Episcopalians, with their large southern membership, fell into line with the Methodists and Congregational Christians in 1940. Before this, in 1937, a prominent Negro clergyman, the Reverend Shelton H. Bishop of New York, asked why the church met in cities where discrimination occurred and pointed out that other denominations and groups did not meet in such places. The 1940 General Convention passed a resolution calling for nondiscrimination at its future meetings.[65] After that General Convention the church carried out this policy, although to do so, even as late as 1954, required dramatic action. In that year the presiding bishop, Henry Knox Sherrill, switched the General Convention from Houston, Texas, to Hawaii when nondiscrimination could not be assured in Houston.[66]

Most southern Protestant denominations did not face the problem of segregated facilities because they had no Negro members to speak of. The one major southern church with Negro members who came to the national conclaves was the southern Presbyterian Church. Of course desegregated facilities were virtually impossible to find in the South, but the southern Presbyterians segregated even their own conference ground at Montreat, North Carolina. When the General Assembly met at Montreat, as it often did, the Negro commissioners stayed in a separate building and ate in the kitchen.[67] In the 1920's, the southern Presbyterians did bring their Negro brethren out of the kitchen, but they ate at separate tables. Not until considerable criticism of the shabby treatment of Negroes was made in the 1940's did the southern Presbyterians hold their first desegregated General

Assembly in 1950, at Massanetta Springs, Virginia. The same General Assembly refused to establish a policy for future meetings.[68] Desegregation of Montreat remained difficult, especially because the commissioners did not have full control over the facilities there. Montreat was governed by the Board of the Mountain Retreat Association, which the General Assembly did not directly supervise. In 1950, the Board decided that future General Assemblies when held at Montreat would be on a desegregated basis but that Negro delegates were not to be allowed to attend the young people's conferences. Although some church leaders agitated for complete desegregation at young people's conferences and at the General Assembly, the church had not committed itself to such a policy as late as 1964.[69] The 1964 Assembly did go a step further when it stated that beginning in 1967 no meeting of the Assembly would be held in churches that normally barred Negroes. In January 1965 the church's moderator, Felix B. Gear, switched the approaching General Assembly meeting from the Second Presbyterian Church of Memphis, Tennessee, to Montreat because of segregation problems at Memphis.[70]

The interracial movement and the efforts of some churchmen to push the churches in the direction of nondiscrimination and nonsegregation in the 1920's and 1930's were counter to the trends that were evident before World War I. Significant though the gains were, they were limited, as witnessed by the attempts to solve the problem of segregation at national church conferences. By 1941, it was becoming increasingly obvious to many Protestants that a more serious appraisal of the American caste system, especially as practiced by Protestant churches, was needed.

5

A Nonsegregated Church and a
Nonsegregated Society?

> The undergirding philosophy of segregation is dia-
> metrically opposed to the undergirding philosophy of
> our Judeo-Christian heritage and all the dialectics of
> the logicians cannot make them lie down together.
> MARTIN LUTHER KING, JR.
> *Race: Challenge to Religion*

During the 1940's a number of leading Protestant denominations
began to attack the American color line and call for an end to
segregation. This was not an anomaly in American society; the
churches were in tune with a growing consensus about the race
problem.

During and immediately after World War II, Negroes as well
as other Americans began to point out discrepancies between the
practice and preaching of democracy in America. The monu-
mental Myrdal study, which clearly described a sore spot in
American life, was completed and published. Moreover, in various areas of American life, Negroes were encountering less discrimination than they had before the war.[1] Militancy on the part
of Negroes during the war was a critical factor in persuading
President Roosevelt to establish the Fair Employment Practices
Commission. By the early 1960's Negro pressure had developed
into a full-scale movement for equality. Because of the rapidly
growing Negro population in northern cities, the movement was
national and not limited to the South. Protestants and non-Protes-
tants alike generally conceded that the race problem was the most
important domestic social issue facing the United States.

One reason Americans paid increasing attention to the race

problem at home during the war was that they were fighting Nazi Germany, the power that glorified fraudulent racist doctrines. Critics of segregation and discrimination in the United States insisted that a war against racism abroad could not succeed unless America practiced genuine democracy at home. Traditional Western colonialism was also challenged during the war. Some political observers noted that most of the world's population was non-white. If peace were to be maintained in the postwar world, they said, racial discrimination and doctrines of racial supremacy must be discarded throughout the world and America must put her own house in order. The sale of Wendell Willkie's *One World*, which discussed some of these ideas, exceeded two million copies. Church leaders reflected this kind of thinking. Dr. Charles T. Leber, secretary of the Board of Foreign Missions of the northern Presbyterian Church, upon returning from a six-month trip abroad, wrote in 1942, "It is my conviction that, as Americans and as a Church, we have not yet learned our lesson from this war. We are still sure of our race superiority and of our reliance upon our materialism. We must eradicate this idea of our superiority or we will have before long a race war in this world." [2]

Within the churches themselves there were pressures for a serious reappraisal of the American color caste system. Many of those individuals and groups who had been working since World War I to promote harmonious race relations began to see that unless segregation were ended it was nonsensical to talk of equality, justice, and democracy. The logical implications of the interracial movement and the attacks upon some aspects of segregation and discrimination touching religious life led many Protestant leaders to conclude that the problem must be met at its roots. If segregation and discrimination at national church gatherings were unchristian, was not any kind of segregation within the churches also unchristian? Was not Race Relations Sunday, occurring once a year, somewhat ludicrous; should not good race relations be practiced every Sunday, indeed, every day? The few Protestants who had asked such questions in the 1930's began to gain adherents during the war. The Christian concept of the brotherhood of man had long been a part of the churches' attitude toward Negroes in America, but in the world of the 1940's it was becoming increasingly difficult for clergymen and lay leaders to reconcile racial segregation with this concept.

Another force within the churches, but related to the changing outside world, was the challenge of the Christian mission abroad. Missionaries began to point to the inadequacy of the old theories of the "white man's burden" and "Christianizing the heathen" for the world of the 1940's. With the Asian and African peoples asking embarrassing questions about race prejudice and segregation in America and with the new social science challenging the old racism, missionaries found themselves in an awkward position. A segregationist God was hardly likely to win adherents in a world predominantly inhabited by non-whites. This argument became even more crucial for the churches in the face of the rising nationalism of former colonial peoples and competition with communism, but it had been present at the time of the war and even before. One of the most famous Methodist missionaries, E. Stanley Jones, had preached in the early 1930's to southern audiences, telling them that the American caste system was the greatest hindrance to the spread of Christianity in the Orient. The veteran missionary to the Far East had even criticized segregation in the churches when he declared that Christ drew no color distinctions. He had suggested Negro membership in "white" congregations as an introductory step toward better racial understanding.[3] The need for Negro missionaries, which was becoming more strongly felt in the 1940's, pointed up the problem of training Negro clergy and stimulated debate over the wisdom of maintaining inadequate Negro seminaries and over the exclusion policies of white southern seminaries.

While Negroes were beginning to demand their rights and were moving slowly up the economic ladder during the war, churchmen, like other Americans, were looking ahead to the postwar world. In 1941 the Federal Council of Churches' Department of Race Relations inaugurated discussions about the race problem in America. Early in 1942, at the Department's urging, the executive committee of the Federal Council established a special committee on race relations in the postwar world.[4]

The Council chose Will Alexander to head this committee. He had left his active post with the Commission on Interracial Cooperation in the 1930's to join the swarm of New Dealers in Washington. He had also broken with organized religion, in part because he felt that the churches as institutions were sluggish on the race question; Will Alexander was a fiercely independent man, who could not adapt to the confinements of a southern church where community pressures limited the freedom of the minister. In spite of his withdrawal from the ministry and his disenchantment with organized religion, Alexander assumed the chairmanship of the new committee. He began to sound out churchmen in the fall of 1942.

After several years of study and discussion, the committee presented a far-reaching program to a special meeting of the Federal Council of Churches in Columbus, Ohio, in March 1946. The report pointed out that churches and church-related institutions were characterized by segregation, which denied democracy and the brotherhood of man. The delegates adopted the report and made this pledge:

> The Federal Council of the Churches of Christ in America hereby renounces the pattern of segregation in race relations as unnecessary and undesirable and a violation of the Gospel of love and human brotherhood. Having taken this action, the Federal Council requests its constituent communions to do likewise. As proof of their sincerity in this renunciation they will work for a non-segregated church and a non-segregated society.[5]

Although the pronouncements of the Federal Council of Churches were binding on no one, this declaration should not be dismissed too lightly. This was the first time in the history of American Protestantism that a major interdenominational group committed itself to fight the traditional practices of racism, practices that had existed since colonial times. It was only a question of time, given the pressures in the United States, before the major denominations would make a similar commitment and try to implement it.

The northern Presbyterians' General Assembly met right after the Federal Council's Columbus meeting; that circumstance gave them the honor of being the first denomination to endorse the resolution.[6] Their position was not necessarily more advanced than those of other northern denominations; immediately after the war the major northern Protestant churches adopted sweeping resolutions condemning discrimination and segregation in church life, and they endorsed the statement of the Federal Council. Perhaps the Congregational Christians and northern Presbyterians were more outspoken and specific than the others. The Congregational Christians approved the Federal Council's resolution at their first opportunity and declared,

> We repent of the sin of racial segregation as practiced both within and outside our churches, and respond to the mandate of the Christian Gospel to promote with uncompromising word and purpose, the integration in our Christian churches and our democratic society of all persons of whatever race, color, or ancestry on the basis of equality and mutual respect in an inclusive fellowship.

Baptists, Methodists, Episcopalians, and others adopted similar resolutions. Even the United Lutheran Church in America, with only a few Negro members and little historical interest in race relations, began to study the race problem and call for integration.[7]

During the 1940's and 1950's and early 1960's the northern churches expanded their pronouncements and sanctioned open housing, F.E.P.C. laws, the Supreme Court's ruling on desegregated schools in 1954, the sit-in movement of the South, and many other steps toward integration and equal rights. Theologians and seminary professors wrote books and articles attacking racism and justifying, in the light of Christian principles, the Negro civil rights movement.[8]

Southern churchmen and denominations moved more slowly in opposing segregation. Pressure from congregations limited the freedom of southern ministers. Some were forced to leave their pulpits because of their views on the race question. Following the Supreme Court's decision on school desegregation, the Reverend Robert Trotman of Lumpkin, Georgia, was asked to resign from the pastorate of the Brownwood Baptist Church for saying in a sermon that the Court's decision was just and right.[9] In the decade following the Court's decision and the Trotman expulsion, the list of southern ministers who were forced to leave their churches grew. The conflicts between congregations and preachers reached mass proportions in early 1963. In January of that year twenty-eight young white Mississippi ministers issued a statement through the *Mississippi Methodist Advocate* proclaiming their belief in freedom of the pulpit and opposing racial discrimination in Mississippi. Although this statement was merely a reiteration of the national Methodist Church's policy on race and freedom of speech, within six months nineteen of the twenty-eight ministers had left their churches under varying degrees of pressure. Twelve of the nineteen had left the state.[10]

Support for segregation came from southern ministers as well as from congregations. During the Montgomery bus boycott of 1957, the Reverend Stanley Frazier, a prominent Methodist minister in Montgomery, was a leading segregationist.[11] In June 1963, when a Negro was denied membership in the First Baptist Church of Houston, Texas, the Reverend Dr. K. Owen White, minister of the church and president of the Southern Baptist Convention, declared that the rejection was "in the best interests of the Lord's work."[12]

Such segregationist positions were becoming less common among the southern clergy by 1964. Most of them, at least the well-educated ones from the "respectable" churches, no longer actively supported segregation as being compatible with Christian

ethics. The situation in the early 1960's was in sharp contrast to
that of a hundred years before, when the southern white ministry supported the South's racial practices.

In spite of opposition to desegregation, southern denominations
gradually accepted it in principle. The General Assembly of the
southern Presbyterian Church passed a declaration against
discriminatory practices in 1954, immediately following the Supreme Court's decision regarding segregation in public schools.
The hesitancy of the southern Presbyterian Church was due
largely to the theological conservatism of that denomination,
its hostility to social Christianity, and its predominantly southern
composition. However, its committee on Social and Moral Welfare, formed during the 1930's and reorganized and renamed
the Division of Christian Relations in the 1940's, increasingly
pointed to the Christian implications of the race question. In a
report given to the General Assembly for study in 1949, the
committee asked, "Are southern Protestants to allow secular, non-
Protestant, and non-southern Christian forces to be the chief
instruments of justice in this realm today, or will they take their
place beside the other forces which are striving to guarantee all
men their basic rights?" [13]

Finally, at the 1954 General Assembly, the delegates approved
the Division of Christian Relations' report supporting the Court's
decision and declaring racial segregation to be contrary to the
ethical and theological teachings of Christianity. The moderator
of the church, Frank W. Price, declared, "I hope and pray that
Christians of the Southland will support and work for the removal of all racial segregation and discrimination because it is
right and democratic and Christian to do so, and because of the
witness we as a nation can thus make to the world." [14]

Although the southern Presbyterians had taken a stand against
segregation, the vote at the General Assembly was far from
unanimous — 236 to 169.[15] The opposition to desegregation in the
church was centered in the group that had begun in 1941 to publish the theologically conservative and lay-oriented *Southern
Presbyterian Journal*. The defenders of segregation generally ar-

gued that it was compatible with Christian teachings; that integration would lead to intermarriage, the ancient southern taboo; and that the church's mission was to preach Christian theology and not to dabble in social or political affairs.[16]

Following the recommendation of the 1954 General Assembly, various synods, presbyteries, and congregations studied the report. Those synods located in the border states approved it quickly, while several synods in the Deep South either voted to ask the General Assembly to reverse its position or tabled approval of the report and called for further study. The Synod of Mississippi called for a reversal; Alabama tabled a resolution calling for an end to segregation and decided to ponder the matter further. The Synod of South Carolina voted 125 to 80 to maintain segregation in the institutions under its authority. One presbytery and a few individual congregations also criticized the report.[17]

However, a majority of those synods and presbyteries voting on the matter supported the report of the General Assembly. Increasingly, larger majorities at the General Assembly endorsed desegregation and more synods and presbyteries sanctioned it.[18] By the 1960's, most of the leadership of the southern Presbyterian Church, especially among the clergy and women, were willing to accept the principle that racial segregation and Christianity were incompatible. Because of the opposition of a sizable minority in the church, however, translating the recommendation of the General Assembly into reality proved difficult.

The Southern Baptist Convention, the largest and most powerful of southern denominations, was more cautious than the southern Presbyterians in its criticisms of segregation. The Convention did not specifically condemn racial segregation in the churches as being incompatible with Christian teachings, and several leading southern Baptists defended segregated churches.[19] On the other hand, the Southern Baptist Convention in 1952 commended its seminaries for desegregating, and two years later endorsed the Supreme Court's decision on school desegregation as being "in harmony with the constitutional guarantee of equal freedom to all citizens, and with the Christian principles of equal justice and love for all men." In 1957, the Convention approved a report noting that Jim Crow laws could not solve the race problem. Two years later, the president of the Convention, Brooks Hays, told the messengers, "Whatever the individual Baptist thinks about legislative policy in this [race relations] field, it is apparent that scriptural support for state segregation laws cannot be claimed." [20] With the qualified support of southern Baptists, the official commitment of Protestantism against segregation was practically complete; the problem lay in implementation.

In an attempt to bridge the gap between Negro and white churchmen and to implement their resolutions, the churches established race relations committees, sometimes in conjunction with their regular social action groups. These committees and their programs had their roots in the interracial movement of the 1920's and 1930's and in the churches' long-standing work for Negro education and evangelism.

The actions of the Congregational Christian Church illustrate the trend toward desegregation. The American Missionary Association in the 1930's had questioned the moral and social effects of segregation. Taking note of Jim Crow in America, the 1939 report of the A.M.A. asserted that the "Fatherhood of God is a mockery and the Brotherhood of Man an unreality under such conditions." [21] Amid growing national interest in the race problem, the Congregational Christians' General Council approved a new program developed by the A.M.A. and the Board of Home Missions in the early 1940's.[22] The A.M.A. schools for Negroes were to be strengthened and adapted to modern needs. Perhaps of greater import was the special program to pioneer in race relations work in local communities. The church established a Department of Race Relations in the A.M.A. headed by the Negro sociologist and future president of Fisk University, Charles S. Johnson. Under the sponsorship of the A.M.A., several books and pamphlets were published, including Johnson's *To Stem This Tide*, an attack upon racial segregation. In co-operation with the Rosenwald Fund, a foundation with a long-standing interest in the Negro, the newly formed Department of Race Relations of the

A.M.A. published and distributed 1000 copies of a bulletin entitled *A Monthly Summary of Events and Trends in Race Relations*. The church aided several interracial churches and sent field workers to racially tense areas.[23]

At the 1946 General Council meeting in Grinnell, Iowa, the Congregational Christian Church voted to place a special emphasis on human relations during the biennium 1946–48.[24] This was the first time that any denomination decided to emphasize such activity. With the help of annual appropriations of $15,000 from the A.M.A. and the Council of Social Action, Congregationalists established the Committee on Church and Race under the Reverend Galen Weaver, who had had experience in interracial work in Hawaii. The director conducted local round-table discussions on the theme of the church and race; sixty-two meetings were held during the biennium. The committee also examined the employment practices of the denomination and questioned church-related colleges about their admission policies. Although the Committee on Church and Race had been intended to operate only for a two-year period, the church made it a permanent committee in 1948.[25] Various other northern denominations followed suit with race relations departments, committees, and commissions.[26]

Race relations work lagged in the South, but even the southern Baptists and Presbyterians began to move. Often they emphasized interracial co-operation rather than desegregation. However, this did represent an increase of interest in the race problem. The southern Presbyterians' Negro evangelistic and educational efforts had always been meager. In 1944, the General Assembly instructed its Home Missions Council to report to the church on the state of Negro work.[27] The resulting report recommended increased effort for Negro evangelism. After some discussion the Assembly created an Ad Interim Committee on Negro Work to make a more thorough study. This committee urged that greater effort should be made in Negro evangelization, that more money should be spent for the improvement of Stillman College, the church's Negro institution, and that Negroes should participate more in directing their own affairs. The program was one upon which liberals and conservatives could and did agree.[28] In 1952–53, the church launched a $2,000,000 fund drive for Negro work. Negroes were given more control over their own affairs as the old paternalism was modified. Eventually the question of segregated presbyteries and synods was raised and debated in the 1940's and 1950's, and, as a result, the southern Presbyterians moved to abolish them.

Southern white Baptists had never had much contact with Negro fellow Baptists. The church did give some money to Negro Baptist church work, and, in 1914, the Southern Baptist Convention had begun to support a Negro seminary. The contribution to this seminary was pitiful; not until the 1940's and 1950's did the southern Baptists take a hard look at Negro religious training and increase contact with Negro Baptists. Yet these modest steps did lead to the desegregation of southern Baptist seminaries. Increasingly, the Southern Baptist Convention's Christian Life Commission concerned itself with the race problem.

The trend toward more active interracial work and desegregation was also evident in the various interdenominational bodies and unofficial denominational agencies. The Race Relations Department of the Federal Council of Churches emphasized the training of community leaders in the interracial clinics that were developed in the 1940's by Dr. George Haynes.[29] In the 1950's the Department became more energetic in promoting desegregation. The Methodist Federation for Social Service, the unofficial social gospel arm of the Methodist Church until its decline in the 1950's, displayed increasing interest in the problems of racial discrimination and segregation. In the past the followers of Harry Ward and Francis McConnell had focused their reforming zeal on economic problems and international relations; the Federation said little about the Negro during the debates over unification of American Methodism in the 1930's. During the war the Federation became interested in the race question in the South, where segregation could scarcely be ignored. Resolutions poured out of the Federation's conferences, and the Federation enlisted Negroes. In 1948, the organization elected Bishop Robert N. Brooks, a Negro, as its president.[30] The Federation repeatedly called for an end to segregation in the church and pointed to particularly embarrassing instances of discrimination in church-related institutions, such as the refusal of the cafeteria in the Methodist Building in Washington, D.C., to serve Negroes, as late as 1947.[31] Small groups, such as the Fellowship of Southern Churchmen, provided interracial contact unobtainable within the denominations themselves. The Fellowship even purchased a camp site where interracial conferences could be held in the South.

In spite of the race relations programs and the many resolutions passed by the churches, Protestants encountered difficulties in implementing the manifestoes for desegregation. The preference for segregation of many local churches, the vested interests of both Negro and white ministers in segregation, the lack of communication between Negro and white Protestants, the voluntary nature of church organization — these and other obstacles lay in the path of integration. Because of these obstacles the color line still presented an agonizing contrast between practice and preaching, even though there was a fair amount of integration at the top levels of church administration.

The denominations with Negro constituencies placed Negroes in positions of responsibility. Frequently, however, the men in these positions dealt only with Negro work. Because of the formula of unification, Negroes in the united Methodist Church were guaranteed participation in the General Conference and in church boards and agencies. In the eight years following the unification of the northern and southern Methodists in 1939, the number of Negroes on the staffs of Methodist boards and agencies doubled and the number of board members increased from 81 to 100.[32] Several Negroes became presidents of church agencies. In 1964, the Council of Bishops elected Bishop Prince A. Taylor president designate of the Council. He was the first Negro chosen for that position.[33] Negro bishops began to preside over predominantly white annual conferences in the 1940's. The first to do so was Bishop Alexander P. Shaw, who by special invitation in 1946 presided over the New Hampshire Conference of

the Methodist Church. With the desegregation of northern Negro Methodist annual conferences in the summer of 1964, two
Negro bishops received regular assignments to predominantly
white conferences.[34]

In the Episcopal Church Negroes witnessed the elevation of
one of their race to a nonracial bishopric in 1962. In the fall of that
year, the Diocese of Massachusetts elected the Reverend John
Burgess suffragan bishop on the first ballot from a field of five
candidates. A Negro archdeacon who had already worked among
both Negro and white churches, Burgess's duties as suffragan were
to include supervision of both Negro and white congregations.[35]
This was ironic, for the position of suffragan had been created
nearly a half century before partly to allow for Jim Crow bishops.

Northern Presbyterians, having begun to elect Negroes to
serve on church boards in the 1930's, elected more during the
1940's. Judge Herbert E. Millen of Philadelphia in 1948 became
the first Negro member of the church's General Council.[36] The
Reverend Edler Hawkins, also a Negro, reached the top of the
hierarchy in the northern Presbyterian Church in 1964. In 1960,
the Presbytery of New York had nominated him for moderator
of the church. At the General Assembly, meeting in Cleveland in
May, he lost by a close vote, 471 to 469, to the Reverend Dr.
Herman Lee Turner, a white liberal minister of Atlanta, Georgia.
At the 1964 General Assembly, Hawkins ran again for moderator; this time the delegates elected him.[37]

Other Negro Protestants recorded similar "firsts" during the
1940's, 1950's, and early 1960's. In the Congregational Christian
Church, Dr. Percy Julian, the distinguished Negro scientist, in
1952 became a member of the executive committee of the board
of directors of the Board of Home Missions.[38] Protestant Episcopalians appointed the Reverend M. Moran Weston, a Negro
priest, assistant secretary in the Department of Christian Social
Relations. This was the highest administrative Episcopal office,
not limited to Negro affairs, ever held by a Negro.[39]

In the major southern church with mixed membership, the
southern Presbyterian Church, the barriers did not drop so easily,

though Negroes did receive more control over their own affairs. One embarrassing incident occurred at the 1942 General Assembly in Knoxville, Tennessee. The moderator of the church had appointed a Negro minister, the Reverend William C. Bouchelion, chairman of the Standing Committee on Thanks. His committee, however, refused to allow him to present its report. At the next General Assembly, held in 1943, several presbyteries expressed their disapproval of the committee's action, and the delegates expressed their formal regret that discrimination had occurred and called for every commissioner "regardless of race or color" to be "accorded the full rights and privileges of the Assembly." At that Assembly a Negro became chairman of the Standing Committee on Bible Cause and gave the report of his committee.[40] Negroes were elected moderators of the southern Presbyterian Church's presbyteries and synods, but as of 1964 no Negroes had been elected to the church's boards.[41]

When the churches tackled segregation in state conferences, presbyteries, synods, and associations in the South, they were less successful than they had been in desegregating their top administrative levels. When the Congregational Church and the Christian Church merged in 1931, southern Negro and white churches were placed in separate conferences, which remained separate as of 1965. The Methodist Church, to which more than half of the Negro Protestants in mixed denominations belong, was not able to achieve desegregation of its southern regional and state conferences.[42]

During the 1940's, the southern Presbyterians discussed the possibility of integrating the churches of their all-Negro Snedecor Memorial Synod into the regular presbyteries and synods. In the spring of 1950, Dr. Walter Lingle, president emeritus of Davidson College, urged integration.[43] The next year the General Assembly voted to dissolve Snedecor Synod. Its dissolution was carried out by the time of the 1952 General Assembly.[44]

In terms of church administration, however, the dissolution of Snedecor Synod did not mean the end of segregation. When the Snedecor Synod disappeared, the Snedecor "Region" appeared, under which Negro churches fell for purposes of women's work, student work, Sunday school work, and a variety of other church activities. When the church in 1952–53 began its $2,000,000 fund drive for Negro work, it was thinking in terms of developing all-Negro congregations.[45] In 1964 the church voted to abolish the all-Negro presbyteries, but left the implementation of the resolution to the local presbyteries and synods.[46]

Northern Presbyterians moved more slowly than did their southern brethren in dissolving their all-Negro synods in the South, of which they had four. In 1953 the all-white Oklahoma Synod recommended that it be merged with the small Synod of Canadian, a Negro synod overlapping the same area. The General Assembly approved the request, and the two synods became one in 1955. The 1954 General Assembly established the Special Committee on Segregated Synods and Presbyteries to work for desegregation of the other segregated synods and presbyteries. Although the committee made progress, its task was not completed a decade later.[47]

As of 1965 the Protestant Episcopal Church was the only major denomination with a sizable membership of both Negroes and southern whites that had achieved desegregation of its southern dioceses. The question of segregation in the South had been linked to the problem of Negro bishops; it had been "settled," though unsatisfactorily, in the second decade of the twentieth century. The solution permitted Negro suffragan bishops limited to Negro churches and segregation in some of the southern dioceses, but rejected racial missionary districts.

Negro Episcopalians in the 1920's revived the agitation for missionary districts in the South so that they could have the right to send delegates to the General Convention and bishops with more power than the Negro suffragan bishops possessed. Nothing came of these requests. The issue was brought up again at the 1931 General Convention, but the delegates postponed a decision and appointed a committee to study the status of Negroes in the Episcopal Church.[48]

The committee discovered disagreement among Negroes over

the best arrangement for accommodating them in the church, though the suffragan plan was found to be unpopular. Moreover, the committee questioned whether there was "some limitation in the Negro which makes him ineffective in the Episcopate," and recommended disapproval of the racial missionary district plan.[49] A study by Bishop Frederick Bartlett in 1935 for the National Council of the Episcopal Church revealed another explanation for the ineffectiveness of the Negro bishops:

> He [Bishop Demby] has been hampered in his work by circumstances beyond his control. At present he is not even consulted by Bishop Saphore [of the Diocese of Arkansas] on matters pertaining to the Negro work. I found that he did not even know what appropriations had been made by the National Council for Negro work in Arkansas. He may be lacking in initiative, but there has been little opportunity for him to demonstrate initiative in Arkansas. What chance has a Suffragan anyway? . . . The treatment [including a salary of only $1625 per year] of Bishop Demby has been nothing less than shameful. . . . We certainly cannot expect results when the Church hampers one of its principal leaders in this manner.[50]

Although the 1934 General Convention defeated the missionary district plan, it was reintroduced in 1937 and referred to the newly established Joint Commission on Negro Work. The Joint Commission noted that the suffragan arrangement could not be regarded as a "sufficient and satisfactory form of episcopal supervision," but it unanimously opposed the racial district idea, believing "that the ideal of the Church is not a policy of segregation, but a living principle of integration." [51]

Southern white churchmen, in whose region the missionary districts would probably have been established, continued to disagree on the plan's merits, but gradually they leaned toward acceptance of the idea. In 1938, the bishops of the southeastern United States rejected the missionary district plan. The next year they reversed themselves. Southern churchmen were apparently coming to the conclusion that it was best for the church to grant equal though separate rights to Negro churchmen. The church's voice in the South, the *Southern Churchman,* also endorsed the plan.[52]

The southeastern bishops carried their proposal to the 1940 General Convention. Although the Conference of Church Workers Among Colored People still supported the plan, the interracial Joint Commission on Negro Work registered its disapproval; and Bishop Demby, the only surviving Negro suffragan, argued against it on one of the few occasions in his career on which he spoke in the House of Bishops. Bishop Edwin A. Penick of North Carolina, one of the Southerners opposed to the scheme, said that the opposition of the Joint Commission on Negro Work was based on a survey revealing that most Negroes opposed the plan.[53] When the House of Bishops defeated the proposal by a vote of 54 to 37, the church finally rejected legalized diocesan segregation.

Negro Episcopalians were in a dilemma, hence their divided mind. In opposing the missionary district plan, they opposed a scheme providing them with Negro bishops and representatives at the General Convention. Yet if they favored the plan, it meant favoring constitutional segregation. The situation frustrated many Negro churchmen. After 1940, however, they did not resurrect the missionary district plan.

The defeat of the racial missionary district scheme increased the pressure to desegregate southern dioceses, although the General Convention in the 1930's declined to take legal action against southern dioceses that discriminated against Negroes. A commission of the General Convention reported in 1934:

> Whatever may be our differing opinions as to the equity or legality of his position [of disfranchisement] in the South, it must be recognized that there are practical difficulties which cannot be remedied by legislation. The question is a sectional one. It is not necessary to assume that this condition is hopelessly irremediable, or indicates any unfriendliness to the

Negro, or lack of interest in his spiritual welfare. May it not be assumed as possible that time will produce a status in which this condition will improve and finally be remedied? Not indeed, within a few years, but even if time is long and progress may be slow, no situation is hopeless under the guidance of the Holy Spirit. It would seem to be questionable wisdom to insist in our legislation upon a remedy for what is considered a defect in the Church's policy, but which exists only in so small a part of the Church. Is it wise to pass general laws to apply only to special and sectional conditions? [54]

Several southern dioceses removed their restrictions on Negroes in the 1930's; several more followed suit in the 1940's.[55] By 1953, the Diocese of South Carolina was the only diocese of the Episcopal Church still restricting the rights of its Negro churches. The diocese had tried on several occasions to amend its constitution to allow Negro participation, but the second reading, required for constitutional changes, proved an impossible hurdle. When it was pointed out that an amendment was unnecessary because the constitution did not use the words "white" or "colored," the delegates to the 1953 convention issued an invitation to Negro churches to participate in the diocesan conventions on the same basis as white churches, thus ending the restrictions on Negro churches in all the dioceses of the Episcopal Church.[56]

The matter of Negro participation at the church's General Convention was also resolved in the 1940's and 1950's. Increasingly, dioceses in both the North and South sent Negroes as part of their delegations to the triennial meetings.[57]

The question of segregation and discrimination in church-related institutions was another testing ground for church pronouncements, but denominational control over church-related institutions varied. Perhaps the institutions most directly controlled by the denominations were their seminaries. In desegregating their seminaries the churches demonstrated their involvement in the social environment, for desegregation of higher education in the South was a movement affecting public and private, religious and secular, institutions alike. Beginning in the 1930's, the National Association for the Advancement of Colored People won cases in the Supreme Court opening the doors of public higher education in the South. At the same time a few private schools dropped their bars against Negroes. Seminaries were in this category.

Related to desegregation of white seminaries was the problem of justifying the existence of all-Negro theological schools. Several northern denominations had seminaries in the South, dating back to Reconstruction days, for the education of Negro clergymen. Some churchmen maintained that because of the cultural conditions peculiar to the Negro church and community, Negro ministers required special training available only in these exclusively Negro seminaries. Then, too, if white divinity schools in the South opened their doors to Negroes, the question remained whether Negroes, with their generally poor academic backgrounds, could meet the entrance requirements. Church leaders were unable to ignore the fact that the educational level of Negro ministers was below that of white ministers. The disparate educational levels made it hard to develop a truly interracial ministry. To close the Negro seminaries would be to eliminate a source of trained clergymen, who were badly needed. Thus, even churchmen interested in desegregation of theological schools found strong arguments against closing the all-Negro seminaries.

In the 1930's, when pressure began, on a modest scale, to desegregate higher education in the American South, several white seminaries dropped their color bars. Eden's Seminary of the Evangelical and Reformed Church in St. Louis became the first private school of higher education in Missouri to admit Negroes. The southern Presbyterian Church's Union Theological Seminary at Richmond, Virginia, admitted a few Negroes for graduate study.[58] A full-scale effort to change the admission policies of southern seminaries did not begin, however, until the 1940's.

Southern Presbyterians discussed desegregation of their divinity schools in the 1940's, and one by one the church's seminaries began to admit Negro students. By 1951, all of them were deseg-

regated. Another southern denomination, the Southern Baptist
Convention, also dropped racial barriers in the 1940's and 1950's.[59]
The admission of Negro students did not necessarily mean that
they were entitled to use all the facilities of the school immediately; it was only a step in that direction.

One factor hastening desegregation among southern Baptists
and Presbyterians was the lack of alternatives for training Negro
ministers. The southern Baptists did support a Negro theological
school in conjunction with the all-Negro National Baptist Convention, Inc., but this was hardly adequate to train a large number
of Negro ministers. The southern Presbyterians supported Stillman Institute for the training of Negro ministers. Stillman, never
an accredited divinity school, was also inadequate.

Episcopalians encountered knotty problems in desegregating
their seminaries. All-Negro Payne Divinity School at Petersburg,
Virginia, was the Episcopal Church's only southern school of
religion open to Negroes. In 1938, the bishops of the southeastern
section of the United States, dissatisfied with the facilities and
training offered by Payne, recommended its removal to the vicin-
ity of Saint Augustine College, an Episcopal college for Negroes in
Raleigh, North Carolina. As the seminary had only twelve pupils
and was ill-equipped, some thought it should be closed. Although
Negroes were increasingly critical of the facilities of Payne and
of the whole concept of segregated education, the church decided to keep Payne at Petersburg.[60] However, little was done to
help it financially.

The question arose again immediately after the war, when
Episcopalians slated $200,000 from their postwar Reconstruction
and Advance Fund for Payne. As criticism mounted, as various
parties disagreed over Payne's future, and as Payne's enrollment
dropped, the church's National Council decided to investigate the
whole matter.[61] In the end, the fate of Payne was decided by the
Negroes themselves. When no new students entered the school in
1948, the whole question became academic. Upon the recommendation of the American Church Institute for Negroes, the
National Council suspended the funds allocated for Payne. After

further negotiations with the parties involved, the church decided to close the school and to grant the lone remaining student
a scholarship to another seminary. Two students, the last gradu-
ating class of Payne Divinity School, received their bachelor of
divinity degrees in 1949.[62]

In part the loss of Negro ministerial candidates from Payne
was compensated for by the increasing Negro enrollment in the
northern divinity schools of the church; in part it was made up by
the admission of Negroes into the southern Episcopal theological
schools. About the same time that Payne was withering away, Virginia Theological Seminary in Alexandria opened its doors to Negroes.[63]

Eliminating racial barriers at the school of theology at the University of the South in Sewanee, Tennessee, proved a more
formidable task and required forceful action on the part of the
faculty and several important Episcopalian leaders. As more and
more institutions of higher education throughout the South desegregated, the school of theology at Sewanee remained one of
the few major seminaries still barring Negroes. Perhaps it was
appropriate that Sewanee stood as a monument to segregation,
for it had been founded by Leonidas Polk, the fighting Confederate bishop, as a symbol of the South and its system of Negro
slavery.

The problem of desegregation was raised in the fall of 1951,
when the Province of Sewanee, composed of the dioceses of the
Southeast, declared it was desirable and advisable to open the
seminary to all without regard to race. But at a meeting held on
June 6, 1952, the board of trustees of Sewanee voted 45 to 12 not
to admit Negroes.[64]

The Episcopal press, various church leaders, and several dioceses criticized the trustees' decision. In a dramatic step, Dean
Francis Craig Brown, himself a product of the University of the
South and Virginia Theological Seminary, and seven of the eight
faculty members of the school of theology announced that they
would resign unless the trustees altered their position. When the
board of trustees, which included conservative laymen as well as

clergy, stuck to their decision, the eight resigned, effective as of June 1953.[65]

In the fall of 1952 the board of trustees appointed a special committee to investigate the issue and report to its spring meeting. The Reverend James Pike, then Dean of the Cathedral of Saint John the Divine of New York, never one to avoid taking a controversial stand, delivered a final blow to the sagging prestige of the school when he declined an invitation to give the baccalaureate sermon at the 1953 commencement. He declared that if he accepted the invitation he would be taking sides with the trustees, with whose position he disagreed.[66] The report of the special committee revealed strong church opinion, especially among those connected with the school of theology, favoring the admittance of Negroes. In a meeting held on June 4, 1953, which lasted more than six hours, with nearly all present, the board reversed its position of the previous year and voted 78 to 6 to admit qualified Negro students.[67] The first Negro student was enrolled that summer, thus ending racial barriers to admission to Episcopal theological schools.

Northern Presbyterians had no white seminaries in the South, but they did have two all-Negro seminaries: one at Johnson C. Smith University in Charlotte, North Carolina, and one at Lincoln University in Pennsylvania. The problem for the northern Presbyterians was that of justifying the continuance of the Negro seminaries, especially the one on northern soil. As in other denominations, the issue of segregated Presbyterian theological education became sensitive in the 1940's.

The 1938 General Assembly asked a special committee to investigate the relation of theological education to the work of the church. After two years of study the committee recommended that the Negro seminaries be given further scrutiny, in the hope that only one would be necessary.[68] Three years later, in 1943, the special Committee on Theological Education reported to the General Assembly that the seminary at Lincoln University, with its part-time faculty, low enrollment, and segregated nature, could not be justified. Although both Negro divinity schools were unaccredited, the committee felt that maintenance of Johnson C. Smith's seminary was necessary to train Negro ministers in the South. The committee recommended that future planning for the two should look toward the day when only Johnson C. Smith's divinity school would be maintained.[69]

Yet the need for Negro ministers was great; hence, the committee was willing to go along with the efforts of the theological school at Lincoln University to raise its standards. By 1946, the committee, while condemning segregation, maintained that both Negro seminaries provided special training for Negroes which was unobtainable elsewhere.[70] The reprieve for Lincoln University's theological school was temporary, however; during the 1950's, with training available for Negroes in northern Presbyterian seminaries, with a decreasing enrollment at Lincoln's divinity school, and with little hope of accreditation, the committee reverted to its original position. In 1958, when the board of trustees of Lincoln University decided to close the seminary, the committee and the General Assembly concurred; this left only one all-Negro seminary operated by the northern Presbyterian Church.[71]

Methodists also encountered opposition to desegregation of their southern seminaries. When pressure mounted for integration, Bishop John M. Moore of Georgia, long a defender of segregation, argued that Methodist unity would be injured by such action and that since the church operated the Gammon Theological Seminary for Negroes there was "no reason for opening the white schools to Negroes unless for social purposes." In spite of this opposition, the Perkins School of Theology of Southern Methodist University admitted Negroes as regular students in 1951 after several years of offering special classes for them.[72] The faculty and students of the divinity school at Duke University on several occasions urged the trustees to admit Negroes, and the trustees finally agreed in 1961. The Candler School of Theology and Gammon Theological Seminary in Atlanta co-operated on some projects, and Candler admitted Negroes in the winter quarter of 1963.[73]

There are still several all-Negro seminaries in the South.

However, these schools will admit whites. As the need for theological training for Negro clergy is great and as these schools give special training for Negro ministers that is sometimes not available in other seminaries, they probably will not go the way of Lincoln and Payne for years to come. When the churches are thoroughly interracial from top to bottom and when Negroes' educational backgrounds approach those of whites, these schools will undoubtedly disappear or become interracial.

Admitting Negro students was not the only requisite of real integration. Often the desegregation of southern seminaries was "tokenism." As in the case of Sewanee, only one or two Negroes enrolled. The total Negro enrollment in "white" southern seminaries remained low. Real integration with all facilities open to both Negro students and faculty was not achieved by 1965 in any southern seminary. There still remained matters such as segregation in dormitories and eating facilities and the hiring of Negro faculty. Seminary facilities were gradually desegregated as Negroes were admitted, but not without a struggle. At times forceful action by militant churchmen was required to open certain facilities to Negroes. Such was the case with the restaurant operated at the Episcopal University of the South. Although the theological school and the university admitted Negroes, the restaurant there refused to serve them. Several Episcopal churchmen argued that since the church-related university owned the property leased by the privately run restaurant, the university should force the restaurant to serve all without regard to race. Sit-ins in the fall of 1961 by the Episcopal Society for Cultural and Racial Unity, a militant civil rights group formed in 1959, led to a partial change in policy by April 1962. Not until 1963 was the restaurant reported to be desegregated.[74]

There were no Negroes on the regular faculties of predominantly white southern seminaries in 1965, but in the North, several seminaries had begun to hire Negroes as faculty members. The Philadelphia Divinity School of the Episcopal Church hired a Negro professor in 1948. Boston University's School of Theology (Methodist) in the 1940's had Negroes as lecturers for entire academic years and in 1953 appointed the Reverend Howard Thurman, formerly pastor of the interracial Church for the Fellowship of All Peoples of San Francisco, as Professor of Spiritual Resources and Disciplines, to develop a special interracial and interdenominational program at the university. Garrett Biblical Institute (Methodist) in Evanston, Illinois, employed Negroes on the summer school faculty. In 1952 Dr. George D. Kelsey, a Negro, was appointed to the theological faculty as an associate professor at the Methodists' Drew University in New Jersey.[75]

The changing attitudes toward seminary education could be seen, too, in the curricula of the schools. Will Alexander's experience at Vanderbilt University just before World War I, when the race problem was rarely discussed, was probably typical for that day. Although sociology courses crept into the seminaries in the 1920's and 1930's, they remained a small part of the over-all program and special courses on race relations were rare. They became more common in the 1940's and 1950's, and study of the race problem could scarcely be avoided in the 1960's.

When meeting problems of desegregation within church organizations or within church-related institutions, the churches often were slow in implementing their resolutions. It is obvious that social pronouncements were not accurate reflections of Protestant attitudes, but goals to be striven for. Moreover, when churchmen looked at the race problem, it became clear that segregation had to be met on the local level, in the local congregation. With interracial congregations there would be few segregation problems within the churches' organizations. A further dimension of the problem of race relations was the growing realization on the part of many Protestants that an interracial church could not be achieved without an interracial community. Segregation and discrimination had to be faced on both the local church and local community levels.

6

Church Unity and the Negro

> There is neither Jew nor Greek, there is neither bond
> nor free, there is neither male nor female: for ye are
> all one in Christ Jesus.
>
> GALATIANS, III: 28

Division among American Protestants can be traced to many causes. When the first colonists settled in America they brought with them the Reformation tradition of a divided Christendom, which meant not only the Catholic and Protestant separation, but also divisions among the reformers themselves. The American environment in the passage of time proved to be fertile for further divisions. Different theologies and nationalities, class structure and the frontier — these and other factors added to the splintering.[1] In contemporary America there are hundreds of sects ranging from the major denominations to those consisting of a handful of storefront churches with only a few hundred members.

The diversity of Protestantism was well established by the end of the colonial period when the question of race added a new dimension to it. Then the racial discrimination encountered by Negro Protestants led to the formation of the all-Negro denominations. Race in the form of the slavery issue also helped to promote division between northern and southern white denominations, especially among the Presbyterians, Baptists, and Methodists.

Around the turn of the twentieth century there developed a movement within Protestantism to reunite the denominations and to promote co-operation among them. In the nineteenth century the churches had co-operated through voluntary societies, such as the American Bible Society and the American Tract Society, whose membership was open to individuals, local congregations, and various organizations. In the late nineteenth and early twentieth centuries, the denominations themselves began to assume the functions of these old voluntary agencies and to co-operate with one another through interdenominational organizations. The most important of these was the Federal Council of Churches, formed in 1908 and reorganized in 1950 as the National Council of Churches. Another fruit of the movement for unity was the actual merger of various denominations.

The unity movement encountered the race problem in two ways. First, the movement influenced race relations within the churches, and second, Protestants encountered the race problem in their attempts to unite one church with another.

Although the interdenominational agencies did not end the color line within Protestantism, they did foster Negro-white co-operation. Leading Negro and white denominations often worked together through these groups. The Federal Council of Churches, for example, included Negro denominations from the beginning. Moreover, the Federal Council's Commission on Race Relations, formed in 1921, facilitated interracial co-operation.

For several reasons, however, this interracial co-operation was limited. In the first place, during the early years Negro churches took a secondary position within the interdenominational groups. Not until the 1940's and 1950's did these agencies begin to provide a greater role for Negro churchmen. In the 1940's Dr. Benjamin Mays, the Negro president of Morehouse College and a leading American clergyman, served as vice president of the Federal Council of Churches. Later the National Council of Churches chose Negroes for other positions of responsibility. On the state and local levels a number of interdenominational church councils elected Negroes to high offices, in both the North and South. In the South the first step toward co-operation usually was desegregation of the local ministerial alliances. The Washington,

D.C., Ministerial Alliance, after refusing several times to admit
Negro clergymen, opened its ranks in 1935 and became interracial. In the 1940's and 1950's several southern ministerial organizations followed Washington's example and dropped their color
bars, and several newly organized associations included Negroes
from the beginning. The Virginia Council of Churches, formed
in 1944, not only was interracial, but it also had a department of
race relations.[2] In the Deep South progress was slower than in
the rest of the country.

Apart from the fact that real interracial co-operation within interdenominational agencies was a relatively late movement, there
was a second limitation on the effectiveness of such co-operation.
Contact between Negro and white Protestants within these
agencies was largely confined to the leadership, leaving the rank
and file untouched.

A final consideration should be kept in mind about the interdenominational organizations — they did not encompass all of
American Protestantism. The southern Baptist Church, one of the
two largest Protestant denominations in America, did not belong
to the National Council of Churches. Other important groups
were unaffiliated, especially among the Pentecostal and Holiness
sects. Some of these theologically conservative groups formed
their own agencies, the most notable being the National Association of Evangelicals. These groups tended to be critical of the
liberally oriented National Council of Churches' view on the race
question and tended to do little to foster integration.[3]

The race issue also was a factor in the movement to unite
northern and southern Protestants into national churches. After
the Baptists split in 1845 into northern and southern denominations, they made little effort to reunite. There were many reasons
for the continuing division between the northern and southern
Baptists, but certainly the race problem was a barrier to unity.
On the other hand, the Methodists and Presbyterians both moved
toward reunion following the Civil War. Northern and southern
Methodists joined to form a united Methodist Church in 1939.
The Cumberland Presbyterian Church and the Presbyterian

Church in the United States of America (the northern Presbyterian Church) succeeded in uniting in 1906, but a plan to unite the northern Presbyterians and the southern Presbyterians was defeated in 1954, after long discussions. In each case a critical issue in the projected unification was the race problem.

Following the Civil War, in 1869, the Cumberland Presbyterian Church, predominantly a southern and border state church, organized its Negro membership into a separate Colored Cumberland Presbyterian Church. On the other hand, the northern Presbyterians did not intend to organize their Negro membership into a separate denomination, nor even into segregated presbyteries and synods. The General Assembly in the 1870's refused to allow transfers of Negro or white churches into separate organizations because such moves violated the requirement that presbyteries and synods be organized along geographical lines. In 1888, the Presbytery of Cincinnati, along with others, suggested that the church establish racial presbyteries and synods. The General Assembly rejected this proposal. The *Presbyterian* remarked of it: "The Presbyterian Church will never add to its constitution a provision by which a color line, 'pale' or otherwise, may be established or perpetuated." [4]

In spite of the *Presbyterian*'s insistence that northern Presbyterians would never draw the color line, the church did draw it. Apart from the general historical context of the rise of racism and the North's languishing interest in the southern race problem, there were two specific reasons within the church for the change in policy. In the first place, the northern Presbyterians wanted to expand their influence and white membership in the South; such expansion was impossible if they insisted upon integrated presbyteries and synods. Several southern presbyteries and one synod petitioned the General Assembly of 1903 to investigate the possibility of changing the church's constitution to permit segregated presbyteries and synods. This was the same proposal the church had rejected fifteen years before. Second, the church wanted to unite with the smaller Cumberland Presbyterian Church. Although doctrine was the key question in the union struggle, the race issue also had to be settled. The Cumberland Presbyterians insisted as a *sine qua non* of union that the Presbyterian Church in the United States of America change its constitution to provide for segregation in presbyteries and synods.[5] The joint committee on union pondered the problem and in 1904 produced a proposal allowing "a particular race" to form its own presbytery or synod within the bounds of the regular geographical ones. The phrase "a particular race" was important; for it permitted whites, if Negroes would not do so, to withdraw from the regular organization and form an all-white presbytery or synod.[6]

The matter came to a head at the northern church's General Assembly in 1904. The Special Committee on Territorial Limits of Presbyteries recommended the change and argued that the current policy meant a color line in the South because southern whites would not join a mixed church. "Are we by our laws to draw the color line in that portion of the country, and exclude the whites from our community?" queried the committee.[7] The committee was saying that the way to keep whites from drawing a color line against themselves was to draw one against Negroes! Several churchmen questioned the logic involved and the ethics of segregation. Negro leaders and presbyteries generally voted against the change, but the church overrode their protests.[8] With its eyes turned toward southern expansion and union with the Cumberland Presbyterians, the General Assembly approved the amendment, and the presbyteries assented the next year.

In sanctioning the change in the church's constitution, the General Assembly declared, "That in approving the Overture looking to a change in the Form of Government concerning the territorial bounds of Presbyteries and Synods, this Assembly affirms its complete freedom from prejudice against any race and from any desire or purpose to bring about a separation from our Church, or from representation in the General Assembly, of any class or race of Presbyterians; but, on the other hand, our purpose is to bring together in one Church members of all races and classes." [9] With the change in the constitution, union was made possible and segregation became the church's policy in the South. As one Negro leader put it, "No alternative was left for the colored churches." [10] The new church born of this union took the name of the old northern church.

Although the northern Presbyterians and Cumberland Presbyterians united, the merged church's attempt to unite with the southern Presbyterian Church failed in the South.[11] When the merger plan was voted down by southern Presbyterians in 1954, little was said about the race problem; but there is reason to believe that it was extremely important in the defeat of the plan in the South. Two sociologists, perhaps exaggerating, have concluded that it was the key factor in the failure of union.[12] In 1955, the moderator of the southern church told the General Assembly of the North that he felt the Negro question, in particular the Supreme Court's decision on school desegregation, had affected the vote. The organ of the northern church, *Presbyterian Life*, and the often perceptive *Christian Century* agreed with this opinion.[13]

Certainly the Negro had figured prominently in the historical relations of the northern and southern Presbyterians. Slavery was one factor causing the split of Presbyterians into northern and southern churches before and during the Civil War. When discussions about reuniting them began after the war, the race question was a prime consideration and was one reason why little was accomplished for decades.[14]

The plan that was defeated in 1954 had originated in discussions held between northern and southern Presbyterians in the 1930's. Committees from the two churches began in 1937 to work on a series of guiding principles and a scheme of organic union. A meeting held in Washington, D.C., in February 1939, produced eight basic principles of union. Among them was the proposal that "Negro congregations, Presbyteries, and Synods are to continue as at present except where they may be combined." [15] The segregated Negro churches and church administration, which prevailed in both denominations in the South, were to be continued. Negotiations between the committees finally produced, in 1943, an actual plan of union that was submitted to the churches for comment. The plan provided for regional synods, among them two for Negroes in the South.

Negroes in the northern Presbyterian Church objected to this provision. Although it took no official action on the merger proposal, the Afro-American Presbyterian Council, consisting of Negro Presbyterians of the North and West, was reported to be against the plan on two counts. First, it objected to the omission of a Negro from the northern committee devising the plan. Second, the Council felt that to perpetuate segregated presbyteries and synods was to lose an opportunity to take a step forward in race relations. As one Negro critic wrote, "If there is one purely Negro presbytery or synod in the reunited Church, the Northern Church would have merely succeeded in waiting eighty-odd years to declare that — after all the Southern Church has a right point of view of the race question and now we declare unequivocally victory to her which has been long overdue. This is the equivalent of saying, though paradoxically, that we reach Christ the better way by moving away from Him." [16]

While the plan was being discussed and revised, the Negroes' objections were met. At the 1947 General Assembly of the northern church the commissioners enlarged the Committee on Church Cooperation and Union from eighteen to nineteen members and elected the Reverend James W. Smith to be the first Negro member.[17] In meetings held in 1945 the negotiating teams agreed that in the synod structure there would be no requirement of separate regional synods for Negroes.[18]

The southern General Assembly voted in 1948 to hold the plan in abeyance for five years and to explore areas of co-operation. This was a compromise between the proponents and opponents of union. The foes of unity naturally did not care to see the church approve the plan, and its supporters felt that the required three-quarters majority in the presbyteries would be impossible to obtain at that time; hence, they preferred to postpone a showdown until they might be in a stronger position.[19] When the

United Presbyterian Church in North America joined the negotiations the projected united church became a three-way merger.

The plan of union presented to these denominations in 1954
proposed to leave the existing presbyteries and synods intact.
Consolidations and readjustments were to be made later. Segregated presbyteries and synods were not required, but language
and cultural groups were to be allowed the privilege of erecting
their own presbyteries if they so desired.[20] In the early 1950's,
both the northern and southern Presbyterians took steps to abolish their all-Negro synods and presbyteries in the South. The
Southerners moved even faster than the Northerners.[21] Hence,
little conflict occurred over this point.

Little was said about desegregated church administration
during the debates over union. Indeed, the race question was
scarcely discussed at all. The most frequently mentioned reasons
why Southerners opposed merger with the northern church were
the laxity of northern doctrine, the difference of opinion over
the roles of women and elders in the church, the alleged greater
efficiency of the southern church, and the general uniqueness of
the southern Presbyterian Church. These issues, some of which
dated back to the nineteenth century, certainly played a role in
the defeat of union. Yet there were vital differences between the
two denominations on the race question, even though they were
not emphasized in the debate over union.

In the first place, the northern church was more outspoken on
the matters of segregation and discrimination. As noted above, in
the 1940's and 1950's northern church groups and leaders called
for an end to segregation and discrimination in church life.
Among the many pronouncements passed by the northern General Assembly was an endorsement of the Federal Council of
Churches' declaration for a "non-segregated church and a non-
segregated society." On the other hand, when the National
Council of the Churches of Christ in America in 1952 called for
an end to segregation, the two representatives of the southern
Presbyterian Church disassociated themselves from the statement.

The southern Presbyterians finally did condemn segregation at their 1954 General Assembly, but not without a sizable opposition.[22]

The northern church was also moving toward desegregation in various areas of church life. Beginning in the 1930's Negroes were elected to church boards, and by 1954 Negroes had been represented on all of the church's boards and on the General Council. Predominantly white presbyteries and synods also elected Negro moderators. In the southern church, on the other hand, there were no Negroes on church boards. Only in the late 1940's and early 1950's did the Southerners begin to end their traditional policy of paternalism and grant Negroes a degree of control over their own affairs.

In the 1940's northern Presbyterians insisted upon holding General Assemblies only in cities where desegregated facilities were available. The southern church did not hold its first desegregated General Assembly until 1950. Even this did not mark a permanent change in policy, for in the 1950's when the church met at its own conference grounds at Montreat, North Carolina, facilities were not completely desegregated.

Probably the sharpest difference between the two denominations concerned the local church congregations. In the 1940's the northern church adopted a deliberate policy of developing interracial congregations. The number of truly interracial congregations was not large, and most such churches were in the North. Actually, the two churches had similar records in the South, where there were few racially mixed congregations of any denomination in 1954. Undoubtedly many other northern Presbyterian congregations in the South had open-door policies, but these were not translated into practice overnight. However, the northern church had adopted a conscious policy of congregational desegregation, while, when the southern church in 1953 began a drive to increase its work among Negroes, the emphasis was upon building exclusively Negro churches, not interracial ones.

The southern church had been growing more liberal on many

social issues, including the race problem, since the end of World War I; nevertheless, it still contained a strong conservative wing. The conservatives opposed both the liberal trend in the church and unification with the northern Presbyterians. In the case of unification the conservatives had one advantage: three-quarters of the presbyteries had to approve union for it to be consummated.

The conservative wing of the southern Presbyterian Church had led an attack on the Federal Council of Churches and in 1931 succeeded in forcing the church to withdraw from the Council. In part its opposition was due to the Federal Council's "meddling in civil affairs." [23] The church re-entered the Council in 1941 and joined its successor, the National Council of Churches, in 1950. At nearly every General Assembly various presbyteries urged disassociation from the Council. In the 1940's and 1950's, "meddling in civil affairs" increasingly meant meddling in the race issue. Some of the attacks upon the Council specifically criticized its liberal position on race relations.[24] As one conservative group put it,

> Urging the elimination of all racial segregation is both unwise and improper and is not desired by the best informed and wisest members of either the white or colored races in the Southland. . . . We hold . . . that the [Federal] Council's programs, urging the intermingling of white and colored young people socially and in religious conferences cannot successfully be effected without far reaching dangers and that any premature program to that end will seriously set back and deter the splendid progress being made for a better understanding and cooperation between the white and colored races.[25]

In 1934 the southern Presbyterian Church established a permanent Committee on Social and Moral Welfare, which in effect was the social gospel arm of the church. The Division of Christian Relations, as the committee was later renamed, recommended firmer pronouncements on race discrimination to the church and finally issued its controversial 1954 report condemning segregation in the church and endorsing the Supreme Court's decision on school desegregation. The conservatives attacked the Division and especially this report, but the General Assembly refused to rescind it.

Alarmed by the church's growing liberalism, including its stand on race, and in particular by the activities of the Federal Council of Churches, a group of southern Presbyterians founded the *Southern Presbyterian Journal* in the 1940's to combat what they considered unsound trends in the church. The *Journal* and its supporters took an anti-unification and pro-segregation point of view. Periodically articles and editorials appeared in the *Journal* about the northern Presbyterian Church's sponsorship of "race mixing." [26] In pointing to the differences beween the two denominations, the editor noted, "One of these Churches believes that 'brotherly love' demands the abrogation of segregation, and the allowing of races to intermingle without any adherence to racial lines. The other branch believes that Christian love and helpfulness can be shown and be given while preserving racial integrity." [27]

As sentiment in favor of union grew, the supporters of the *Southern Presbyterian Journal* organized a committee to fight it. This group expanded and launched a full-scale attack as the plan of union neared completion.[28] It warned against the agitation of the northern church on the race question. A meeting of the Association for the Preservation and Continuation of the Southern Presbyterian Church held in August 1954 at Weaverville, North Carolina, where the *Journal* was published, adopted a series of resolutions, among them one declaring, "We fear the outcome of agitation of this vexed [race] question by professional leaders, and the pronouncements of some major denominations. Let eager enthusiasts be reminded that changes in the social patterns are of slow growth if they are to endure, and that happy and lasting benefits are not produced by either ecclesiastical resolutions or civil edict." [29]

The 1954 General Assembly approved the plan of union by a vote of 283 to 169. At the same General Assembly the Division of

Christian Relations' report calling for an end to segregation in the church and for support of the Supreme Court's decision on school desegregation also received 169 negative votes. Although voting lists are unavailable, many of the commissioners probably voted the same way on both resolutions. In spite of the General Assembly's approval, the plan was defeated in the presbyteries. Union needed the approval of three-quarters of the presbyteries. Of 86 presbyteries, 43 voted against union; 42 voted for it. In one presbytery there was a tie. The vote against union was strongest in the Deep South, especially in rural areas with a large Negro population, where feeling on the race question was intense.[30] Many of the anti-union presbyteries were the same ones that through the years had criticized the church's and the National Council of Churches' liberalism on race matters. Conversely, those synods and presbyteries that gave immediate approval to the 1954 General Assembly's stand on segregation were also centers of pro-union sentiment.[31]

It is true that in the southern Presbyterian Church the most frequently stated reasons for the failure of union, theological conservatism and strong regional feeling, ran hand in hand with pro-segregation opinion. Thus, if race played a vital role in the defeat of union, as it apparently did, as an issue it was certainly not debated publicly. Sentiment for closer ties and possible union with the northern church and more liberal attitudes on the race question had been growing in the southern church. But the conservative group was able to defeat union in 1954–55. The merger proposal certainly came at an unfortunate time for those favoring unity; in 1954 feeling in the South against the North was intense. Union probably would have been defeated anyway, but, at such a critical moment, the race issue undoubtedly helped to account for the decisive nature of the defeat. Not until the two denominations agree on how to handle the race problem will their unification become possible.

Although the northern and southern Presbyterians failed to unite, the Methodists achieved unity. The price paid for a national Methodist Church, however, was racial segregation.

Following the Civil War, the northern and southern Methodists exchanged fraternal delegates and occasionally discussed union. After years of general discussions, the Methodists began serious negotiations in 1910. Several issues were involved, but the Methodists had split over slavery in 1844 and the status of the Negro loomed as the major stumbling block in the way of reunification. The northern Methodists had capitulated to segregation in their southern churches in the 1870's. Even so, their practices differed from those of the Southerners; for the Northerners still had Negro members, while the southern Methodists had organized their Negroes into a separate denomination.

During the negotiations the southern Methodists expressed their desire for an all-white united church, with Negroes placed in a separate denomination. Bishop James Cannon, Jr., the "dry messiah" who later supported union, expressed this attitude when he wrote, "All facts indicate that it would be better for them [the Negroes] to be separate from white membership. . . . Their own voluntary retirement would remove the greatest stumbling block to unification." [32]

Although some northern white Methodists said they were willing to accept such a church, most wanted the northern church's Negroes, who comprised about one-tenth of the membership, to be included in a united Methodism. [33] The Negro Methodists also insisted that they be part of the united church.

For over a decade the two churches wrestled with the various problems relating to union, but the issue that came up again and again was the status of the Negro members. [34] By the 1920's the two branches were willing to compromise. The Southerners had shifted from their stand that Negroes should be excluded to acceptance of a plan including them, provided the North accepted the jurisdictional or regional conference system. This scheme provided for regional conferences in addition to the General Conference, which decentralized the power of the national church. An ecclesiastical version of states' rights, it offered protection to those Southerners fearful of engulfment by the North.

The Negroes accepted the plan because their rights were protected. The Negro *Southwestern Christian Advocate* remarked, "It was generally accepted and freely stated in private among members of the [negotiating] commission that the Negro question was regarded as settled, and that in the case of any unification, the Negro membership of the Methodist Episcopal Church would be part of union, with powers and prerogatives in the united church and the General Conference of said church the same as all members. . . . Nothing was said as to separation." [35] The northern church as a whole echoed the Negroes' assent, and the General Conference of 1924 approved the plan by a vote of 802 to 13. The annual conferences subsequently returned a heavy majority for union, well over the two-thirds required. [36]

Although the trend in the southern church seemed to be running toward a willingness to have Negroes in the church with equal ecclesiastical rights, a vociferous minority opposed the new plan on racial as well as other grounds. Most of the church hierarchy favored the plan, but among the minority were some capable leaders. Spearheading the opposition were Bishops Warren Candler and Collins Denny. Bishop Denny, a southern diehard who later refused to join the united church in 1939, objected to the plan, among other reasons, "because it establishes a relation with the negro race not best for him, not possible for us. . . . The proposed plan, if adopted, will increase the difficulties of our race problem and produce conditions that will weaken the foundation of our social structure and impair the fabric of our Southern Civilization." [37] The minority also opposed the plan on the ground that it gave too much power to the General Conference, but the especially assembled session of the southern church's General Conference in 1924 approved it by a vote of 297 to 75. [38]

Bishop James Cannon, Jr., led the southern hosts battling for a united Methodism. The obstacle in the way of the unity-minded Southerners was that three-quarters of the annual conferences had to give their consent. The total number of approving conferences, while a majority, was far less than the three-quarters required for adoption. As an indication of the influence of southern bishops and the importance of leadership — in those conferences presided over by opponents of union, the vote generally went against unification; in those presided over by supporters of union, the vote went for it. Also, the border state conferences tended to favor union while those in the Deep South tended to oppose it.[39]

Certainly factors other than the race issue influenced the vote on unification. The traditional southern fear of the North and of a strong national church undoubtedly affected it. Although Methodists generally agreed on theology, the North was more liberal than the South. This liberalism touched upon social questions. Southern bishops had more power than northern ones, and the power of bishops would have been reduced in the united church. Not even the regional conference system, which was designed to protect southern rights, allayed the fears of some Southerners.

Although these issues were important, the race factor was critical for unification; an agreement had to be reached on this issue before union could be achieved. The debates of the commissioners designing the plan, the debates in the General Conferences, and the discussions in the church press clearly indicate that the settlement of the status of the Negro was probably the most important factor in union.[40] Commenting after the debates in the South, the Colored Methodist Episcopal Church's official journal declared, "The 'bloody shirt' has been waved and 'Nigger, Nigger' has been used in a way that suggests the extreme to which race prejudice can go." [41]

Although the merger plan was defeated and although the two denominations agreed to forgo negotiations during the remainder of the decade, significant developments had occurred during the debates. First, southern Methodists were moving toward acceptance of Negroes with equal constitutional rights in a segregated church, much like the northern one. Second, the suggestion of the regional or jurisdictional conference system provided an important framework for the future formulation of a plan of union. Third, after some wavering, northern white Methodists came to the defense of equal ecclesiastical rights for Negroes in the church. The difficulty for Northerners lay in the future, when Negroes would find the 1924 plan outdated.

The southern and northern wings of American Methodism renewed negotiations for unification in 1934, when the southern church appointed a commission to discuss unity with the northern church's commission, which had been established two years before. The smaller Methodist Protestant Church also joined the talks. The second formal meeting of the commissioners devised a jurisdictional conference system that made unification possible.[42]

This system divided the church into six jurisdictional conferences: two in the North; two in the South; one in the West; and one for Negroes, the Central Jurisdiction. The few Negro churches in mixed annual conferences were to remain in those conferences; hence, they would be in a jurisdiction other than the Central. In establishing the jurisdictional system the northern church was making a concession to the South, for the jurisdictional conferences protected Southerners from northern domination by granting some of the powers formerly held by the General Conference to the jurisdictional conferences. Bishops, for example, were no longer to be elected by the General Conference but were to be chosen by the jurisdictional conferences for work in their respective jurisdictions. And, above all, the establishment of the Central Jurisdiction ensured enough racial segregation for Southerners to agree to union.

The two Negro delegates on the northern commission, Bishop Robert E. Jones and Willis King of Gammon Theological Seminary, favored the proposal. They were agreeing to a plan similar to the one defeated in the South in 1924 and generally accepted by Negroes at that time.[43] By the 1930's, however, most Negroes were asking more of their church, and a majority of them opposed the scheme of unification, calling it a step backward in race relations and labeling it racial segregation.

When the General Conference of the northern church pondered the merger proposal at its 1936 meeting, the only issue dis-

cussed was the role of the Negro. Speaking for the Negro delegates, who voted 36 to 11 against the plan, David D. Jones, Negro
educator and brother of Bishop Robert E. Jones, declared:

> Everyone knows the Plan is segregation, and segregation in
> the ugliest way, because it is couched in such pious terms. My
> friends, what does segregation do for a people? It sets them
> aside, it labels them, it says that they are not fit to be treated
> as other people are treated. My friends, you have the priv-
> ilege of saying that to us, but surely you will expect us to be
> men enough not to say it ourselves. This Plan turns its back
> on the historic attitude of the Methodist Episcopal Church.[44]

The proposal received the overwhelming approval of the General Conference and the annual conferences, but it failed to win
even a majority of the votes of the Negro annual conferences.[45]

Although the vast majority of white northern Methodists approved the unification scheme, some criticized it on the ground
that it fostered racial segregation. The protest was centered in the
Northeast under the leadership of Lewis Hartman, editor of
Zion's Herald, which was published in Boston. Hartman took the
position that the Central Jurisdiction represented a retreat in
race relations, especially in view of Negro opposition to it. Several annual conferences, mainly in the Northeast, endorsed union
with the proviso that the settlement might be altered in the future to facilitate greater contact between Negro and white
churches.[46]

Also embarrassing for the northern church was the outspoken
opposition of Methodist youth. In 1936, even before Negro criticism had become pronounced, the executive committee of the
National Council of Methodist Youth questioned the plan and
said segregation of Negroes was a "vicious compromise and
policy which is unethical, anti-social, and anti-Christian." At the
interracial National Conference of Methodist Youth held the following year at Berea College, Kentucky, the young delegates
voted 464 to 14 against the proposal.[47]

Those defending the plan generally argued that since the
church already had separate local churches and annual confer-

ences for Negroes, the proposal merely recognized the existing
fact of ecclesiastical segregation. They also claimed that Negro
churches could easily be transferred into predominantly white
conferences after union, and that rigid segregation was not being
written into the constitution. Others argued that Negroes would
gain new opportunities for leadership in the united church because the Central Jurisdiction would elect its own bishops and
would have more than its proportionate share of representation
on church boards and in the General Conference. In a remarkable
reply to the protest of the Methodist youth, the church's leading
journal, the *Christian Advocate*, asserted that a racial jurisdiction
was being established to give Negroes leadership opportunities
and not because of feelings of racial superiority; hence, it was not
segregation. Said the editor:

> Again, I say, however, this is not a question of racial supe-
> riority. It is merely a question of racial understanding; and it
> should not be seen as discriminatory. . . . Negro organiza-
> tion for purposes of racial leadership is not segregation. It is
> a practical measure which definitely serves the best interests
> of the Negro race. Segregation as a principle of race inferi-
> ority in Methodism is definitely excluded by the circumstance
> that all races sit as equals in our church's great legislative
> gathering, in its college of bishops, in its benevolent boards,
> and in many other gatherings.[48]

If there were any doubt about why the Central Jurisdiction
was being established, southern churchmen provided the answer.
The southern Methodists would not have entered into union
without some form of racial segregation that kept Negro congregations and annual conferences apart from southern white congregations and conferences. Since their rejection of unification in
1924, southern churchmen had become more willing to accept
Negroes in a united denomination. Nevertheless, they were willing to have integration only at the very top level of the church.
Methodists devised the jurisdictional system not only to protect
southern rights, but also to maintain segregation. Some Southerners, particularly in the Deep South, opposed the plan, but the

southern church approved it overwhelmingly. The southern Methodists' General Conference voted 434 to 26 for union, and only one annual conference, in Mississippi, voted against it. Several laymen's groups fought unification, but they had little strength.[49]

A few Southerners were apprehensive about having Negroes in the united church. When the plan was debated, several churchmen pointed out that the northern church's stand on nonsegregated facilities at General Conference meetings precluded holding them in the South. Others warned that Negroes and northern liberals would press for abolition of the Central Jurisdiction and that the united church's boards would distribute literature that conflicted with southern racial teachings. However, these arguments mustered few votes against union.[50]

While some Northerners were asserting that the plan did not provide for racial segregation, the southern proponents of unity maintained that the jurisdictional system protected the South and that the all-Negro jurisdiction was being written into union.[51] Southerners seemed to be more candid than Northerners. The influential *Christian Advocate* of Nashville remarked, "No opponent of the present plan has been able to suggest a plan more in harmony with what the Southern Church has asked for than the present plan of a separate jurisdiction for the Negro. . . . If the proposed plan would be defeated by the Southern Church, it would be evident before the world that the measure was defeated as a result of sectional enmity and racial prejudice." [52]

One group in the southern church criticized the unification scheme as being a step backward in race relations; as might have been expected, it was the women. The Woman's Missionary Council set up a committee to investigate the place of the Negro in a unified Methodism and to discern whether the plan met "the test of Christian principles." The special committee reported:

> Your committee agrees that this plan is less than ideal; that it leaves much to be desired if the Methodist Church is fully to represent the Kingdom of God on earth. For Methodist

churches in the same city to be related to each other only
through a General Conference that meets once in four years
seems consistent neither with Methodist connectionalism nor
with Jesus' concern that "they all may be one." . . . The inadequacy of the plan lies in its failure to provide for cooperation between white and colored Methodists in annual and
jurisdictional conferences and in local communities.

The committee concluded by urging women to take the lead
in bringing about co-operation between Negro and white
churches.[53]

The three denominations sealed their merger at a uniting conference held in Kansas City in 1939. The Negro spokesman stated
that though Negro conferences had generally opposed the plan,
Negroes would be loyal and support the church.[54] Loyalty
to the church did not mean the end of criticism, however; the
Methodists entered into an uneasy union.

In the decade following reunion, Methodist youth continued
to attack the settlement and Negro Methodist leaders sometimes
called attention to its inadequacy. The Negro bishops declared in
1944, "We consider it expedient only on account of the Christian
childhood of some American Methodists who need a little cod-
dling until they can grow into full grown manhood and woman-
hood in Christ Jesus. We are hopeful that in the near future our
Methodism may become sufficiently Christian in character and
maturity to find a more excellent way." A few white Methodists,
mainly in the Northeast and West, also criticized segregation
within the church, but a full-scale attack did not begin until the
1950's.[55]

The first attempt to abolish the Jim Crow Central Jurisdiction
occurred at the 1952 General Conference, when Chester A.
Smith of the New York Conference, a perennial critic of the
Central, urged an amendment to the constitution to abolish it.
This proposal was defeated.[56]

Several white annual conferences in the North suggested gradual abolition of the Central Jurisdiction when they invited Negro

churches in it to join their conferences. According to a Judicial Council decision given to the 1952 General Conference, this required approval of the various churches, district conferences, annual conferences, and jurisdictional conferences involved, as well as that of the General Conference.[57] Consequently, such transfers of Negro churches into predominantly white annual conferences were cumbersome and time-consuming. The 1956 General Conference passed an amendment to the constitution to simplify the process by eliminating the requirement of General Conference approval.[58] More than the required number of annual conferences quickly agreed to this constitutional change, commonly called Amendment IX, and it became law. Southerners could vote for the amendment without fear of integrated conferences in the South because all parties involved would still have to approve a transfer by a two-thirds vote before it could be effected. No Negro church could be transferred into a white southern annual conference without that conference's approval, and Southerners were well aware of this fact.[59]

Gradual elimination of the Central Jurisdiction was difficult to achieve not only because it required white approval in the South where most Negro churches were located, but also because of problems in the North. There the predominantly white annual conferences tended to invite those Negro churches that were large and relatively well off financially to join them. If these churches had moved out of the Negro annual conferences, leaving behind the smaller and poorer Negro churches, those remaining would have found it difficult to finance the work of their conferences. Furthermore, unless white congregations were willing to accept Negro ministers, the few Negro ministers in predominantly white conferences would have had limited opportunities to rotate to new charges in accordance with denominational tradition. Because of the problems in both North and South and because of the time required to effect transfers, less than 1 per cent of the membership of the Central Jurisdiction had taken advantage of the amendment by the time the 1960 General Conference met.[60]

While Amendment IX was being pondered at the 1956 General

Conference, considerable debate occurred over the Central Jurisdiction, with Southerners advocating its retention and such
Northerners as Chester A. Smith urging its abolition and the integration of the Negro churches into the nonracial annual and
jurisdictional conferences. The bishops and many other churchmen favored appointing a commission to investigate the entire
jurisdictional system and report to the 1960 General Conference.
This proposition was carried.[61] The commission recommended
no change in the jurisdictional system and the General Conference of 1960 approved its report, thus leaving the *sine qua non*
of reunion intact.

Although Negro and white leaders who supported the Central
Jurisdiction pointed to the various problems of integration in the
North and to the representation on church boards and agencies
that the Central guaranteed to Negroes, the major reason for the
continuance of the Jim Crow jurisdiction was that the southern
wing of the Methodist Church opposed any major change in the
jurisdictional system. While criticism of the all-Negro jurisdiction
was growing among various groups within the church, southern
opposition to change remained firm. The two southern jurisdictions had developed the system and had made it an integral part of
the church's administration. This was not done in the North and
West, where many churchmen felt the system was unnecessary.[62]
The development of the system in the South gave southern Methodists an additional incentive for wanting to maintain it. Said the
bishops of the South Central Jurisdictional Conference to their
1952 meeting:

> The racial element did play its inescapable part in the for-
> mulating of the Plan of Union, but only to the extent of
> recognizing existing situations and patterns within the frame-
> work of which all three constituting churches were operating
> in certain parts of the country at the time of Union. If the
> racial issue were the sole or chief reason for the creating of
> the jurisdiction, that reason would not have justified its birth
> and would not justify its continued existence.

Similar views came from the bishops of the Southeastern Jurisdiction, who went on record as looking "with disfavor on any
proposal that would radically change our Jurisdictional Plan." [63]

Several southern conferences in the 1950's passed resolutions
supporting the jurisdictional system and segregation and urging
that no basic changes be made.[64] The heart of opposition to
change in the system lay in the states of the Deep South, particularly in Georgia, Alabama, and Mississippi. With the approach of
the 1956 General Conference and the growing agitation to abolish the Central, southern Methodists, especially laymen, in the
Deep South organized groups dedicated to the preservation of
segregation in the Methodist Church.[65] Although not large
in numbers and perhaps more outspoken than the average
southern Methodists, these groups did demonstrate the depth of
feeling about segregation in the Deep South. The 1956 General
Conference kept the Central Jurisdiction, and shortly before the
1960 General Conference new groups appeared, again devoted to
the cause of segregation.[66]

With open support of the existing jurisdictional system by the
southern bishops and southern jurisdictional conferences, and
with an almost fanatical unofficial support from the laymen's
groups, it was difficult to abolish the Central Jurisdiction without
splitting the church. However, in 1963 and early 1964 white
Americans felt additional counterpressure from the civil rights
organizations and a sense of urgency about ending racial segregation. This triggered a new assault on the Central. At the 1964
General Conference the Methodists voted to abolish the Negro
jurisdiction within the next four years. The precise manner of
abolishing the Central was left to the jurisdictional and annual
conferences. In the North, Negro churches in the Central began
to be integrated into the regular annual conferences in the summer of 1964, while in the southern states no action was taken.
There remained the possibility, if Negro churchmen agreed, that
southern jurisdictional conferences would receive Negro annual
conferences intact and not integrate their churches into the regular annual conferences.[67]

Abolition of the Central Jurisdiction by the 1964 General Conference did not end segregation in the Methodist Church. It still left all-Negro and all-white congregations, Negro ministers caring only for Negro churches, the possibility of all-Negro annual conferences in the South, the possibility of Negro bishops presiding only over southern Negro annual conferences, and some church-related institutions that practiced segregation and discrimination. As the Negro bishops noted in 1952:

> Whether or not the Central Jurisdiction is continued as such within the church, whether or not jurisdictions will continue as part of the church, certainly the race problem belongs not alone to the top levels, such as the jurisdictional boundaries. The race problem is most intense and at its worst on the level of the local community, especially the small community in many sections of our land. . . . It is here that the problems will ultimately come; whether the solution starts here or ends here it will not be achieved until it is achieved on the local level.[68]

7

The Local Church

All Christian churches should in fact be open to all
regardless of race, and should publicly so declare.
Similarly it should be affirmed that all qualified
ministers should have access to pulpits or other church
positions regardless of race or color.

GENERAL ASSEMBLY OF THE NATIONAL
COUNCIL OF CHURCHES, DECEMBER 6,
1963.

"Whites Only" was never carved over the doors of any white
Protestant church in America; it was understood. For the local
church was the most segregated major institution in American
life. At the time Protestants began to attack segregation in the
local churches, there was little contact between Negro and white
Protestants on Sunday mornings. Of course some white congregations always had a few Negro members. In ante-bellum days
the southern churches had slave galleries for the plantation hands.
Such churches would scarcely be classified as truly interracial by
modern-day standards and would seem to be a mockery of Christianity, at least to the Negroes attending them. In the ante-bellum
North some Negroes attended white churches, though often in
the "Negro Pews." After the Civil War and Reconstruction, the
races, for the most part, worshipped at separate churches. Only
rarely in both North and South did they worship together.

Occasionally a Reverend William Blackshear caused a stir by
openly telling Negroes to attend their own churches and not his
"white" one. But Blackshear only said bluntly what was generally
accepted tacitly. Seven years before the Blackshear incident of
1929, the Chicago Commission on Race Relations had summa-

rized the situation in that city when it stated, "A few white churches have several Negro members, usually of long standing. There are instances of white churches accepting particular Negro members, with some apprehension that they might bring friends." [1] A study by the Federal Council of Churches in 1930, prompted by the Blackshear incident, revealed little Negro participation in local white churches.[2]

In 1946, Frank Loescher, a sociologist, made the first extensive survey of interracial practices of local congregations. Of the eight million Negro Protestants, seven and a half million were in congregations connected with the all-Negro denominations. Of the remaining half million connected with mixed denominations, the vast majority were in separate congregations. From his data Loescher estimated that approximately eight thousand Negroes in the whole country were in congregations with mixed membership. This figure was less than one-tenth of 1 per cent of Negro Protestants. Most of the Negroes who were members or attenders of predominantly white churches lived in the North or Far West, notably in New England and such states as California, New York, New Jersey, and Pennsylvania. Negro membership in white churches in the border state regions or in the South was rare.[3] Nor were the few Negroes in mixed churches necessarily well integrated into the social life of the church.

One of the major obstacles to local church desegregation was the northern residential pattern, yet Loescher could not find a single white church with an open or mixed membership in an area beginning to undergo transition; only when Negroes reached a majority in a neighborhood did membership in local white churches become open. "The customary pattern in Protestantism," reported Loescher, "is to resist the Negro invasion and then when transition has occurred, to sell the property to a Negro group." [4] Added to Loescher's revelations was the fact that, at that time, no Negro minister was pastor of a predominantly white church. The pattern of segregation in local churches and church administration and the discriminatory practices of many church-related institutions led Loescher to conclude, "Protestantism, by its policies and practices, far from helping to integrate the Negro in American life, is actually contributing to the segregation of Negro Americans." [5]

Such was the picture when the churches began to advocate an end to the segregation of Negroes in religious life. During the 1940's, a few Protestants consciously followed the social teachings of their denominations and developed local congregations open to all. The movement for truly interracial congregations — that is, churches in which all aspects of church life were open to all races — was still extremely limited by 1965. A larger number of congregations became desegregated or racially inclusive; that is, they demonstrated willingness to accept Negroes in some phases of church activity.

In some cases open churches were deliberately planned interdenominational ventures. In other cases individual ministers, sensitive to the contradictions of a Jim Crow Christianity, made their congregations racially inclusive, and eventually fully interracial. In still other instances regular white congregations opened their doors to their Negro neighbors rather than flee in the face of Negro migration. Finally, some Negro and white congregations combined. In short, churchmen employed a variety of methods, some frankly experimental, to achieve racially inclusive churches. In the early 1960's the initiative was taken by Negroes themselves with kneel-ins and other attempts to attend or join southern white churches.

It was the primarily northern denominations or northern wings of national denominations that began to develop racially inclusive congregations. Southern branches of national denominations or primarily southern denominations, such as the southern Presbyterian and southern Baptist Churches, made little effort in this direction. As late as 1959, the usually reliable Southern Regional Council reported no more than twenty white churches with Negro participants in eleven southern states; three-quarters of them were affiliated with the liberal American Unitarian Association.[6] Although the figure was probably too low and although more Negroes were admitted to southern white congregations after

1959, by 1964 there was scarcely any movement to encourage the development of interracial congregations in the American South, unless the kneel-ins are viewed in this light.

Apart from the few white churches that included Negroes, either as members or as attenders, Protestants found few opportunities for interracial contact. Perhaps the major occasion for some form of interracial worship was Race Relations Sunday. The Race Relations Sunday program, started by the Federal Council of Churches in 1922, provided for pulpit exchanges between Negro and white preachers and for Negro and white congregations to worship together. Begun on a small scale, Race Relations Sunday was increasingly observed during the 1930's and 1940's.[7] Even this form of interracial worship was extremely limited, however, occurring only once a year, on the Sunday nearest Lincoln's birthday. Individual denominations supported the Race Relations Sunday and Brotherhood Week programs and sometimes had similar programs of their own. In the late 1940's, for example, six Protestant Episcopal dioceses promoted special interracial communion services in several cities, mainly in the North. The purpose of this venture was to stimulate Negro lay participation in the church and to promote better race relations.[8]

The periodic and special interracial worship services led to the establishment of special interracial churches. In the mid-1930's a group of Protestants organized the Fellowship Church of Philadelphia. Sponsored by the Interracial Committee of the Philadelphia Federation of Churches and the Committee on Race Relations of the Society of Friends, the church was interdenominational and interracial in character. The Fellowship Church differed from the ordinary neighborhood congregation in that it allowed members to attend both its services and their own regular ones. Holding services on one Sunday a month from fall until spring, the church offered an opportunity for people of various races and religious persuasions to worship together, an opportunity unavailable in the usual denominational church. The services were held in Baptist, Episcopal, and other churches, and both Negro and white ministers preached to the mixed audiences.

Mixed teams of ushers and a mixed choir were other features of the Fellowship Church.[9]

Other groups emulated the Philadelphia experiment. In several large northern cities during the 1940's, churchmen formed inter-denominational and interracial fellowships that met monthly at special services. Perhaps the most notable of these was the Inter-racial Fellowship of Greater New York, founded in 1943 to promote "a church of all peoples and a society free from racial barriers." Some of these special churches also sponsored interracial projects of various kinds.[10] However, only a small number of people participated in such churches. They were by no means regular neighborhood churches; hence, they lacked the functions of the normal Protestant church. Their significance lay not in their numbers but in their pioneering nature.

Of a more enduring and everyday nature, though also inter-denominational and experimental, were other kinds of fellow-ship churches that developed in northern and west-coast cities during the war years. Unlike those described above, these fellow-ship churches met every Sunday, had a regular church program, and were served by regular full-time pastors. They were the fruits of Protestants' growing awareness of the race problem's importance and of individual Protestants' belief that segregated churches were a violation of basic Christian precepts. Individual ministers and laymen were often instrumental in developing these churches.

The first and most notable of these churches was the Church for the Fellowship of All Peoples of San Francisco. During the war, Dr. Alfred G. Fisk, a white Presbyterian minister and professor at San Francisco State College, gathered a small group of followers and began to hold worship services in a Negro area of San Francisco. The northern Presbyterians provided Fisk with a place to hold these interracial worship services, and a young Negro theological student assisted him in running "The Neighbor-hood Church," as it was called at that time.[11]

Although Dr. Fisk was the original mover in the church, much of the credit for its later development belongs to the dynamic

Negro minister, the Reverend Howard Thurman. Because of his teaching duties Dr. Fisk decided to secure a full-time Negro minister to handle the church. Through the Reverend A. J. Muste, the noted pacifist and leader of the Fellowship of Reconciliation, word of the project reached Thurman. After several unsuccessful attempts to secure a Negro minister, Thurman decided to take the position himself, thinking it possible "that this may be *the* opportunity toward which my life had been moving." [12] Consequently Howard Thurman became pastor of the church in the summer of 1944. At that time it had fifty members.

The Board of National Missions of the Presbyterian Church in the United States of America continued to give financial aid to the Church for the Fellowship of All Peoples, but its membership was interdenominational. The Methodist Church also helped secure a place to worship. Eventually the church voted to remain independent of denominational affiliation, and aid from the Presbyterians ceased.[13] Nevertheless the church grew, and the donations of the members in addition to contributions from sympathizers scattered throughout the United States made possible an expanding church program. An interracial, interdenominational, and international quality characterized the church.[14] Although Thurman was the regular pastor, Dr. Fisk served as co-pastor and preached on alternate Sunday mornings, thus keeping the ministry interracial. After Dr. Fisk resigned from the church, a succession of assistant ministers aided Thurman. When Thurman left in 1953 to develop an interracial program as Dean of Marsh Chapel and Professor of Spiritual Disciplines and Resources at Boston University, he was succeeded by the Reverend Francis Geddes, who was white.

Throughout its history the Church for the Fellowship of All Peoples remained interracial in its membership. When Thurman left, the membership was about 60 per cent Caucasian and 35 per cent Negro.[15] Although many regular denominational churches desegregated after the founding of the Church for the Fellowship of All Peoples, this church was unique. It was a frankly experimental church designed to cross racial, cultural, and denomina-

tional lines. It held regular Sunday worship services and conducted a church program. The church also developed a special
type of dual membership that permitted people to belong to it as
well as to their own denominational church. Moreover, persons
living outside the San Francisco Bay area were allowed to become
members-at-large; groups even held "collective memberships-at-
large." In short, the church offered an opportunity for those in
the area to enjoy an active interracial and intercultural experience
and an opportunity for those not living in the area to support the
venture morally and financially.[16] Finally, the church was unusual in that it had a special creed or commitment that symbolized
its purpose and significance.

Several other racially inclusive congregations were organized
in the 1940's. In 1943 the Congregational Christian Park Church
of Berkeley, California, voted to disband. Members had been leaving the congregation as the community rapidly became Negro.
The Congregational Christians then made the church available
for an interracial congregation; it was placed under a Negro minister, the Reverend Roy Nichols, and renamed the South Berkeley Community Church. The church maintained an interracial
ministry, with the Reverend Buell Gallagher of the Pacific
School of Religion, onetime president of a Negro college, serving
as co-pastor without pay and preaching once a month. Although
originally aided by the Congregational Christians, the church was
interdenominational as well as interracial. The South Berkeley
Community Church, like the Church for the Fellowship of All
Peoples across the Bay, had a covenant that welcomed "all persons without regard to race, class, nation, or creed." [17] In Los
Angeles the Reverend Harold Kingsley, formerly of the Negro
Congregational Church of the Good Shepherd in Chicago, became minister of a similar church. The Reverend Dan Greuning,
a Disciples of Christ clergyman, founded the All Peoples' Christian Church and Community Center, also in Los Angeles.[18]

Taking their cue from these ventures on the West Coast,
churchmen in northern cities launched similar projects. In 1944
the Detroit Council of Churches declared that Negroes should be

admitted to all churches in the city. A year later, under the sponsorship of the Detroit Council of Churches, the Detroit Church of All Peoples was launched. In June 1946 the Church of All Peoples of Cleveland opened its doors.[19]

Another case of an interracial and interdenominational ministry serving an area without regard for race was the East Harlem Protestant Parish in New York City. Three students at Union Theological Seminary started the Parish in 1948 in the East Harlem section of Manhattan, an area predominantly inhabited by Puerto Ricans and Negroes. Although the purpose of the founders was to serve a depressed area where the conventional church had been unsuccessful, it was also an interracial venture. This was true of both the membership of the Parish and the staff; one of the three ministers, Archie Hargraves, was a Negro. Beginning with practically no facilities — the churches themselves were "storefronts" — the three built a religious and social program in spite of great obstacles. Once the project was under way, funds were provided by a variety of denominations.[20] After the success of the East Harlem Protestant Parish, churchmen inaugurated similar ventures in Chicago, Cleveland, and New Haven.

The denominations aided the various interdenominational and interracial fellowship churches by making ministers, members, and money available. During the 1940's churchmen also developed racially inclusive denominational churches in several northern communities. This movement was stimulated partly by the success of the fellowship churches, but some of these denominational churches appeared at about the same time as the interdenominational ones.

One of the first racially inclusive denominational churches was the South Congregational Church in Chicago. Although the church eventually disbanded, it was an important pioneering venture. In the early 1940's, Negroes began to move into the area around the church. Meetings held between the church and the Chicago Congregational Union led to the appointment of the Reverend Howard Spragg as minister and the Reverend William Lovell as associate pastor of the church. Both ministers were

white. The church voted not to sell or move. The Chicago Congregational Union said that the church should not be used either
to break down or to enforce the restrictive covenants in the
neighborhood even though some of the church members were active in the groups promoting them. The church was to be open
to all, and some leaders felt that it might be possible to maintain
an interracial congregation for several years.[21]

In 1944, Negroes first attended the South Congregational
Church. Two years later the congregation faced the issue of Negro membership and after a heated debate voted by a close mar-
gin to reaffirm its policy of keeping membership open to all.[22]
On Palm Sunday, 1946, the first Negroes joined. The next year
Negroes were elected to several church offices for the first time.
In the fall of 1948, the Reverend Robert Johnson, a Negro graduate of the Colgate-Rochester Divinity School, was appointed associate pastor. William Lovell replaced Howard Spragg as head
minister. When Lovell left the church several years later, Johnson became pastor. The shift from white to Negro leadership was
accompanied by a similar shift in the composition of the church's
membership. Eventually the church became practically all Negro
and was sold to a Negro congregation.

The problems of the church were many, and they illustrate
some of the difficulties facing congregations that attempted to
become interracial. It was difficult to have a racially mixed church
in a neighborhood whose residents were of one race. Such was
the case with South Congregational Church, for as whites moved
away from the neighborhood, they found it difficult to attend
the services of worship on Sundays. Protestant churches perform
a social function, often being the center of their members' social
lives. Social mixing is one of the most sensitive aspects of the
race problem, for it touches upon many of the fears, taboos, and
prejudices of both the white and Negro communities. Protestant
churches may have admitted Negroes as members, but they did
not include them in all phases of church life, so the churches
were not truly interracial. The South Congregational Church
faced this problem and met it with mixed success; not all of its

activities were interracial. Perhaps the significance of this church was that it attempted to meet the problem of the church in a changing neighborhood and that it brought to light some of the concrete obstacles to developing interracial congregations.[23]

A more successful venture, also located on the south side of Chicago, was that of the First Presbyterian Church. Once a fashionable, flourishing congregation of over two thousand members, the church faced a declining membership and a changing neighborhood in the 1940's. This church had confronted similar situations in the past. Its response to a Negro influx in the 1920's had been to sell its building and move to a new location just south of the University of Chicago. Faced with a changing neighborhood again in the 1940's, the congregation established a committee of church officers to study the problem and its effect on the future of the church. The committee weighed various alternatives and decided both against remaining an all-white church in a Negro neighborhood and against moving. Instead, it favored ministering to the neighborhood without regard to race.[24]

The congregation did not hold a meeting to decide the issue of Negro membership, but the church elders concluded that no sincere Christian could be refused membership on account of his race. A good deal of credit for the church's decision belongs to the forceful minister, the Reverend Harold Bowman. Bowman preached on race relations, stressing a progressive Christian approach to the race question, and he counseled individual church members.

In 1949, after the committee's report, Negro children began to attend the Sunday school and Negroes began to appear at the Sunday services of worship. The first Negro joined the church in the fall of 1953. After that time many Negroes became members and the church's various programs became interracial. In the fall of 1957, the Reverend Ulysses Blakeley, who was Negro, and the Reverend Charles Leber, who was white, became co-pastors of the church, with equal responsibility, salary, and title, thus bringing an interracial ministry to the church.[25]

An example of a Negro congregation's receiving white mem-

bers was the Bidwell Presbyterian Church of Pittsburgh. Although Negro churches were generally willing to receive whites,
few whites availed themselves of the opportunity. In 1952, when
the Negro congregation of the Bidwell Church was seeking a
new pastor, the Reverend Virgil P. Moccia, a young white minister, announced that he would like to have his name placed among
those being considered for the position. The church voted to accept the white minister, who became its pastor in June 1952. The
next year the congregation voted to work for a racially inclusive
church. Within one year the church reported twenty-five white
members in a total membership of almost four hundred. In some
church activities roughly one-fourth of the participants were
whites.[26]

Another way of achieving a racially inclusive congregation was
by merging a Negro and a white congregation to form one
church. In some cases this was effected by a white congregation
absorbing a smaller Negro mission church. In November 1954,
the four thousand-member downtown Hennepin Avenue Methodist Church of Minneapolis voted to welcome all regardless of
race. Two years later when the Negro Border Methodist Church
of Minneapolis, which had about two hundred members, was
forced to move to make way for a city redevelopment project,
the Hennepin congregation invited the members of the Border
Church to combine with them. Similar mergers took place among
Episcopalians and Presbyterians.[27]

One interesting interracial church was the result of a co-
operative project between the Episcopalians and the Presbyterians. In the mid-1940's the Saint Barnabas Episcopal Church in
Cincinnati found its neighborhood changing. Saint Barnabas combined with a new interracial Presbyterian congregation, the
West Cincinnati Presbyterian Church, and the two became the
West Cincinatti–Saint Barnabas Church, an interracial church
under the Reverend Maurice F. McCrackin, who had promoted
the interracial congregation at West Cincinnati Presbyterian
Church. The Episcopal church building served as the community
center and the Presbyterian edifice as the church. As in other

cases, various church programs became interracial before the first
Negroes were received into membership.[28]

For many Protestant congregations, becoming racially inclusive was difficult, if not impossible, because of residential segregation, especially in northern communities. These churches could
achieve at least a degree of racial inclusiveness by accepting Negro ministers, co-pastors, and associate ministers. Some predominantly white churches in neighborhoods undergoing change in
racial composition, rather than abandon their buildings, appointed
Negro ministers in an effort to encourage Negroes to join. The
appointment of Negro ministers to nearly all-white congregations
in areas of stable population was rare. In the early 1950's a few
Protestant churches took up this challenge. In 1950, the Congregational church in Staffordville, Connecticut, called the Reverend
Roland T. Heacock, a Negro who had had some experience with
white churches, to be its regular pastor. A few other churches
made similar appointments after that, but the number was
small.[29] Still others declared their willingness to accept a Negro
minister. In 1952, Methodist Bishop John Wesley Lord told the
New England Conference of the Methodist Church that white
churches should consider the appointment of Negro ministers
when vacancies occurred. Following Bishop Lord's statement,
Zion's Herald suggested that churches pledge themselves to be
willing to accept Negro ministers. A number of New England
Methodist churches agreed to accept ministers without regard to
race, color, or national origin.[30]

Students of the Union Theological Seminary made an effort to
stimulate interracial pastorates in the spring of 1960, when the
Student Interracial Ministry was organized. Beginning in the
summer of 1960, a number of seminarians served summer pastorates without regard to race. By 1962, as a result of the experiment, the Reverend James Forbes, a Negro, had served as assistant minister in a predominantly white southern church, the Olin
T. Binkley Memorial Baptist Church of Chapel Hill, North Carolina.[31]

The examples cited above of racially inclusive congregations or attempts to form them could be multiplied for most major northern Protestant denominations and the northern wings of national Protestant churches. Beginning on a modest scale during World War II, a movement was well under way by the early 1960's to desegregate local churches. Yet it was primarily a northern and western movement; the South was left largely untouched. Here and there a few southern churches did begin to desegregate. One did so under the lead of the Reverend Charles M. Jones of the Presbyterian Church of Chapel Hill, North Carolina. Jones, who was theologically in the liberal camp, had had some experience with labor problems and unions in western North Carolina and Tennessee before coming to Chapel Hill in the early 1940's. His modernist and humanist views on the theology of southern Presbyterianism fitted him for the university-oriented and liberal Presbyterian Church at Chapel Hill, among whose members was Frank Graham, president of the University of North Carolina. When faced with the possibility of Negroes' attending his church, Jones, with the support of his congregation, declared, "This church does not encourage Negroes to desert their own churches for membership or worship in this church. On the other hand, we do not close our doors or discriminate against or receive with aught but the spirit of Christian brotherhood any sincere worshipper who may present himself." [32]

In 1947, an interracial group from the Fellowship of Reconciliation traveled through several southern states to discover whether those states were complying with the Supreme Court's decision in Morgan *v.* Virginia, which prohibited segregation on motor buses engaged in interstate commerce. When the group reached Chapel Hill a near-riot occurred. The usually soft-spoken and casual-appearing Reverend Mr. Jones hustled several members of the group away in his automobile and offered them the protection of his home. Eventually the police had to guard his residence, though students, among whom Jones was popular, offered to protect it. The Jones family left town for several days, though Jones himself stayed. No violence occurred except for a few rocks thrown at Jones's house.[33]

Although Jones was supported by his congregation, eventually the Orange Presbytery forced him out of his pastorate and out of the southern Presbyterian Church for alleged nonconformity with basic Presbyterian doctrine. Some critics charged that Jones's theological divergencies from established dogma were used as an excuse to purge him because of his liberal views on labor and race relations.[34] Whatever the real reason, certainly his views on both theology and social issues differed from those of the conservative Orange Presbytery. Following his expulsion from the southern Presbyterian Church in 1953, Jones founded a community church in Chapel Hill which, like his Presbyterian church, was open to all races.

There were other southern white churches that admitted Negroes. Some, like the church in Chapel Hill, were in university towns, which seemed to be more liberal on the race question than the average community. Others in less liberal areas voted an open membership policy. Beginning in 1960, with the challenge of the kneel-ins accompanying the sit-in movement, a number of churches were tested on the meaning of "everyone welcome." In some instances the Negroes attempting to attend white services were turned away; in others they were allowed to worship. The fact that the kneel-ins were tests caused some complications for southern white churches. At the Oklahoma City First Baptist Church under the Reverend Herschel H. Hobbs, president of the Southern Baptist Convention, such a test led to the denial of membership to a Negro in January 1962. When a fifteen-year-old Negro, Glendale Brown, applied for membership after attending for a few months, the members rejected his application. The rejection was supposedly on the ground that his application was not offered in good faith.[35] Whether or not kneel-ins eventually lead to desegregation, as of the early 1960's the vast majority of southern congregations were still racially segregated.

A variety of factors affected the development of racially inclusive and interracial congregations. The most important was the custom of the region where the churches were located. The South was more segregated than the North; hence, the southern churches were more segregated than their northern counterparts. Of the mixed congregations with Negro members or attenders, the majority had only a few Negro members.[36] These churches were located primarily in the Northeast, along the West Coast, and to some extent in the Midwest, usually in communities where the Negro population was small.[37] The Congregational Christian Church seems to have had relatively many racially inclusive congregations, but churches of this denomination were located mainly in the North, especially in the Northeast. Churches of other denominations in the Northeast reported a similar degree of racial inclusiveness.[38]

The evidence also suggests that urban churches were more desegregated than rural ones.[39] This factor was related to the regional one. Most rural Negroes lived in the South, where the race problem was worse. So few northern Negroes lived in rural areas that the opportunities for integration there were limited.

Residential segregation hindered the development of mixed churches. Many white churches would have welcomed Negroes, but Negro attendance was difficult to achieve because of residential segregation and the custom of the local church serving the local neighborhood. Nevertheless, many churches in areas with Negro populations did not accept Negroes; and many white Protestants fled to the suburbs in the face of a Negro influx. The Congregational Christians, in a survey conducted in 1956–57, reported that of 371 churches that had moved for various reasons, 22 indicated that race was a prominent cause.[40] The evidence suggests that when an area became 40 per cent Negro, white Protestant churches either had moved or disbanded. The optimum situation for the development of a desegregated congregation probably occurred when the population surrounding the church was between 5 and 40 per cent Negro.[41]

As the trend toward a more open policy on the part of local congregations grew, residential segregation became an increasingly important barrier to further development of racially inclusive churches. Many such congregations were so only as a transi-

e in a changing neighborhood and eventually became
as the neighborhood did.

class also influenced the development of interracial con-
ns. Racial inclusiveness seemingly occurred more readily
rches of middle-class or upper-class composition. Some-
these were the large downtown churches. This factor helps
in some of the success of northern Presbyterians, Congrega-
al Christians, Episcopalians, and certain churches of other de-
minations in achieving desegregation.[42]

The cultural difference between the Negro and white churches
and communities also affected the growth of racially inclusive
and interracial congregations. As the local church formed such an
important social unit, a cultural gap between members of a congregation was important. Negro churches generally tended to be
more evangelic than white churches, and Negro ministers less
educated than white ministers. The shortage of trained Negro
ministers created a problem in developing an interracial ministry.
The Negro church also tended to be more important in the Negro community than its counterpart was in the white community. Then, too, lower educational and economic levels among
Negroes created problems for those desiring mixed churches.
Lower-class Negroes and middle-class whites did not feel at home
together. In some cases, the situation worked in reverse. The fir
Negroes moving into a white neighborhood were sometimes o
higher socio-economic level than their white neighbors and
not feel at home in their churches.[43]

Furthermore, the existence of segregated congregations
times created suspicions and reinforced myths between th
The congregations that developed racial inclusiveness in
ade after World War II were pioneering in a new field
to fight myths as well as prejudice. Many well-mea
Protestants believed that Negroes preferred their ov
Whites sometimes feared Negro participation in
affairs, and Negroes feared rejection or insults.

In the face of the various obstacles to the devel

interracial congregations, vigorous ʼ
important roles. On occasion a sn
kept the church's racial barriers intac.
wanted to desegregate.[44] On the other i.
careful planning and forceful leadership,
of the minister, were able to overcome tradh.
development of racially inclusive churches. Mo.
members actually left their churches because ot
actions.[45]

It is difficult to assess precisely the extent of racial in.
in local congregations because of the scarcity of data.
gational Christians, northern Presbyterians, United Luth.
southern Presbyterians, and southern Baptists made studie.
their local congregations and some scholars investigated the pra
tices of other denominations and of churches in particular areas.
The value of such studies varied, however, and some were fragmentary.

In 1945 the Congregational Christian Church studied its
churches, and in 1956–57 the boards and agencies involved with
race relations conducted another survey of the extent of racial
inclusiveness among its congregations. Data gathered in the early
1950's by Alfred Kramer of the Department of Race Relations of
the National Council of Churches added to the knowledge of the
Congregational Christians. The study completed in 1957 was of
churches in metropolitan areas — that is, urban communities con-
taining at least one city with a population of 50,000 or more.
Approximately 12 per cent of the predominantly white congregations had some Negroes participating in their church life. This
showed some progress over the situation revealed in the 1945
study.[46]

Racially inclusive churches were proportionately more numerous in the urban East and especially in the urban West. The Midwest lagged behind; and no white churches in the South were
found to have Negro members, though some stated that they
would accept Negroes. Examination of the churches' activities
nd officers revealed that Negroes participated in a wide range of

activities, but conspicuous gaps occurred where positions of professional leadership were involved.[47]

At about the same time that the Congregational Christian study of 1956–57 was being made, the northern Presbyterians' Department of Social Education and Action conducted a survey of racial inclusiveness among congregations of that church. Of those returning the questionnaire, 609, or about 13 per cent, of the predominantly white churches had at least one Negro present in their life.[48] About half of these had at least two Negro members or six Negroes in attendance at worship services or some Negroes in leadership positions. Of the 119 Negro churches responding, 28 reported having at least one white member and several more reported having whites in attendance. Thus, Negro churches accepted other races more often than did predominantly white churches, a fact also revealed by the Congregational Christian analysis.[49]

The results of the survey made by the Presbyterians resembled those of the Congregational Christians in showing the relationship of geography to racial inclusiveness. In the South no white congregations were found that had two or more Negro members. Only three predominantly white churches in the South, in a survey covering about half of the denomination's congregations, had one Negro participating in some manner; none of these were in the Deep South. Considerably fewer churches in the South than in the rest of the country expressed willingness to accept Negroes. The areas in which the highest rates of acceptance of Negroes occurred were the Northeast, the West, and some parts of the Midwest. Other parts of the Midwest lagged, and still fewer instances of Negroes' participating in predominantly white churches were found in the border states.[50] The data concerning Negroes in positions of leadership and Negro participation in the social, educational, and policy-making life of the church again resembled those of the Congregational Christians. Less than half of the churches that had at least one Negro as a member or attender reported having Negroes in active roles.[51]

After 1956–57 other Presbyterian and Congregational Christian churches became racially inclusive; perhaps close to one-fifth of the churches of these two denominations claimed racial inclusiveness by 1965. The overwhelming majority of these congregations had only nominal Negro participation; hence, they were not truly interracial.

Detailed data on other denominations, except perhaps the United Lutherans, are unavailable; hence, conclusions about racially inclusive and interracial churches among them are merely guesses. The United Lutheran survey of 1950 and the work of Kramer a few years later revealed that the Lutherans had proportionately fewer racially inclusive churches than did Presbyterians and Congregational Christians. Historically, the Lutherans never had many Negro members either in all-Negro congregations or in predominantly white churches; consequently the results are not surprising. The Lutherans had different cultural and language traditions from those of American Negroes. Though these patterns were breaking down in the twentieth century, the Lutherans had only a small link to the Negro community. Some Lutheran slaveholders converted their slaves, and after the Civil War Lutherans gathered in a few Negroes in missionary work in the South. Missionary work in the North in the twentieth century added to the numbers.[52] If the small size of the Negro community within the United Lutheran Church is taken into account, the data on racially inclusive congregations were similar to those for northern Presbyterians and Congregational Christians in several respects. Most of the white churches with some non-white participation included only a few Negroes. Most were in the same geographical areas where the northern Presbyterians and Congregational Christians achieved some success in racial inclusiveness. And the presence of a few Negroes did not mean that they were accepted in all phases of church life.[53]

The Methodist Church undoubtedly had proportionately fewer racially inclusive congregations than did the northern Presbyterians and Congregational Christians.[54] In the first place, a large section of Methodist membership was in the South where there was resistance to desegregation, especially among Alabama, Mississippi, and Georgia Methodists. More important was the influence of the Central Jurisdiction on racial practices throughout the Methodist Church. The Central Jurisdiction offered all-Negro churches and Negro ministers certain advantages in the church in terms of leadership possibilities and representation on church boards and at the General Conference. These opportunities for Negroes in the church depended upon their separate annual conferences and jurisdiction, which were based upon separate local congregations. This tended to discourage mixed congregations even though the overwhelming majority of Negro Methodists were undoubtedly opposed to a Jim Crow church. Moreover, the church had geared its thinking to separate congregations, conferences, and jurisdictions to a greater extent than had the other denominations with Negro membership. Unification, with its concomitant institutionalization of segregation, was achieved just at the time when the movement in Protestantism for racially inclusive congregations was beginning.

The record of northern Baptists and Protestant Episcopalians was probably similar to that of northern Presbyterians and Congregational Christians, though data are lacking.[55] Certainly these denominations developed a number of racially inclusive congregations in the North.

Among southern denominations, such as the southern Baptists and Presbyterians, the number of desegregated churches was small. In a sketchy survey made by the Baptist press in 1962–63, 90 per cent of the congregations were revealed to be all-white. Detailed information about the Negro participation in the other 10 per cent was not given, but it was probably minimal.[56] Southern Presbyterians also surveyed some of their congregations in 1962–63. Of the nearly 1200 reporting, slightly over half indicated they would welcome Negroes at the Sunday morning worship service, some on a segregated basis. Only one-fourth indicated they would not welcome Negroes. As for membership, only 2 per cent said they would welcome Negro members and 4 per cent indicated that Negroes had been members at some time; 5 per cent said that Negroes attended regularly. Information as to whether Negroes would be accepted in all phases of church life, including leadership positions, was unavailable. However, probably only a handful of either southern Baptist or Presbyterian congregations would have accepted Negroes in positions of authority.[57]

In Protestantism as a whole, probably 10 per cent, perhaps slightly more, of the predominantly white congregations had either Negro members or attenders by the early 1960's. Most of these included only a few members or attenders, however, and close to ninety-nine of every hundred Negro Protestants worshipped in segregated congregations on Sunday mornings. Many more white Protestant churches, even in the South, indicated that they would welcome Negroes, but obstacles, such as residential segregation and reluctance of Negroes to attend white churches, stood in the way. Certainly the existence of long-established all-Negro denominations was a barrier to desegregation. Sometimes Negro ministers from these denominations had a vested interest in segregated churches. And certainly their members, long accustomed to distrust the white community, were reluctant at times to bridge the caste system.

Yet the white churches themselves were a powerful block to the development of interracial churches. They may have welcomed Negroes to the Sunday morning service, but they did not invite Negroes to join in all phases of church life; hence they were not fully interracial. The evidence, though fragmentary, suggests that in some instances Negroes attended services but were not welcome as members, or if they were members they were not selected for leadership positions in the church. A church may have accepted Negro members but not a Negro minister; the ministry was one of the most segregated professions in America. In addition, many white churches still closed their doors and fled to the suburbs rather than face the problems of a changing neighborhood. In short, Protestantism was often passive and sometimes actually resistive to the development of an interracial Christianity, rather than active in promoting it. The movement toward inter-racial congregations with all areas of local church life open to Negroes was well under way by the early 1960's, but the over-whelming majority of both white and Negro Protestants were untouched by it.

Conclusion

In an article in the *Christian Century* in 1931, William E. B. Du Bois declared, "The church, as a whole, insists on a divine mission and guidance and the indisputable possession of truth. Is there anything in the record of the church in America in regard to the Negro to prove this? There is not. If the treatment of the Negro by the Christian Church is called 'divine,' this is an attack on the conception of God more blasphemous than any which the church has always been so ready and eager to punish." [1] Du Bois's stricture had been made before, and it has certainly been made since. Some of the abolitionists had assailed the white churches as bulwarks of slavery, and in the early 1960's numerous church conferences produced speakers who attacked the churches for their race relations practices.

The critics of white Protestantism's treatment of the Negro had much evidence to support their strictures. But Protestantism's treatment of the Negro was no better and no worse than that of American society as a whole. Fundamental to an understanding of the race problem in Protestantism is the fact that the churches are social institutions that are shaped by the culture in which they exist. There were experiments in American history that attempted to build a holy society, but often these experiments were sharply modified by the very environment and people they sought to mold. This was especially true after the end of the colonial era.

Church members, whether in the pre-twentieth century days, when they represented only a minority of the community, or in the twentieth century, were also members of a variety of social groups and were pressured and influenced by many social forces. Hence, the attitudes and practices of white Protestant churches regarding the Negro were those of white America generally.

In the colonial era some efforts were made to convert Negro slaves. Once a Negro, slave or free, became a Christian the question of race relations within the church became a problem. Sometimes Negroes were received equally in the churches; sometimes they were segregated in "Negro Pews." In the years following the American Revolution, new institutions appeared, the all-Negro denominations. These denominations were born of race prejudice and discrimination. All-Negro congregations and segregationist practices in mixed congregations developed in the northern churches in the decades before the Civil War. Not even the Society of Friends, the pioneer in the antislavery movement, escaped without some taint of discrimination. These practices were not novel; as Leon Litwack in *North of Slavery* showed, segregation and discrimination were the major characteristics of Negro-white relations in the North during those years. There were some religious critics of those practices, but they were in a minority.

In the South slavery determined the relations of Negro to white. Slaves were allowed in white churches, but only in slave galleries. If Negroes were permitted to hold their own worship services, it was under the watchful eyes of whites.

Slavery was the prime social and moral issue in the three decades before the Civil War. The Protestant churches could not avoid it. In the South the clergy gave slavery their moral support. On the eve of the Civil War scarcely a southern clergyman could be found who would attack the South's peculiar institution. The Biblical defenses were the ones most frequently cited to justify slavery. Clergymen and secular leaders used the curse on Ham and numerous scriptural references to defend the institution. This is not to say that the churches were uninterested in the soul of the Negro or in his welfare. They often insisted upon religious training for Negroes and urged planters to treat their slaves kindly. But slavery as an institution was accepted. Other clergymen dodged the question by insisting that it was a political or civil issue; hence, the churches should not tamper with it. These religious leaders in effect sanctioned the status quo. In short, the southern churches responded to the slavery controversy as did the South generally.

While the southern churches were tacitly or overtly defending slavery, the antislavery crusade enlisted the support of many northern churchmen, especially the evangelic ones. Actually not many clergymen were abolitionists, but one by one most of the leading northern denominations took antislavery positions. Although the militants among the clergy were in a minority and although the northern churches sometimes hedged on the slavery issue, the position of the churches north of the Mason-Dixon Line was strong enough to divide American Protestantism into sectional branches. Perhaps the greatest contribution of religion to the antislavery impulse was not the work of the churches as institutions but rather the religious motivation behind many individuals' attacks on slavery.

During the Civil War northern and southern ministers rallied to their respective causes. Even before the end of the war, northern churchmen began to discuss the plight of the ex-slave. Driven by a vision of the Kingdom of God on earth and by an equalitarian and religious fervor, northern missionaries departed for the South to build a new social order and to carry the gospel to the freedmen. In the 1860's these missionaries, many of whom had been abolitionists, set up schools and churches for Negroes. In some cases they supported the Radical Republicans, defended the Negro's civil rights, and insisted upon racial equality.

The activities of the northern churches and the self-righteous attitude of Northerners did not endear them to southern white Protestants. During Reconstruction co-operation between northern and southern churches was nil. The southern white churches, like the South generally, began to erect a social order to replace slavery. The result was segregation, discrimination, and a philosophy of white supremacy. For the southern Protestant churches the transition from slavery to segregation and white supremacy came easily. Under slavery whites had presumed Negroes to be innately inferior and had segregated them in the churches; this attitude and this condition were simply carried over into the postwar years. As C. Vann Woodward has pointed out, while segregation in many public areas was not instituted until the 1890's, the churches did not wait that long; segregation was established in Protestantism by the end of Reconstruction. Indeed, the evidence suggests that white southern Protestantism helped prepare the white South for the full capitulation to racism.

Racism triumphed in the South in the latter part of the nineteenth century, and the northern churches condoned it. Though northern congregational life was generally segregated before the Civil War, when the northern churches went south they maintained integration in some phases of church life. Compromises came in the 1870's, 1880's, and 1890's as the churches gave in to segregation in their southern schools and church administration. The pressures for northern capitulation — racism, imperialism, political bargains, economics, and desire to heal the wounds of the war — all left their marks on the churches. The tragedy of the northern white churches' surrender was that the voice of moral protest was silenced. The social gospel movement scarcely considered the plight of the American Negro. The great revivalistic tradition of the early nineteenth century, sometimes sensitive to the Negro's civil rights and the slavery issue, gave way to the revivalism of Dwight L. Moody and Billy Sunday. This new evangelism did not protest the American practice of race relations. The northern churches did not abandon their southern schools for Negroes, but the schools became training grounds for second-class citizenship, hardly adequate to train needed leaders for the Negro race. Booker T. Washington became northern white Protestantism's hero. The whole race problem, in the eyes of both the northern and southern churches, became the problem of the personal defects of the Negro; hence, the solution became one directed toward Christian uplift of the Negro. A few church-men still protested against this "solution," and the churches, especially in the North, did attack special problems such as lynch-ing, but basically the churches agreed with American practices and attitudes.

During and after World War I, a few church leaders began to feel that Christian education and evangelism were inadequate to solve the race problem. These churchmen and women, working through church groups, in the Y.M.C.A. and Y.W.C.A., or on the secular interracial committees that developed in the 1920's, sought to foster better relations between the races and to secure equal, though usually separate, facilities for Negroes. The Federal Council of Churches' Department of Race Relations was founded during this period, and churchmen connected with domestic mis-sionary work and southern churchwomen were particularly ac-tive. During the years between the world wars, however, church-men rarely examined their basic ideas about race relations. Both northern and southern white Protestants accepted segregation, the Southerners more readily than the Northerners. On the eve of World War II, the Methodist Church, America's largest Protestant denomination, with more Negro members than all other mixed Protestant sects combined, segregated its Negro membership in the cause of unity. Some Methodists even told the Negroes that segregation was not really segregation, but a way of giving Negroes opportunities in the united Methodist Church.

During World War II, under the leadership of the Federal Council of Churches, the churches began to question their con-ceptions of race relations. By the end of the 1940's the major northern denominations were calling for a "non-segregated church and a non-segregated society." Acceptance of the idea that segregation and Christianity are incompatible was more diffi-cult for white southern churches. Many fundamentalist ministers, especially in rural areas, still could not give up the centuries-old belief that the Christian God was a God of segregation. On the extreme Right of Protestantism there existed, too, the "apostles of discord" who stirred up race hatred. For the most part, however, the "respectable" southern white Protestant churches followed the trend toward condemning segregation as unchristian. Southern Presbyterians and southern Baptists issued statements to this effect in the 1950's.

In attacking segregation, Protestantism was in the mainstream of American life. It was no accident that the call for a "non-segregated church and a non-segregated society" came at about the same time as the threatened Negro march on Washington, Myrdal's *American Dilemma*, and President Truman's Commission on Civil Rights.

With the new goal, pronouncements covering almost every aspect of the race problem came from church conferences and religious leaders. But it is doubtful if many of the laity and even some of the leadership were fully aware of their denomination's position on the race problem. Thus the problem lay in implementation. Protestant churches are voluntary associations, and their social pronouncements are binding upon no individual or congregation. Rather, they serve as guideposts for social behavior.

By the early 1960's the white churches had made some progress in implementing their desire for truly interracial churches. Negroes were occupying leadership positions they had never filled before, church administration and church-related institutions were being desegregated, and even local congregations were becoming racially inclusive. At best, however, practice fell considerably short of preaching. Much of the desegregation within the churches stopped short of full integration. Southern seminaries, for example, admitted Negro students but did not hire Negro deans and faculty. Negroes became bishops, but their work was generally confined to Negro churches. Local white congregations admitted Negroes to membership but did not allow them to serve in the pulpits or in other leadership positions. Full integration, in which all phases of church life were open to all without regard to race and in which Negroes served in nonracial capacities, was far from being achieved by 1965. In 1959 Liston Pope of the Yale Divinity School wrote of Protestantism,

> Its record indicates clearly, however, that the church is the most segregated major institution in American society. It has lagged behind the Supreme Court as the conscience of the nation on questions of race, and it has fallen far behind trade unions, factories, schools, department stores, athletic gatherings, and most other areas of human association as far as the achievement of integration in its own life is concerned.[2]

Whether or not Pope's comment was entirely fair, the fact is that Protestantism had not been in the vanguard of integration.

Congregational Christians were generally more progressive in their attitudes on the race question than the churchmen of other denominations. They were usually a jump ahead of the other groups in social pronouncements, in establishing race relations programs, and in church practices. Moreover, the Congregationalists' American Missionary Association, founded as an antislavery organization, fought more vigorously than other groups against the pressures for segregation in the last quarter of the nineteenth century. But this denomination's strength lay in the northeastern states, and in this region the other denominations behaved much like the Congregational Christians. The traditional voice of Methodist liberalism on the race question, for example, was *Zion's Herald,* published in Boston and run by Northerners. The Congregational Christian Church had no more success than other denominations in desegregating its few local churches in the South. In 1964 it still maintained the Convention of the South, an all-Negro unit. The Episcopalians were the only group to desegregate their southern dioceses by that year; but in contrast to other national and southern denominations, most Negro Episcopalians were in the North, and the southern Negroes could more easily be "swallowed up" by the white southern Episcopalians.

If southern denominations were the last to challenge old con-ceptions and practices in race relations, the southern wings of national denominations exhibited similar behavior. Viewed in this light, it would seem that the explanation of the denominations' various attitudes and practices regarding the Negro lies in regional rather than religious differences.

Nevertheless, denominations sometimes differed within a given region. If a denomination was more advanced in one respect, however, it lagged in others. The Episcopal Church was the least segregated in the South because it sometimes chose unofficial exclusion or disfranchisement of Negroes rather than constitutionally separate dioceses. Negroes paid a price for this arrangement over the years; they were virtually excluded from the church's General Conventions until the 1950's and had fewer leadership positions in the church. The Methodists, on the other hand, allowed Negroes the greatest participation at the top levels of church administration, but the price for this representation was constitutional separation in the form of the all-Negro Central Jurisdiction and segregated annual conferences, even in the North.

It is difficult to assess the role of theology as a factor in the history of race relations. In the colonial era, the Quakers' theology directly affected their humanitarianism and views on slavery. During the decades before the Civil War, the new theology of evangelic Protestantism gave impetus to the antislavery movement. In the post-Civil War period, the theologically more conservative groups, such as the southern Baptists and southern Presbyterians, were also more conservative on the race question. But this theological conservatism tended to have greater strength in the South. How much of the churches' conservatism on race was due to their theology and how much to regional mores would be difficult to determine. Moreover, there was in post-Civil War conservative theology a tendency to shun social issues on the ground that the church's mission was to preach the gospel and not meddle in such questions. In the 1950's, however, many southern ministers, though theologically conservative, moved into the liberal camp on race relations. An important factor retarding change in the churches' practices was the resistance to desegregation among laymen.

If the white churches on the whole were slow in climbing to the high plateau established by their own social pronouncements, many individual Protestants over the years were ahead of institutionalized religion. Some were in the antislavery movement or active during Reconstruction. Some protested against the churches' own segregationist and discriminatory practices. Some worked in associations such as the women's missionary groups or the National Council of Churches' Department of Race Relations. The distinction between the social institution and the individuals and groups within it is an important one, for these individuals and groups acted as the moral voice of the churches when the churches themselves practiced segregation and discrimination.

The individuals who fought slavery, segregation, and discrimination were often torn between conflicting loyalties. On the one hand, their Christian consciences drove them to seek justice, which at times meant denouncing the church for its racial practices. On the other hand, their roots and loyalties lay with the church, which for all its imperfections was still the carrier of the word of God. Some of these people were forced out of the church or left it voluntarily, as was the case with Will Alexander. Others remained within the church and formed such groups as the Episcopal Society for Cultural and Racial Unity to correct the faults of the church and to reconcile Negroes and whites.

Another contribution of the white churches to the development of a truly democratic society was made inadvertently. After the Civil War, they talked of evangelism and Christian education to uplift the American Negro. Although the educational programs of northern missionaries smacked of paternalism and Booker T. Washington's philosophy, they also propagated the Christian gospel. The churches and their schools talked long and loud of Christianity, and many Negro ministers absorbed these teachings. In the 1950's these Negro clergymen made themselves heard. Whether Ralph Abernathy or Martin Luther King, Jr., in the South, or James H. Robinson in the North, these Negro churchmen began to lead their people in demanding the fulfill-ment of the democratic and Christian ideals that white churches had taught them. It may well be that these Negro churchmen will yet teach the white Protestant churches the full meaning of the gospel of the brotherhood of man they espouse.

Notes

CHAPTER I, PAGES 3–24

1 Thomas E. Drake, *Quakers and Slavery in America* (New Haven: Yale University Press, 1950), *passim.*

2 Dwight L. Dumond, *Anti-Slavery: The Crusade for Freedom in America* (Ann Arbor: University of Michigan Press, 1961), pp. 341–6.

3 Owen D. Pelt and Ralph L. Smith, *The Story of the National Baptists* (New York: Vantage Press, 1960), pp. 27–8.

4 Alice Adams, *The Neglected Period of Anti-Slavery, 1808–1830* (Boston: Ginn & Co., 1908), *passim;* John R. Bodo, *The Protestant Clergy and Public Issues, 1812–1848* (Princeton: Princeton University Press, 1954), pp. 112–24; P. J. Standenraus, *The African Colonization Movement* (New York: Columbia University Press, 1961), *passim.*

5 Eric L. McKitrick (ed.), *Slavery Defended* (Englewood Cliffs: Prentice-Hall, 1963), p. 94.

6 William Jenkins, *Pro-slavery Thought in the Old South* (Chapel Hill: University of North Carolina Press, 1935), chap. 5; Walter Posey, *The Presbyterian Church in the Old Southwest* (Richmond: John Knox Press, 1952), chap. 7.

7 Clement Eaton, *Freedom of Thought in the Old South* (Durham: Duke University Press, 1940), *passim.*

8 Gilbert Barnes, *The Anti-Slavery Impulse, 1830–1844* (New York: D. Appleton Century, 1933), *passim;* Charles Cole, *The Social Ideas of the Northern Evangelists, 1826–1860* (New York: Columbia University Press, 1954), chap. 7; Timothy L. Smith, *Revivalism and Social Reform* (Nashville: Abingdon Press, 1957), chaps. 12–13; Bodo, op. cit., chap. 5.

9 Benjamin Thomas, *Theodore Weld* (New Brunswick: Rutgers University Press, 1950), chaps. 5 and 6; Robert Fletcher, *A History of Oberlin College,* I (Oberlin, Ohio: Oberlin, 1943), chaps. 18 and 19.

10 For the role of Parker in the antislavery movement, see Henry Steele Commager, *Theodore Parker* (Boston: Beacon Press, 1947).

11 John Norwood, *The Schism in the Methodist Church 1844* (Alfred, N.Y.: Alfred Press, 1923), *passim;* Willis D. Weatherford, *American Churches and the Negro* (Boston: Christopher Publishing House, 1957), chap. 3. The antislavery Wesleyan Methodist Church had broken with the Methodist Episcopal Church over slavery shortly before the split of 1844.

12 C. Bruce Staiger, "Abolitionism and the Presbyterian Schism of 1837–1838," *Mississippi Valley Historical Review*, XXXVI (December 1949), pp. 391–414; Lewis Vander Velde, *The Presbyterian Churches and the Federal Union, 1861–1869* (Cambridge: Harvard University Press, 1932), chaps. 2–3.

13 Weatherford, op. cit., chap. 4; Mary Putnam, *The Baptists and Slavery, 1840–1845* (Ann Arbor: George Wahr, 1913), pp. 46–87.

14 Robert Fortenbaugh, "American Lutheran Synods and Slavery, 1830–1860," *Journal of Religion*, XIII (January 1933), pp. 72–92; Abdel Wentz, *A Basic History of Lutheranism in America* (Philadelphia: Muhlenberg Press, 1955), pp. 148, 163–72.

15 Dumond, op. cit., chap. 41; Adelaide Lyons, "Religious Defense of Slavery in the North," *Historical Papers*, XIII (Durham: Trinity College Historical Society, 1919), pp. 1–34; Philip S. Foner, *The Life and Writings of Frederick Douglass*, II (New York: International Publishers, 1950), p. 197.

16 Samuel May, *Some Recollections of Our Anti-Slavery Conflict* (Boston: Fields, Osgood & Co., 1869), p. 329.

17 For the slavery controversy in the American Tract, Bible, and Home Missionary Societies, see Clifford S. Griffin, *Their Brothers' Keepers* (New Brunswick: Rutgers University Press, 1960), chap. 10.

18 Clifton Johnson, "The American Missionary Association, 1846–1861: A Study of Christian Abolition" (Unpublished Ph.D. dissertation, University of North Carolina, 1958), pp. 41–57, 184–5; Lewis Tappan, *The Life of Arthur Tappan* (New York: Hurd & Houghton, 1870), pp. 317–21.

19 Carter G. Woodson, *The History of the Negro Church* (Washington: Associated Publishers, 1921), chaps. 1 and 2.

20 Lorenzo Greene, *The Negro in Colonial New England* (New York: Columbia University Press, 1942), pp. 281–5.

21 Clifford M. Drury, *Presbyterian Panorama* (Philadelphia: Board of Christian Education, 1952), pp. 15, 24.

22 Richard Allen, *The Life, Experience and Gospel Labors of the Rt. Rev. Richard Allen* (Nashville: Abingdon Press, 1960), pp. 24–5.

23 Leonard Haynes, Jr., *The Negro Community Within American Protestantism, 1619–1844* (Boston: Christopher Publishing House, 1953), pp. 125–39.

24 Pelt and Smith, op. cit., pp. 49–52, 68–9; Woodson, op. cit., pp. 107–22.

25 George Bragg, *History of the Afro-American Group of the Protestant Episcopal Church* (Baltimore: Church Advocate Press, 1922), pp. 61–4.

26 William Jay, *Miscellaneous Writings on Slavery* (Boston: J. P. Jewett & Co., 1853), pp. 449–50.

27 Leon Litwack, *North of Slavery* (Chicago: University of Chicago

Press, 1961), pp. 199–201; *Journal of the Proceedings of the Annual Convention of the Protestant Episcopal Church in the State of New York,* 1846, p. 73.

28 Ibid., 1853, p. 45.

29 Bragg, op. cit., p. 68; *Journal of the Convention of the Protestant Episcopal Church in the State of Pennsylvania,* 1795, p. 30; ibid., 1843, p. 33.

30 Woodson, op. cit., pp. 188–92.

31 *Journal of the General Conference of the Methodist Episcopal Church,* 1848, pp. 42, 130; ibid., 1852, p. 65.

32 Ibid., 1860, p. 308.

33 Ibid., 1864, pp. 485–8; ibid., 1868, p. 130.

34 Ibid., 1864, p. 488. See also Chapter 3, pp. 56–7.

35 *Christian Advocate,* XL (April 27, 1865), p. 130; ibid., XLI (November 8, 1866), p. 356; ibid., XLIII (April 2, 1868), p. 108.

36 Litwack, op. cit., p. 209.

37 Ibid., pp. 196–9; James Birney, *The American Churches: The Bulwark of Slavery* (Concord, N.H.: Parker Pillsbury, 1885), pp. 10–11, 45; Harvey Newcomb, *The Negro Pew* (Boston: Isaac Knapp, 1837), pp. 79–86; William Chambers, *American Slavery and Caste* (London: W. & R. Chambers, 1857), pp. 129–31.

38 Henry J. Cadbury, "Negro Membership in the Society of Friends," *Journal of Negro History,* XXI (April 1936), pp. 151–213; Thomas Drake, "Joseph Drinker's Pleas for the Admission of Colored People to the Society of Friends, 1795," ibid., XXXII (January 1947), pp. 110–12; *Friend,* XVI (August 19, 1843), pp. 374–5; Sarah Douglass to William Basset in Gilbert Barnes and Dwight Dumond (eds.), *Letters of Theodore Dwight Weld, Angelina Grimke Weld and Sarah Grimke,* II (New York: D. Appleton Century, 1934), pp. 829–31.

39 May, op. cit., p. 269.

40 Litwack, op. cit., pp. 201–3; Jay, op. cit., pp. 442–3; DeGrasse to Weld in Barnes and Dumond, op. cit., I, pp. 445–6.

41 For the free Negro in the North, see Litwack, op. cit., *passim.* For Prudence Crandall, see Edwin and Miriam Small, "Prudence Crandall: Champion of Negro Education," *New England Quarterly,* XVII (December 1944), pp. 506–29.

42 Pelt and Smith, op. cit., pp. 37, 46–8.

43 Woodson, op. cit., chap. 7; Stiles B. Lines, "Slaves and Churchmen: The Work of the Episcopal Church Among Southern Negroes, 1830–1860" (Unpublished Ph.D. dissertation, Columbia University, 1960), *passim.*

44 James W. Silver, *Confederate Morale and Church Propaganda* (Tuscaloosa: Confederate Publishing Co., 1957), *passim.*

45 See Charles F. Dunham, *The Attitude of the Northern Clergy Toward*

the South, 1860–1865 (Toledo: Gray Co., 1942); Oliver S. Heckman, "Northern Church Penetration into the South, 1860–1880" (Unpublished Ph.D. dissertation, Duke University, 1939), chap. 2.

46 *Christian Advocate*, XLII (September 19, 1867), p. 300.

47 Richard Drake, "The American Missionary Association and the Southern Negro, 1861–1880" (Unpublished Ph.D. dissertation, Emory University, 1957), pp. 7–9.

48 Woodson, op. cit., pp. 202–11; Heckman, op. cit., *passim;* Mason Crum, *The Negro in the Methodist Church* (New York: Board of Missions and Church Extension of the Methodist Church, 1951), pp. 64–7.

49 Bell Wiley, *Southern Negroes, 1861–1865* (New York: Rinehart, 1953), chap. 14; Henry Swint, *The Northern Teacher in the South, 1862–1870* (Nashville: Vanderbilt University Press, 1941), *passim.*

50 Richard Drake, op. cit., chap. 4; Ralph Morrow, *Northern Methodism and Reconstruction* (East Lansing: Michigan State University Press, 1956), chap. 5.

51 Richard Drake, op. cit., pp. 58–60.

52 *Southern Christian Advocate*, XXVIII (November 16, 1865), p. 2.

53 *Journal of the General Conference of the Methodist Episcopal Church, South*, 1874, p. 459.

54 George Prentice, *The Life of Gilbert Haven* (New York: Phillips & Hunt, 1883), p. 22; Wade C. Barclay, *History of Methodist Missions*, III (New York: Board of Missions of the Methodist Church, 1957), p. 303.

55 Prentice, op. cit., pp. 298–302, 410–17, 441; Morrow, op. cit., pp. 181–5, 193–4.

CHAPTER 2, PAGES 25–50

1 The standard work on Social Darwinism is Richard Hofstadter, *Social Darwinism in American Thought* (Boston: Beacon Press, 1955). For the ideology of white supremacy, see Guion Johnson, "The Ideology of White Supremacy, 1876–1910," in Fletcher Green (ed.), *Essays in Southern History* (Chapel Hill: University of North Carolina Press, 1949), pp. 125–56.

2 *Churchman*, LXXVI (September 25, 1897), p. 353. See also Kenneth M. MacKenzie, *The Robe and the Sword* (Washington: Public Affairs Press, 1961), pp. 9, 110–12.

3 See, for example, Benjamin F. Riley, *The White Man's Burden* (Birmingham: B. F. Riley, 1910). Riley was a prominent southern Baptist.

4 *Christian Advocate* (Nashville), LX (February 23, 1899), p. 1.

5   Charles Carroll, *The Negro A Beast* (St. Louis: American Book and Bible House, 1900).

6   *Baptist Standard*, XIV (November 20, 1902), p. 3.

7   William Brown, *The Crucial Race Question* (Little Rock: Arkansas Churchman's Publishing Co., 1907).

8   *Presbyterian Quarterly*, I (July 1887), p. 153.

9   *Proceedings of the Church Congress of the Protestant Episcopal Church*, 1882, p. 100. The speaker was the Reverend Henry Dunlop of Savannah, Georgia.

10 Rev. W. M. Leftwich, "The Race Problem in the South," *Quarterly Review* (Methodist Episcopal Church, South), VI (April 1889), p. 94.

11 *Western Recorder*, LXXVI (November 14, 1901), p. 8.

12 *Proceedings of the Southern Baptist Convention*, 1888, p. 19.

13 Ray Stannard Baker, *Following the Color Line* (New York: Doubleday, Page & Co., 1908), p. 35.

14 Rufus B. Spain, "Attitudes and Reactions of Southern Baptists to Certain Problems of Society, 1865–1900" (Unpublished Ph.D. dissertation, Vanderbilt University, 1961), pp. 86–91.

15 Ibid., p. 99.

16 Hunter Farish, *The Circuit Rider Dismounts* (Richmond: Dietz Press, 1938), pp. 166–76.

17 *Southern Christian Advocate*, XXIX (May 11, 1866), p. 4.

18 *Journal of the General Conference of the Methodist Episcopal Church, South*, 1874, p. 543; ibid., 1898, p. 22.

19 *Minutes of the General Assembly of the Presbyterian Church in the U.S.*, 1866, p. 35.

20 Rev. Robert L. Dabney, *Ecclesiastical Relations of Negroes*, pamphlet (Richmond, 1868), p. 16; Thomas C. Johnson, *The Life and Letters of Robert Lewis Dabney* (Richmond: Presbyterian Committee of Publication, 1903), pp. 319–20.

21 *Minutes of the General Assembly of the Presbyterian Church in the U.S.*, 1874, pp. 516–18. See also B. W. Moseley, "The Evangelization of the Colored People," *Southern Presbyterian Review*, XXV (April 1874), pp. 230–33; John L. Bell, "The Presbyterian Church and the Negro in North Carolina During Reconstruction," *North Carolina Historical Review*, XL (Winter 1963), pp. 115–36.

22 *Minutes of the General Assembly of the Presbyterian Church in the U.S.*, 1882, pp. 530–34, 541, 567.

23 *Presbyterian Quarterly*, IX (July 1895), pp. 481–2.

24 C. R. Vaughan, "The Southern Assembly," ibid., I (July 1887), p. 147.

25 *Minutes of the General Assembly of the Presbyterian Church in the U.S.*, 1916, pp. 33–4. A few Negro congregations had opposed the separate denomination and never left the southern Presbyterian Church.

There were also a few Negro churches in white presbyteries after 1916.

26 Bragg, op. cit., pp. 150–53; Albert Thomas, *A Historical Account of the Protestant Episcopal Church in South Carolina* (Columbia: R. L. Bryan Co., 1957), pp. 88–99.

27 *Churchman*, XLVIII (August 25, 1883), p. 205. The Sewanee Conference suggested that the question of admitting Negro churches in the proposed Negro districts to regular dioceses be left to the decision of the regular dioceses. The Negro districts themselves were not to have the right of representation at the General Convention, which made them separate and unequal.

28 *Journal of the General Convention of the Protestant Episcopal Church*, 1883, pp. 251–2, 595–9. The Sewanee proposal was defeated in the House of Deputies.

29 Ibid., 1889, pp. 57–9.

30 *Churchman*, LVII (May 12, 1888), p. 562.

31 Ibid. (May 19, 1888), p. 593; ibid., LX (October 19, 1889), p. 433.

32 Bishop Robert Strange, "Missionary Districts for Negroes — The Case Stated," ibid., XCVI (September 14, 1907), pp. 369–70.

33 Several small southern denominations also organized their Negro churches into separate denominations. Negro Cumberland Presbyterians were organized into the Colored Cumberland Presbyterian Church in 1869, and Negro Primitive Baptists were organized into the Colored Primitive Baptists of America in 1865. Woodson, op. cit., p. 192.

34 *Southern Presbyterian*, XXII (September 1, 1887), p. 2; *Proceedings of the Church Congress of the Protestant Episcopal Church*, 1888, p. 93. See also Spain, op. cit., pp. 151–4; Farish, op. cit., pp. 218–21.

35 *Religious Herald*, IX (January 8, 1874), p. 2.

36 *Christian Advocate* (Nashville), LXVI (August 10, 1905), p. 3.

37 *Southern Presbyterian Review*, XIX (April 1868), p. 292.

38 Rev. James C. Hinton, "Educational Problems in the South," *Quarterly Review* (Methodist Episcopal Church, South), V (October 1883), p. 706.

39 Ibid., VII (January 1885), p. 14. See also Spain, op. cit., pp. 133–7.

40 R. N. Shield, "A Southern View of the Race Question," *Quarterly Review* (Methodist Episcopal Church, South), VIII (July 1890), p. 335.

41 *Christian Advocate* (Nashville), LXVI (February 2, 1905), p. 2; Rev. J. M. Hawley, "Factors Underlying the Race Problem," ibid., LXV (January 14, 1904), p. 3; John Stagg, "The Race Problem in the South," *Presbyterian Quarterly*, XIV (July 1900), p. 332; *Baptist Standard*, XIV (December 4, 1902), p. 4.

42 *Alabama Baptist*, XVIII (June 11, 1891), p. 2.

43 *Quarterly Review* (Methodist Episcopal Church, South), VII (January 1885), p. 15.

44 Rev. W. T. Poynter, "The Church and the Black Man," *Methodist Review* (South), XX (March–April 1896), p. 79.

45 *Proceedings of the Southern Baptist Convention*, Appendix B, 1891, p. xxxvi.

46 *Southern Methodist Review*, III (November 1887), p. 250.

47 *Proceedings of the Southern Baptist Convention*, 1890, p. 19.

48 Ibid., 1891, pp. 26–7; Rev. C. P. Atkinson, "Negro Evangelism," *Christian Advocate* (Nashville), LVIII (December 2, 1897), p. 3.

49 *Southern Presbyterian*, XXIV (August 8, 1889), p. 2. Italics in the original.

50 Elam F. Dempsey, *Atticus G. Haygood* (Nashville: Methodist Publishing House, 1940), pp. 150–51. Biographical information is drawn from Marion L. Smith, "Atticus G. Haygood: Christian Educator" (Unpublished Ph.D. dissertation, Yale University, 1929).

51 Marion Smith, op. cit., *passim;* Atticus G. Haygood, *Our Brother in Black* (New York: Phillips & Hunt, 1881); Haygood, "The Negro Problem: God Takes Time — Man Must," *Methodist Review* (South), XLII (September–October 1895), pp. 40–53.

52 *Christian Advocate* (Nashville), XL (March 6, 1880), p. 8.

53 W. C. Dunlap, "Clark University and Paine Institute," ibid., XLVI (June 26, 1886), p. 13.

54 *Minutes of the General Assembly of the Presbyterian Church in the U.S.*, 1895, p. 443.

55 William G. McLoughlin, *Modern Revivalism* (New York: Ronald Press, 1959), pp. 306–7.

56 *Annual of the Southern Baptist Convention*, 1905, p. 6.

57 *Proceedings of the Church Congress of the Protestant Episcopal Church*, 1882, p. 92.

58 *Minutes of the General Assembly of the Presbyterian Church in the U.S.*, 1896, p. 605.

59 *Southern Churchman*, LX (November 14, 1895), p. 9.

60 Farish, op. cit., pp. 227–9; *Alabama Baptist*, X (October 25, 1883), p. 2; *Christian Advocate* (Nashville), LII (September 26, 1891), p. 1; Spain, op. cit., pp. 186–90.

61 *Christian Advocate* (Nashville), LIII (May 12, 1892), p. 1; G. S. Tumlin, "Concerning Mob Violence," *Baptist Standard*, XIII (March 28, 1901), p. 1

62 Rev. D. W. Foster, "Mobocracy," *Christian Advocate* (Nashville), LV (February 15, 1894), p. 4; *Western Recorder*, LXVI (June 16, 1892), p. 4.

63 Spain, op. cit., pp. 185–6.

64 *Western Recorder*, LXVIII (November 2, 1893), p. 4; D. E. Jordan, "Mob Law," *Presbyterian Quarterly*, IV (October 1890), pp. 591–613.

65 *Southern Churchman*, LX (October 19, 1893), p. 4.

66 *Proceedings of the Church Congress of the Protestant Episcopal Church*, 1882, p. 114.

67 *Churchman*, XLVIII (October 20, 1883), p. 451.

68 Rev. O. Sievers-Barten, "The Colored Question," ibid., LXX (July 7, 1894), pp. 10–11.

69 See Arlin Turner (ed.), *The Negro Question* (Garden City: Doubleday & Co., 1958). Biographical material is drawn from Arlin Turner, *George W. Cable* (Durham: Duke University Press, 1956), and Philip Butcher, *George W. Cable: The Northampton Years* (New York: Columbia University Press, 1959).

70 Rev. W. M. Leftwich, "The Race Problem in the South," *Southern Methodist Review*, VI (April 1889), pp. 88–9; *Christian Advocate* (Nashville), XLVII (June 25, 1887), p. 1; *Alabama Baptist*, XVII (July 3, 1890), p. 2.

71 *Christian Advocate* (Nashville), LXV (May 26, 1904), p. 4.

72 Rev. Arthur J. Barton (Corresponding Secretary, Educational Board, Baptist Convention of Texas) in *The South Mobilizing for Social Service* (Nashville: Southern Sociological Congress, 1913), pp. 467, 471.

73 Riley, op. cit., p. 55.

CHAPTER 3, PAGES 51–83

1 For a more extensive discussion of the Methodists' reunion, see Chapter 6.

2 George Mowry, *Theodore Roosevelt and the Progressive Movement* (Madison: University of Wisconsin Press, 1946), pp. 266–9; Arthur Link, *Woodrow Wilson and the Progressive Era* (New York: Harper & Bros., 1954), pp. 64–5; C. Vann Woodward, *Origins of the New South* (Baton Rouge: Louisiana State University Press, 1951), chap. 14.

3 Charles Hopkins, *The Rise of the Social Gospel in American Protestantism, 1865–1915* (New Haven: Yale University Press, 1940), p. 319; Guy and Guion Johnson, "The Church and the Race Problem in the United States" (Unpublished monograph for the Myrdal study, Schomburg Collection, New York, 1940), chap. 6; Rayford Logan, *The Negro in American Life and Thought* (New York: Dial Press, 1954), pp. 165–7, 271–4. For Lyman Abbott's comment on the Niagara Movement, see *Outlook*, LXXX (July 29, 1903), pp. 795–6.

4 Josiah Strong, *Our Country* (New York: Baker & Taylor Co., 1885), pp. 174–5.

5 Johnson and Johnson, op. cit., pp. 88–9; William D. P. Bliss (ed.), *The Encyclopedia of Social Reforms* (New York: Funk & Wagnalls, 1898),

pp. 927–9; Bliss (ed.), *The New Encyclopedia of Social Reform* (New York: Funk & Wagnalls, 1908), pp. 818–20.

6   Walter Rauschenbusch, "Belated Races and the Social Problems," *Methodist Review Quarterly* (South), LXIII (April 1914), pp. 252–9.

7   Washington Gladden, *Recollections* (Boston: Houghton Mifflin Co., 1909), chaps. 11 and 24.

8   For Abbott, see pp. 79–80.

9   Elias B. Sanford (ed.), *Church Federation* (New York: Fleming H. Revell Co., 1906), pp. 286–7. One Negro, Bishop W. B. Derrick, spoke at the meeting. He completely ignored the political aspects of the race problem and made a plea for white sympathy. Ibid., pp. 520–24.

10   Elias Sanford (ed.), *Federal Council of the Churches of Christ in America* (New York: Revell Press, 1909), p. 238.

11   McLoughlin, *Modern Revivalism*, pp. 306–7, 354–5, 361–3; McLoughlin, *Billy Sunday Was His Real Name* (Chicago: University of Chicago Press, 1955), pp. 271–6.

12   Prentice, op. cit., pp. 415–17.

13   *Christian Advocate*, XLIII (April 2, 1868), p. 108; *Journal of the General Conference of the Methodist Episcopal Church*, 1868, p. 307.

14   Ibid., 1876, p. 331.

15   Rev. W. P. Thirkield, "The Race Crisis and the Methodist Episcopal Church in the South," *Christian Advocate*, LXV (January 30, 1890), p. 68. See also Barclay, op. cit., pp. 309–21; Morrow, op. cit., chap. 7.

16   Woodson, op. cit., pp. 259–60.

17   Pelt and Smith, op. cit., pp. 93–4; J. M. Frost, "Mr. Johnson–Dr. Griffith Correspondence," *Western Recorder*, LXV (October 16, 1890), p. 5. See also Lewis Jordan, *Negro Baptist History, U.S.A.* (Nashville: National Baptist Convention, 1931 ?), pp. 122–4.

18   *Minutes of the National Council of the Congregational Churches*, 1886, p. 129; Rev. Joseph E. Roy, "Parallels to the Georgia Case," *Congregationalist*, XLI (August 15, 1889), p. 273.

19   Horace Bumstead, "The Color Line," ibid., XXXV (March 8, 1883), p. 82.

20   *Annual Report of the American Missionary Association*, 1889, p. 34.

21   Rev. W. Hayne Leavell, "The Color Line," *Congregationalist*, XXXV (April 26, 1883), p. 144; ibid. (December 20, 1883), p. 443.

22   Turner (ed.), *The Negro Question*, p. 221.

23   *Minutes of the National Council of the Congregational Churches*, 1889, pp. 27, 278–81. There was precedent for accepting overlapping groups in New England, but there the race question was not present.

24   Ibid., 1892, p. 26; ibid., 1898, p. 34.

25   *Congregationalist*, LXXX (April 18, 1895), p. 618; ibid., LXXXI (April 9, 1896), p. 605; ibid., LXXXIII (April 21, 1898), p. 594; ibid.,

LXXXIX (December 3, 1904), p. 837; ibid., LXXXVIII (December 5, 1903), p. 851.

26 *Minutes of the National Council of the Congregational Churches*, 1917, pp. 163, 167.

27 For an example of some Negroes in mixed churches, see John Daniels, *In Freedom's Birthplace* (Boston: Houghton Mifflin Co., 1914), pp. 230–33. See also Baker, op. cit., pp. 121–3.

28 *Journal of the General Conference of the Methodist Episcopal Church*, 1884, p. 334.

29 *Daily Christian Advocate*, XIV (May 10, 1900), p. 120.

30 For northern seminaries that did not admit Negroes, see W. E. B. Du Bois, *The Negro Church* (Atlanta: Atlanta University Press, 1903), pp. 195–6.

31 *Minutes of the General Assembly of the Presbyterian Church in the U.S.A.*, 1876, p. 41.

32 *Journal of the General Conference of the Methodist Episcopal Church*, 1880, p. 293.

33 Ibid., 1884, pp. 334, 366.

34 Ibid., 1888, pp. 696–9; Morrow, op. cit., pp. 197–200; Gilbert Govan and James Livingood, *The University of Chattanooga* (Chattanooga: University of Chattanooga, 1947), pp. 35–48.

35 *American Missionary*, XI (May 1867), pp. 109–10.

36 Richard Drake, "Freedmen's Aid Societies and Sectional Compromise," *Journal of Southern History*, XXIX (May 1963), pp. 181–5; Richard Drake, "The American Missionary Association and the Southern Negro 1861–1880," pp. 104–5, 237–8.

37 *Annual Report of the American Missionary Association*, 1883, pp. 23, 51–2; *American Missionary*, XXXIX (November 1885), p. 311.

38 Rev. C. L. Woodworth, "Atlanta University and the Glenn Bill," *Congregationalist*, XXXIX (August 11, 1887), p. 269.

39 *Annual Report of the American Missionary Association*, 1888, p. 34.

40 *Congregationalist*, LXXX (October 31, 1895), p. 661; ibid., LXXXI (October 29, 1896), p. 635; *Christian Advocate*, LXXI (May 21, 1896), p. 341.

41 *American Missionary*, X (December 1866), pp. 279–80; ibid., XI (October 1867), pp. 217–18.

42 *Journal of the General Convention of the Protestant Episcopal Church*, 1874, pp. 255, 362–3. Unlike the districts proposed by the Sewanee Conference, Bishop Whittingham's projected racial districts had the same rights as other missionary districts.

43 Ibid., 1877, p. 529.

44 Ibid., 1883, pp. 251–2, 175–6.

45 Bragg, op. cit., pp. 152–3.

46 *Journal of the General Convention of the Protestant Episcopal Church,*
    1907, pp. 518–22.

47 In the early history of the church suffragan bishops had been utilized
    on several occasions, but they had been prohibited by church canon
    before the Civil War.

48 *Journal of the General Convention of the Protestant Episcopal Church,*
    1907, pp. 157, 160–61.

49 *Church Advocate,* XVI (May 1907), p. 3; ibid., XXV (November 1916),
    pp. 3–4.

50 Ibid., XVI (May 1907), p. 2.

51 Ibid., XXV (November 1916), pp. 3–4; ibid., XXIV (July 1916), p. 2.

52 Ibid., XVIII (June 1909), p. 2; E. C. Gaillard, "A Negro Suffragan
    Bishop — A Puppet Bishop," ibid., XXI (January 1912), p. 3.

53 *Churchman,* CIX (May 23, 1914), pp. 665–6.

54 Herbert Woodward, *The Negro Bishop Movement in the Episcopal
    Diocese of South Carolina* (Savannah: Broid & Hutton, 1916), pp. 12,
    30, 36. See also Thomas, *A Historical Account of the Protestant Epis-
    copal Church in South Carolina,* pp. 131–2.

55 In the southeastern dioceses, where discrimination was greatest against
    Negroes, the majority of the bishops did not favor the missionary
    district plan. *Journal of the General Convention of the Protestant
    Episcopal Church,* 1916, p. 495; *Church Advocate,* XX (April 1911),
    p. 2. For an example of the opinion of these bishops, see Bishop Guerry's
    statement, ibid., XXIII (November 1914), p. 2.

56 Ibid., XXI (March 1912), p. 1.

57 For a statement by Bishop Johnston of West Texas, see ibid., XIX
    (January 1910), p. 1. See also Bishop Robert Strange, "Missionary Dis-
    tricts for the Negro — The Case Stated," *Churchman,* XCVI (Septem-
    ber 14, 1907), pp. 369–70. Bishop William Brown of Arkansas advocated
    a third scheme. His plan called for placing Negroes in a separate Epis-
    copal denomination, but this proposal did not have much support.
    Brown, op. cit.

58 *Journal of the General Convention of the Protestant Episcopal Church,*
    1916, pp. 484–5.

59 Ibid., pp. 76, 96, 491–3.

60 For a further discussion of the missionary district plan, see Chapter 5,
    pp. 123–6.

61 *Journal of the General Conference of the Methodist Episcopal Church,*
    1872, pp. 91, 253; *Christian Advocate,* LI (June 22, 1876), p. 194. These
    bishops were to work within the United States. Several Negroes had
    been bishops for foreign missionary work.

62 Daniel Cury, "The Colored Bishop Question," ibid., LV (August 5,

1880), pp. 498–9; *Journal of the General Conference of the Methodist Episcopal Church*, 1880, pp. 282–4.

63 Ibid., 1896, p. 226.

64 *Zion's Herald*, LXXXV (June 10, 1907), pp. 870–71.

65 *Daily Christian Advocate*, XIV (May 10, 1900), p. 117.

66 Ibid., XV (May 31, 1904), pp. 376–7.

67 For representative opinions of Negro leaders concerning the amendment, see *Southwestern Christian Advocate*, XLI (September 12, 1907), pp. 1–8.

68 Ibid. (March 21, 1907), p. 2.

69 *Daily Christian Advocate*, XVI (May 23, 1908), p. 1.

70 *Journal of the General Conference of the Methodist Episcopal Church*, 1912, p. 774.

71 *Southwestern Christian Advocate*, XLI (August 22, 1912), p. 1.

72 Ibid., XLIII (October 29, 1914), p. 1.

73 *Daily Christian Advocate*, XIX (May 4, 1920), p. 55.

74 Ibid. (May 11, 1920), p. 210; ibid. (May 12, 1920), pp. 220–23.

75 *Journal of the General Conference of the Methodist Episcopal Church*, 1928, p. 393.

76 See, for example, *American Missionary*, XII (October 1868), p. 227; *Christian Advocate*, XLI (August 9, 1866), p. 262; Rev. R. M. Hatfield, "Outrages in the South," ibid., LI (October 5, 1876), p. 313.

77 *Journal of the General Conference of the Methodist Episcopal Church*, 1904, pp. 143, 320–21. See also ibid., 1892, pp. 459–60.

78 *Minutes of the General Assembly of the Presbyterian Church in the U.S.A.*, 1892, p. 217; *Minutes of the National Council of the Congregational Churches*, 1892, p. 39; ibid., 1907, p. 429.

79 *Baptist Home Mission Monthly*, XI (October 1889), p. 271. See also *Christian Advocate*, LIV (May 1, 1879), p. 281; *Congregationalist*, XXX (December 4, 1878), p. 388.

80 *Christian Advocate* (Nashville), XLIV (June 14, 1884), p. 8; ibid., LII (May 12, 1892), p. 1; *Western Recorder*, LXVIII (May 10, 1894), p. 2; Samuel M. Smith, "The Negro in Ecclesiastical Relations," *Presbyterian Quarterly*, III (October 1889), pp. 481–507.

81 Rev. J. C. Hartzell, "The Negro Exodus," *Methodist Quarterly Review*, LXI (October 1879), p. 747.

82 *Minutes of the National Council of the Congregational Churches*, 1913, p. 391.

83 *Baptist Quarterly Review*, XII (April 1890), pp. 232–9.

84 *Churchman*, LIII (May 22, 1866), p. 564. See also *Christian Advocate*, LVII (September 21, 1882), p. 593.

85 Ibid., LXIV (March 23, 1889), p. 193; *Baptist Home Mission Monthly*,

XVI (November 1894), p. 437; speech of President E. A. Ware of Atlanta University in *Congregationalist*, XXXIII (November 9, 1881), p. 361.

86 Ibid., XXX (December 4, 1878), p. 388; ibid., LXXXIV (January 5, 1899), p. 7; speech of Professor J. C. Long of Crozier Theological Seminary, *Proceedings of the Baptist Congress*, 1890, pp. 101–5; *Pacific Christian Advocate*, XLVIII (February 5, 1902), p. 2; statement of Bishop Edwin S. Lines of the Diocese of Newark, *Proceedings of the Church Congress of the Protestant Episcopal Church*, 1905, p. 23.

87 Lyman Abbott, *Reminiscences* (New York: Houghton Mifflin Co., 1915), pp. 270, 424.

88 Ibid., p. 425. See also Ira Brown, *Lyman Abbott* (Cambridge: Harvard University Press, 1953), chap. 4 and pp. 204–7.

89 Richard Drake, "The Freedmen's Aid Societies and Sectional Compromise," pp. 175–86.

90 *Churchman*, CXIII (February 12, 1916), p. 203.

91 *Congregationalist*, LXXXIV (September 14, 1899), p. 339. See also S. F. Fisher, *The American Negro* (Pittsburgh: Presbyterian Board of Missions for the Freedmen, n.d.), pp. 45–51.

92 *Examiner*, LXXXIV (April 19, 1906), p. 483; *Christian Advocate*, LXXX (February 23, 1905), p. 310.

93 *Zion's Herald*, LXXIX (February 13, 1901), p. 197; ibid., LXXX (November 26, 1902), p. 1511; ibid., LXXXV (May 15, 1907), p. 611. See also *Northwestern Christian Advocate*, LXI (March 19, 1913), p. 3; *Examiner*, LXXVIII (August 9, 1900), p. 1.

94 *Northwestern Christian Advocate*, LXII (April 23, 1913), pp. 4–5.

95 Lyman Abbott, *Silhouettes of Contemporaries* (New York: Doubleday, Page & Co., 1922), pp. 258–81. See also, for example, *Churchman*, XCII (August 26, 1905), p. 310; *Congregationalist*, LXXXVIII (August 8, 1903), pp. 184–5.

96 See U.S. Department of the Interior: Bureau of Education, *A Study of the Higher and Private Schools for Colored People in the U.S., 1916*, 2 vols. (Washington: Government Printing Office, 1917).

CHAPTER 4, PAGES 84–108

1 John Hope Franklin, *From Slavery to Freedom* (New York: Alfred Knopf, 1956), pp. 472–6.

2 Katherine Du Pre Lumpkin, *The Making of a Southerner* (New York: Alfred Knopf, 1947), p. 191.

3   Willis D. Weatherford, *Negro Life in the South* (New York: Association Press, 1910), especially chap. 6.

4   Edward Burrows, "The Commission on Interracial Cooperation, 1919–1944" (Unpublished Ph.D. dissertation, University of Wisconsin, 1954), pp. 11–18, 35–6, 46–53.

5   Biographical material on Alexander is drawn from "The Reminiscences of Will Alexander," Oral History Project, Columbia University, and Wilma Dykeman and James Stokely, *Seeds of Southern Change* (Chicago: University of Chicago Press, 1962).

6   Ibid., pp. 273–5.

7   Burrows, op. cit., pp. 146–51; *Minutes of the General Assembly of the Presbyterian Church in the U.S.*, 1921, pp. 80–81; *Journal of the General Conference of the Methodist Episcopal Church, South*, 1922, pp. 237–8; ibid., 1926, p. 384; *Journal of the General Conference of the Methodist Episcopal Church*, 1924, p. 671; *Annual of the Northern Baptist Convention*, 1926, pp. 168–9.

8   Guy and Guion Johnson, op. cit., p. 212.

9   Burrows, op. cit., pp. 58–71; Mrs. Luke Johnson, "Woman's Interracial Conference," *Missionary Voice*, X (December 1920), pp. 374–5; *Annual Report of the Woman's Missionary Council of the Methodist Episcopal Church, South*, 1919–20, pp. 29, 179–80.

10 *Missionary Voice*, XII (February 1922), p. 46; ibid. (June 1922), p. 175.

11 Dykeman and Stokely, op. cit., chap. 11.

12 Sara J. McAfee, *History of the Woman's Missionary Society in the Colored Methodist Episcopal Church* (Phenix City, Ala.: Harold E. Poor, 1945), pp. 174–8.

13 *Annual Report of the Woman's Missionary Council of the Methodist Episcopal Church, South*, 1924–25, p. 127; ibid., 1928–29, p. 115; *Annual Report of the Woman's Home Missionary Society of the Methodist Episcopal Church*, 1920–21, p. 45.

14 *Annual Report of the Department of Woman's Work of the Presbyterian Church in the U.S.*, 1931, p. 7.

15 Ibid., p. 10; ibid., 1922, p. 11; ibid., 1927, pp. 11, 16.

16 *Minutes of the General Assembly of the Presbyterian Church in the U.S.*, 1935, pp. 46–7.

17 *Federal Council Bulletin*, II (October 1919), pp. 169–70; Minutes of the Commission on Negro Churches and Race Relations of the Federal Council of Churches, July 12, 1921 (in the files of the Commission); George Haynes, "Toward Interracial Peace" (Unpublished monograph for the Myrdal study, Schomburg Collection, New York, 1940), chap. 1, pp. 2–4.

18 *Annual Report of the Federal Council of the Churches of Christ in*

America, 1923, pp. 63–5; ibid., 1928, pp. 111–12; *Quadrennial Report of the Federal Council of the Churches of Christ in America,* 1920–24, pp. 129–30; ibid., 1924–28, pp. 112–16; Haynes, "Toward Interracial Peace," *passim.*

19 *Woman's Home Missions,* XXXIX (August 1922), p. 9; ibid., XLI (December 1924), p. 4; *Annual Report of the Woman's Home Missionary Society of the Methodist Episcopal Church,* 1929–30, pp. 224–33.

20 *Minutes of the National Council of the Congregational Churches,* 1921, p. 385. Later the commission became part of the Social Service Commission.

21 Ibid., 1929, pp. 42–3; *Annual Report of the Congregational Church Extension Boards,* 1929, p. 37; ibid., 1930, pp. 40–41; *Congregationalist,* CXIII (April 26, 1928), pp. 531, 535.

22 For the social gospel movement between the two world wars, see Paul Carter, *The Decline and Revival of the Social Gospel* (Ithaca: Cornell University Press, 1956), and Robert M. Miller, *American Protestantism and Social Issues, 1919–1939* (Chapel Hill: University of North Carolina Press, 1958).

23 *Journal of the General Conference of the Methodist Episcopal Church, South,* 1922, p. 356; ibid., 1930, p. 67; Arthur Raper, *The Tragedy of Lynching* (Chapel Hill: University of North Carolina Press, 1933), pp. 22–3, 71–2, 82, 335–6.

24 *Minutes of the National Council of the Congregational Churches,* 1919, p. 40; ibid., 1923, p. 236; ibid., 1934, p. 111; *Congregationalist,* CVI (May 26, 1921), pp. 631–2; *Journal of the General Conference of the Methodist Episcopal Church,* 1920, pp. 583, 638; *Annual of the Northern Baptist Convention,* 1935, p. 277; *Christian Advocate,* CI (December 23, 1926), p. 1719; *Minutes of the General Assembly of the Presbyterian Church in the U.S.A.,* 1923, p. 205; ibid., 1937, p. 224.

25 *Journal of the General Conference of the Methodist Episcopal Church, South,* 1922, p. 356; *Annual of the Southern Baptist Convention,* 1928, p. 88. For an attack on federal antilynching legislation, see Bishop Warren A. Candler, "Mistaken Advocates of Mischievous Measures," *Southern Christian Advocate,* LXXXVII (March 29, 1923), p. 4.

26 *Journal of the General Convention of the Protestant Episcopal Church,* 1922, p. 164; ibid., 1934, pp. 317–18.

27 *Annual Report of the Woman's Missionary Council of the Methodist Episcopal Church, South,* 1920–21, p. 32.

28 Emerson H. Loucks, *The Ku Klux Klan in Pennsylvania* (Harrisburg: Telegraph Press, 1936), p. 34; *Christian Advocate,* XCVII (June 22, 1922), p. 764; *Churchman,* CXXVII (July 28, 1923), p. 7; *Northwestern Christian Advocate,* LXX (October 4, 1922), p. 1052; Charles Alexander, *Crusade for Conformity: The Ku Klux Klan in Texas, 1920–1930*

(Houston: Gulf Coast Historical Association, 1962), pp. 29–31; Robert M. Miller, "A Note on the Relationship Between the Protestant Churches and the Revived Ku Klux Klan," *Journal of Southern History*, XXII (August 1956), pp. 355–68; Norman Furniss, *The Fundamentalist Controversy, 1918–1931* (New Haven: Yale University Press, 1954), pp. 37–8.

29 *Journal of the General Convention of the Protestant Episcopal Church*, 1922, p. 115; *Minutes of the National Council of the Congregational Churches*, 1923, p. 235; *Congregationalist*, CVIII (September 27, 1923), p. 391; *Living Church*, LXIX (May 5, 1923), pp. 4–5.

30 *Baptist*, II (April 23, 1921), p. 358; *Annual of the Northern Baptist Convention*, 1927, p. 144.

31 *Journal of the General Conference of the Methodist Episcopal Church*, 1924, pp. 187–8, 234, 295; *Epworth Herald*, XXXIII (October 21, 1922), p. 1006; ibid. (October 28, 1922), p. 1034; *Western Christian Advocate*, LXXXVIII (September 13, 1922), p. 5.

32 *Presbyterian*, XCI (September 15, 1921), p. 4.

33 *Presbyterian of the South*, XCVI (November 8, 1922), p. 1; ibid. (June 7, 1922), p. 1.

34 *Annual of the Southern Baptist Convention*, 1923, p. 103; Foy Valentine, "A Historical Study of Southern Baptists and Race Relations, 1917–1947" (Unpublished Th.D. dissertation, Southwestern Baptist Theological Seminary, 1949), pp. 65–6.

35 "The Reminiscences of Will W. Alexander," Oral History Project, Columbia University, pp. 190–93.

36 Ibid., pp. 314–15; *Journal of the General Conference of the Methodist Episcopal Church, South*, 1922, p. 356.

37 *Quadrennial Report of the Federal Council of the Churches of Christ in America*, 1920–24, pp. 82–3, 301; ibid., 1928–32, pp. 245–6.

38 See, for example, *Presbyterian of the South*, CI (September 28, 1927), p. 1; *Christian Advocate* (Nashville), LXXXVI (March 27, 1925), p. 387; *Southern Churchman*, LXXXVIII (May 5, 1923), p. 11; George Kelsey, "The Social Thought of Contemporary Southern Baptists" (Unpublished Ph.D. dissertation, Yale University, 1946), pp. 191–203.

39 "A General Survey of the Commission of Interracial Cooperation for 1922–1923" (in the files of the Commission).

40 *Churchman*, CLV (June 15, 1941), p. 7. See also *Zion's Herald*, CX (October 26, 1932), p. 1348. The strongest pronouncement adopted by any major Protestant denomination during this period was the one by the Congregationalists at their 1934 national meeting. This resolution came close to condemning all forms of segregation. *Minutes of the General Council of the Congregational Christian Churches*, 1934, pp. 110–11.

41 *Congregationalist*, CX (March 12, 1925), pp. 326–7; *Northwestern*

Christian Advocate, LXIX (August 3, 1921), p. 859; Basil Mathews, "New Horizons," *Christian Advocate*, XCVI (November 17, 1921), pp. 1454-5. The church press scarcely mentioned the Garvey movement, which had been creating quite a stir in the Negro community in the early 1920's.

42 *Churchman*, CXL (September 28, 1929), p. 19.

43 *New York Times*, September 18, 22, 23, and October 14, 1929. On October 13, approximately twenty-five members (unhooded) of the Klan were alleged to have attended the church upon hearing an unfounded rumor that a hundred Negroes were planning to attend the Sunday service.

44 *Living Church*, LXXXI (October 5, 1929), p. 752.

45 *Churchman*, CXL (September 28, 1929), p. 8.

46 *New York Times*, September 24, 1929.

47 Ibid., September 25, 1929. The list of churchmen included such notables as Reinhold Niebuhr, John C. Bennett, George Butterick, Henry Sloan Coffin, and Harry Emerson Fosdick.

48 *Baptist*, XIII (January 30, 1932), p. 135.

49 *Living Church*, LXXXV (June 13, 1931), p. 231; *Southern Churchman*, C (February 2, 1935), p. 17.

50 *Minutes of the General Assembly of the Presbyterian Church in the U.S.A.*, 1934, p. 211.

51 Ibid., 1932, p. 98; *Annual Report of the Board of National Missions of the Presbyterian Church in the U.S.A.*, 1933, pp. 12–13; ibid., 1939, pp. 42–3; *Africo-American Presbyterian*, LVI (January 17, 1935), p. 2; ibid. (May 23–30, 1935), p. 2; *Interracial News Service* (May 1939), p. 4; and ibid. (June 1937), p. 2. In 1924 the Reverend James S. Russell, a Negro, was elected to the Episcopal National Council's Social Service Department and became the first Negro member of a National Council department. *Living Church*, XCII (April 6, 1935), pp. 429–30.

52 *Minutes of the National Council of the Congregational Churches*, 1927, p. 230.

53 Ibid., 1931, p. 197; Hubert C. Herring, "Congregationalists and Race Discrimination," *Christian Century*, XLVIII (June 17, 1931), p. 814. An incident of discrimination occurred at the 1956 convention, and the church decided to take the case to court for violation of a Nebraska state law. Ibid., LXXIII (July 11, 1956), p. 820–21.

54 *Journal of the General Conference of the Methodist Episcopal Church*, 1904, p. 249. For an incident involving missionary Bishop Scott, a Negro, at the 1916 conference at Saratoga, N.Y., see *Southwestern Christian Advocate*, XLV (May 25, 1916), p. 8.

55 *Journal of the General Conference of the Methodist Episcopal Church*, 1932, pp. 259–60; ibid., 1936, p. 337; *Michigan Christian Advocate*, LIX

(May 19, 1932), pp. 1, 5; Robert M. Miller, "Methodism, the Negro, and Ernest Fremont Tittle," *Wisconsin Magazine of History*, XLIV (Winter 1960–61), pp. 104–6.

56 *Zion's Herald*, CIV (May 26, 1926), p. 652; Dwight Culver, "Negro Segregation in the Contemporary Methodist Church" (Unpublished Ph.D. dissertation, Yale University, 1948), p. 302.

57 *Zion's Herald*, CXII (October 24, 1934), p. 1021.

58 Minutes of the Church Women's Committee on Race Relations of the Federal Council of Churches, September 29, 1941 (in the files of the Department of Race Relations); *Annual Report of the Woman's Division of Christian Service of the Methodist Church*, 1942 (Minutes of the Executive Committee, June 1941), p. 76.

59 Miller, "Methodism, the Negro and Ernest Fremont Tittle," pp. 108–9; *Journal of the General Conference of the Methodist Church*, 1944, pp. 272, 359–60, 725; ibid., 1948, p. 740.

60 *Chicago Defender*, June 9, 1928; *Minutes of the General Assembly of the Presbyterian Church in the U.S.A.*, 1928, p. 152.

61 *Africo-American Presbyterian*, LIV (June 23, 1932), p. 2; Rev. D. Nance, "The Negro and the Presbyterian Church in the U.S.A.," ibid. (July 7, 1932), p. 1.

62 For discrimination at the 1943 General Assembly, see *Christian Century*, LX (June 9, 1943), pp. 697, 702. Though the church had a policy of nondiscrimination, an incident occurred at the 1959 meeting in Indianapolis. See the *Milwaukee Journal*, May 21, 1959.

63 *Africo-American Presbyterian*, XLIX (May 5, 1938), p. 2; ibid. (May 26, 1938), p. 2.

64 *Annual of the Northern Baptist Convention*, 1935, p. 277; ibid., 1949, p. 143.

65 Rev. Shelton H. Bishop, "Conflicting Loyalties of the Negro Churchman," *Living Church*, XCVI (February 6, 1937), pp. 159–60; ibid., CI (November 15, 1939), p. 15; M. Moran Weston, "Social Policy of the Episcopal Church in the Twentieth Century" (Unpublished Ph.D. dissertation, Columbia University, 1954), pp. 263–5; *Journal of the General Convention of the Protestant Episcopal Church*, 1940, p. 344.

66 *Living Church*, CXXVIII (June 20, 1954), pp. 6, 14–15; ibid. (May 9, 1954), pp. 14–15; ibid., CXXIX (October 17, 1954), p. 18; ibid. (October 24, 1954), p. 15; *Churchman*, CLXVIII (December 15, 1954), p. 15; ibid. (May 15, 1954), pp. 4–5; *Episcopal Churchnews*, CXIX (July 11, 1954), pp. 5–6.

67 *Presbyterian Outlook*, CXXXII (April 10, 1950), pp. 3–4; *Presbyterian Survey*, XVII (February 1927), p. 109.

68 *Presbyterian Outlook*, CXXXII (June 26, 1950), pp. 10–11; *Minutes of the General Assembly of the Presbyterian Church in the U.S.*, 1950, p. 72.

69 *Southern Presbyterian Journal*, IX (June 15, 1950), pp. 2–3; ibid. (July 15, 1950), p. 5; ibid., XIII (September 15, 1954), p. 3.
70 *New York Times*, April 27, 1964, January 27, 1965.

CHAPTER 5, PAGES 109–33

1 See Franklin, op. cit., chap. 29.
2 *Presbyterian*, CXII (March 5, 1942), p. 19.
3 E. H. Raulings, "The South Hears E. Stanley Jones," *Northwestern Christian Advocate*, LXXXI (April 27, 1933), p. 399; John C. Petrie, "Stanley Jones — A Revolution," *Zion's Herald*, CXI (April 5, 1933), pp. 317, 328; John D. Clinton, "We Have Our Negro Member," ibid., CXV (May 19, 1937), p. 625. See also *Federal Council Bulletin*, XXV (September 1942), pp. 8–9.
4 Minutes of the Administrative Committee of the Department of Race Relations of the Federal Council of Churches, February 4, 1942 (in the files of the Department of Race Relations); *Biennial Report of the Federal Council of the Churches of Christ in America*, 1942, pp. 121–4, 169–71; "The Reminiscences of Will Alexander," Oral History Project, Columbia University, pp. 715–23.
5 *Federal Council Bulletin*, XXIX (April 1946), p. 12.
6 *Minutes of the General Assembly of the Presbyterian Church in the U.S.A.*, 1946, pp. 211–12.
7 *Journal of the General Conference of the Methodist Church*, 1948, pp. 739–41; *Journal of the General Convention of the Protestant Episcopal Church*, 1943, pp. 467, 573; *Minutes of the General Council of the Congregational Christian Churches*, 1946, p. 46; *Minutes of the Biennial Convention of the United Lutheran Church in America*, 1952, pp. 790–92; *Year Book of the Northern Baptist Convention*, 1948, p. 125.
8 See, for example, Liston Pope, *The Kingdom Beyond Caste* (New York: Friendship Press, 1957); Everett Tilson, *Segregation and the Bible* (Nashville: Abingdon Press, 1958). For a religious defense of segregation, see H. C. McGowan, *God's Garden of Segregation* (New York: Vantage Press, 1961).
9 *Atlanta Constitution*, June 29, 1954.
10 *New York Times*, June 29, 1963.
11 *Montgomery Advertiser*, May 8, 1957. For the position of Little Rock's clergy during the 1957 school desegregation crisis there, see Ernest Q. Campbell and Thomas F. Pettigrew, *Christians in Racial Crisis* (Washington: Public Affairs Press, 1959).
12 *New York Times*, June 12, 1963.

13 *Minutes of the General Assembly of the Presbyterian Church in the U.S.*, 1949, pp. 190–92.

14 Ibid., 1954, pp. 190–97; *Presbyterian Outlook*, CXXXVI (April 5, 1954), p. 3.

15 Ibid., CXXXVII (June 20, 1955), pp. 6–7.

16 Rev. J. David Simson, "Non Segregation Means Eventual Intermarriage," *Southern Presbyterian Journal*, VI (March 15, 1948), pp. 6–7; ibid., X (August 8, 1951), pp. 4–5; ibid. (November 7, 1951), p. 4.

17 Ibid., XIII (December 8, 1954), pp. 14–15; *Presbyterian Outlook*, CXXXVI (November 22, 1954), p. 3; ibid. (July 12, 1954), p. 4; ibid. (September 27, 1954), p. 10; ibid. (June 28, 1954), p. 3.

18 Ibid. (November 29, 1954), p. 3; ibid., CXXXVII (June 20, 1955), pp. 6–7.

19 *Western Recorder*, CXXXI (December 5, 1957), p. 3; W. M. Nevins, "Segregation and the Bible," ibid., CXXXIII (September 24, 1959), pp. 14–15; Kyle Haselden, "Baptists in Travail," *Christian Century*, LXXX (May 22, 1963), pp. 672–4; *New York Times*, May 24, 1964.

20 *Annual of the Southern Baptist Convention*, 1952, p. 55; ibid., 1954, pp. 55–6; ibid., 1957, p. 366; ibid., 1959, p. 88. See also Brooks Hays, *A Southern Moderate Speaks* (Chapel Hill: University of North Carolina Press, 1959).

21 *Annual Report of the Board of Home Missions of the Congregational Christian Churches*, 1939, pp. 27–8.

22 Ibid., 1942, pp. 28, 38–41; *Minutes of the General Council of the Congregational Christian Churches*, 1942, p. 38.

23 *Annual Report of the Board of Home Missions of the Congregational Christian Churches*, 1942, pp. 28, 38–41; ibid., 1944, pp. 32–5; William E. McCormick, "For Interracial Unity," *Advance*, CXXXV (July 1943), pp. 22–3; Fred Brownlee, "Racial and Interracial Riotings," ibid. (October 1943), pp. 20–21; *Advance Report of the General Council of the Congregational Christian Churches*, 1944, pp. 102–3.

24 *Minutes of the General Council of the Congregational Christian Churches*, 1946, p. 21.

25 *Advance Report of the General Council of the Congregational Christian Churches*, 1948, pp. 54–7.

26 In 1943, the Episcopal Church established a Bi-Racial Committee on Negro Work, and in 1957 the committee was reorganized as the Presiding Bishop's Advisory Committee on Racial Minorities. In the Methodist Church race relations fell under the Board of Social and Economic Relations. In 1948, northern Presbyterians set up an Institute on Racial and Cultural Relations.

27 *Minutes of the General Assembly of the Presbyterian Church in the U.S.*, 1944, pp. 56–7.

28 Ibid., 1945, pp. 130–32; ibid., 1946, pp. 136–40.
29 George Haynes, "Michigan Leaders Face Racial Tension," *Federal Council Bulletin*, XXVIII (April 1945), pp. 7–9; *Annual Report of the Federal Council of the Churches of Christ in America*, 1945, pp. 38–41; ibid., 1947, pp. 38–9.
30 *Social Questions Bulletin*, XXXV (April 1945), pp. 9–10; *Central Christian Advocate*, CXXIV (January 27, 1949), p. 2; Milton John Huber, Jr., "A History of the Methodist Federation for Social Action" (Unpublished Ph.D. dissertation, Boston University, 1949), chap. 8.
31 *Social Questions Bulletin*, XXXVII (October 1947), p. 109.
32 Central Jurisdiction of the Methodist Church: *Report of the Committee to Study the Central Jurisdiction of the Methodist Church*, April 1, 1952, pp. 12–14.
33 *Central Christian Advocate*, CXXXI (February 15, 1956), p. 17; ibid., CXXVIII (July 30, 1953), p. 12; ibid., CXXIII (June 10, 1948), p. 371; *Christian Advocate*, VIII (May 7, 1964), p. 23.
34 *Zion's Herald*, CXXVIII (June 28, 1950), p. 607; *Christian Advocate*, CXXI (May 16, 1946), p. 629; *Central Christian Advocate*, CXXV (May 18, 1950), p. 12; Dwight Culver, *Negro Segregation in the Methodist Church* (New Haven: Yale University Press, 1953), p. 95; *Methodist Christian Advocate*, LXXIV (August 11, 1964), p. 15. For a report on integration at the top levels of the Methodist Church, see *Report to the 1960 General Conference of the Methodist Church by the Commission to Study and Recommend Action Concerning the Jurisdictional System*, January 6, 1960, pp. 20–21.
35 *New York Times*, December 8, 1962.
36 Jesse Barber, *Climbing Jacob's Ladder* (New York: Board of National Missions of the Presbyterian Church in the U.S.A., 1952), pp. 85, 93–4; *Interracial News Service* (September–October 1944), p. 2; *New Advance*, VII (May 1945), p. 11.
37 *New York Times*, May 20, 1960, May 22, 1964.
38 *Advance*, CXLIV (December 8, 1952), pp. 11–12.
39 Tollie Caution, *A Decade of Progress in Negro Work, 1941–1951*, pamphlet (mimeograph, n.d.), p. 18.
40 *Minutes of the General Assembly of the Presbyterian Church in the U.S.*, 1942, p. 95; ibid., 1943, pp. 74, 89.
41 In 1962, the Synod of Kentucky elected the Reverend Lawrence Bottoms, a Negro, as moderator. He had previously been moderator of the Louisville Presbytery. *Christian Century*, LXXIX (August 1, 1962), p. 944.
42 For a more expanded discussion of the Methodists' attempts to desegregate, see Chapter 6.
43 *Presbyterian Outlook*, CXXXIII (June 25, 1951), pp. 11–12, 15. The

Board of Church Extension discovered strong opposition to integration among white churchmen in the presbyteries of Birmingham and Tuscaloosa. See also the comments of lay leader Dr. L. Nelson Bell in the *Southern Presbyterian Journal*, IX (June 15, 1950), pp. 2–3.

44 *Minutes of the General Assembly of the Presbyterian Church in the U.S.*, 1951, p. 84; ibid., 1952, p. 17; *Presbyterian Outlook*, CXXXIII (October 15, 1951), p. 3. When the Synod of Alabama voted to accept Negro churches it noted that the issue was one of administrative policy and "does not affect the present practices in the matter of segregation in the Presbyterian Church in the U.S."

45 *Annual Report of the Board of Church Extension of the Presbyterian Church in the U.S.*, 1952, pp. 35–6; Norman Cook, "Snedecor Gets New Regional Director," *Presbyterian Survey*, LXIII (May 1953), pp. 26–7. See also Sara Barry, "The Role of the Presbyterian Church in the United States in a Segregated Society" (Unpublished M.R.E. thesis, Biblical Seminary in New York, 1955), pp. 67–8.

46 *Minutes of the General Assembly of the Presbyterian Church in the U.S.*, 1964, pp. 80–81.

47 *Minutes of the General Assembly of the Presbyterian Church in the U.S.A.*, 1953, pp. 101–2; ibid., 1955, p. 107; *Minutes of the General Assembly of the United Presbyterian Church in the U.S.A.*, 1964, pp. 134–8.

48 *Journal of the General Convention of the Protestant Episcopal Church*, 1925, pp. 247–8; ibid., 1931, pp. 129, 268, 379–80.

49 Ibid., 1934, pp. 475–8.

50 Bishop Bartlett, "Report on Survey of Negro Work for the National Council" (August 15, 1935), p. 5 (in the files of the Bi-Racial Committee of the Protestant Episcopal Church).

51 *Journal of the General Convention of the Protestant Episcopal Church*, 1937, pp. 33, 333–4; ibid., 1940, pp. 498–9; *Living Church*, CII (January 24, 1940), p. 13.

52 Ibid., XCVIII (February 16, 1938), pp. 203, 212; ibid., CI (November 29, 1939), p. 11; *Southern Churchman*, CVI (January 6, 1940), p. 3.

53 *Churchman*, CLIV (November 1, 1940), p. 13; *Journal of the General Convention of the Protestant Episcopal Church*, 1940, pp. 262–4.

54 Ibid., 1934, p. 176.

55 *Living Church*, CXII (June 9, 1946), pp. 22–3; ibid., CXIV (March 23, 1947), pp. 17–18; ibid. (June 1, 1947), p. 24; ibid. (February 16, 1947), p. 21; *Southern Churchman*, CXIV (May 29, 1948), pp. 11–12; ibid., CXV (May 28, 1949), p. 11.

56 *Episcopal Churchnews*, CXIX (May 31, 1953), p. 7.

57 Minutes of the Bi-Racial Committee on Negro Work, January 17–18, 1956 (in the files of the Bi-Racial Committee).

58   Chester Marcus and Galen Weaver, "Our Beginnings in Race Relations,"
     Advance, CXLIX (November 1, 1957), pp. 16–18; *Presbyterian Out-
     look*, CXXIX (March 17, 1947), p. 3.
59   Henlee Barnette, "Negro Students in Southern Baptist Seminaries,"
     Review and Expositor, LIII (April 1956), pp. 207–10; *Minutes of the
     General Assembly of the Presbyterian Church in the U.S.*, 1954, p. 190;
     Interracial News Service (November–December 1951), p. 4.
60   *Living Church*, XCVIII (February 16, 1938), pp. 203, 212; ibid., XCIX
     (December 28, 1938), p. 703; ibid., CIII (October 29, 1941), p. 6; *Journal
     of the General Convention of the Protestant Episcopal Church*, 1940,
     p. 497; Othello D. Stanley, "Theological Education in Negro Schools,"
     Southern Churchman, CVII (June 14, 1941), pp. 8–9.
61   *Living Church*, CXIII (December 29, 1946), pp. 5–7; Minutes of the
     National Council of the Protestant Episcopal Church, February 11–13,
     1947, pp. 118–20 (in the files of the National Council); Minutes of the
     Bi-Racial Committee on Negro Work, April 9–10, 1946 (in the files of
     the Bi-Racial Committee).
62   *Living Church*, CXVI (January 25, 1948), pp. 6–7; ibid., CXVIII
     (May 8, 1949), p. 8; Minutes of the National Council of the Protestant
     Episcopal Church, February 17–19, 1948, pp. 12–13, 73–4; *Southern
     Churchman*, CXV (June 11, 1949), pp. 11–12. Left over funds from
     Payne Divinity School were to be used to support Negro students at-
     tending other church seminaries.
63   *Episcopal Churchnews*, CXIX (July 12, 1953), pp. 6–7; *Information
     Service*, XXX (April 21, 1951), p. 3.
64   *Episcopal Churchnews*, CXVIII (June 29, 1952), pp. 3–5; *Living Church*,
     CXXIII (November 11, 1951), p. 7.
65   *Episcopal Churchnews*, CXVIII (June 29, 1952), p. 10; ibid. (July 6,
     1952), p. 3; ibid. (November 30, 1952), pp. 3–4; *Living Church*, CXXV
     (December 14, 1952), p. 6; ibid., CXXVI (January 25, 1953), pp. 6, 16.
66   Ibid. (February 22, 1953), pp. 19–21.
67   Ibid. (June 14, 1953), pp. 8–10; *Episcopal Churchnews*, CXIX (June 28,
     1953), p. 7.
68   *Minutes of the General Assembly of the Presbyterian Church in the
     U.S.A.*, 1940, p. 114.
69   Ibid., 1943, pp. 107–10.
70   Ibid., 1946, pp. 89–92.
71   Ibid., 1958, pp. 474, 498. When Dean Andrew E. Murray closed the
     school of theology he reported that small enrollments were plaguing
     Negro seminaries. See Robert Lee, *The Social Sources of Church
     Unity* (Nashville: Abingdon Press, 1960), p. 29.
72   Bishop John M. Moore, "Keeping Union in Good Repair," *Christian
     Advocate*, CXIX (March 2, 1944), pp. 246–7; *Interracial News Service*

(January–February 1951), p. 11; Edward H. Maynard, "The Church in Race Relations," *Zion's Herald*, CXXVII (September 28, 1949), pp. 916–17.

73 *Christian Century*, LXXV (July 30, 1958), p. 885; *New York Times*, July 6, 1961; *Journal of the General Conference of the Methodist Church*, 1952, pp. 697, 1212.

74 *Chattanooga Times*, April 12 and 13, 1962; *Christian Century*, LXXIX (May 16, 1962), pp. 626–7; *Episcopal Society for Cultural and Racial Unity Newsletter*, August 6, 1963, p. 7.

75 *Information Service*, XXXIII (January 23, 1954), p. 2; Culver, *Negro Segregation in the Methodist Church*, p. 130; Minutes of the Bi-Racial Committee on Negro Work, January 4–5, 1950; Report of the Secretary for Negro Work to the Bi-Racial Committee, January 8–9, 1952. In 1951, Dr. Tollie Caution became the first Negro member of the board of trustees of the Philadelphia Divinity School.

CHAPTER 6, PAGES 134–57

1 For a perceptive account of the social sources of denominationalism, see H. Richard Niebuhr, *The Social Sources of Denominationalism* (New York: Meridian Books, 1959).

2 *Federal Council Bulletin*, XVII (November–December 1935), p. 20; *Presbyterian Outlook*, CXIX (January 22, 1945), p. 3; *Presbyterian of the South*, CXVII (September 30, 1942), p. 15; *Interracial News Service* (July 1943), p. 4; *Christian Century*, LX (November 10, 1943), p. 1317.

3 For the extreme Right of Protestantism, see Ralph Roy, *Apostles of Discord* (Boston: Beacon Press, 1953).

4 *Presbyterian*, LVIII (March 31, 1888), p. 10.

5 Hon. E. E. Beard, "Recommendation No. 1," *Cumberland Presbyterian*, LXVII (March 17, 1904), p. 328. In 1869 the Cumberland Presbyterian Church organized its Negro members into a separate denomination, the Colored Cumberland Presbyterian Church.

6 Ibid.; Ira Landrith, "Later Lights on the Buffalo Assembly," ibid. (June 9, 1904), pp. 713–14.

7 *Minutes of the General Assembly of the Presbyterian Church in the U.S.A.*, 1904, p. 146.

8 Ibid., pp. 141–7, 158; *Presbyterian*, LXXIV (May 4, 1904), pp. 4–5; ibid. (November 9, 1904), p. 10; Herrick Johnson, "A Protest Against Separate Presbyteries," *Interior*, XXXV (December 29, 1904), pp. 1699–1700. In some areas of the South the church had no white members; hence, several all-Negro presbyteries existed even before 1904.

9 *Minutes of the General Assembly of the Presbyterian Church in the U.S.A.*, 1904, pp. 119-20.

10 *Assembly Herald*, XIV (March 1908), p. 135. Not all Cumberland Presbyterians joined the united church. A sizable portion remained in the Cumberland Presbyterian Church.

11 The proposed merger also included the smaller United Presbyterian Church in North America, which did unite with the northern Presbyterian Church.

12 Sanford Dornbusch and Roger Irle, "The Failure of Presbyterian Union," *American Journal of Sociology*, LXIV (January 1959), pp. 352-5.

13 *Presbyterian Life*, VIII (June 11, 1955), p. 14; ibid. (February 19, 1955), p. 21. *Presbyterian Life* said the "real" reason for the defeat of union was apathy on the part of the pro-union forces. See also the *Christian Century*, LXXII (February 2, 1955), p. 135.

14 See the author's article, "The Race Problem and Presbyterian Union," *Church History*, XXXI (June 1962), pp. 203-6.

15 *Minutes of the General Assembly of the Presbyterian Church in the U.S.A.*, 1939, p. 63.

16 William Simpson, "Statement of the Proposed Plan of Union of the Presbyterian Church in the U.S.A. and U.S.," *New Advance*, VII (November 1944), p. 8; James Robinson, "Northern Lights," ibid., pp. 6-7.

17 Ibid., IX (September 1947), p. 3.

18 *Minutes of the General Assembly of the Presbyterian Church in the U.S.A.*, 1946, pp. 306-7, 312.

19 *Christian Observer*, CXXXVI (June 16, 1948), p. 2. In the previous year the presbyteries had approved the church's remaining in the Federal Council of Churches by a decided majority, though not by a three-fourths majority. Since unity was less popular than membership in the Federal Council of Churches, the proponents of union realized that union would be defeated at that time. Hence, they were willing to see a vote on unification postponed.

20 *The Plan Providing for the Reunion of the Presbyterian Church in the U.S.A. and the Presbyterian Church in the U.S. and the United Presbyterian Church in North America as the Presbyterian Church of the U.S.*, issued in 1954 as revised in November 1953, pp. 17-18, 132.

21 For a discussion of the attempts of the Presbyterians to desegregate their southern presbyteries and synods, see Chapter 5, pp. 122-3.

22 *Christian Observer*, CXL (July 9, 1952), p. 2. The southern Presbyterian representatives also dissented when the Federal Council of Churches decided to file an *amicus curiae* brief in the Sweatt case, which involved segregation of the Texas University Law School. *Presbyte-*

rian Outlook, CXXXI (October 24, 1949), p. 3. The vote for desegregation at the 1954 General Assembly was 236 to 169.

23 For examples of criticism of the Federal Council's position on the race
issue and the Ku Klux Klan, see *Presbyterian of the South*, LCIII (November 12, 1919), p. 1; ibid., LCVI (November 8, 1922), p. 1.

24 *Minutes of the General Assembly of the Presbyterian Church in the
U.S.*, 1947, pp. 38–9; ibid., 1949, p. 35; Daniel Gage, "The Federal Coun-
cil," *Christian Observer*, CXXXVI (February 4, 1948), p. 10; Charles C.
Dickinson, "Political Activities of the Federal Council of Churches,"
Southern Presbyterian Journal, I (December 1942), p. 12; ibid., IV
(July 1945), pp. 7–8. In 1945, the *Christian Observer* noted that it had
become a General Assembly "custom" to debate the matter of continu-
ing membership in the Federal Council. *Christian Observer*, CXXXIII
(June 13, 1945), p. 2.

25 *Southern Presbyterian Journal*, VI (September 1, 1947), p. 3.

26 Ibid., IV (September 15, 1945), pp. 11–12; ibid., XII (January 20, 1954),
pp. 6–7.

27 Ibid., XI (September 24, 1952), p. 3.

28 The group was reported to have had a budget of $98,000 to finance
a well-organized campaign against union. Although voting on unification
was not to begin until January 1955, presbyteries, particularly the anti-
union ones, began to ballot before that date. *Christian Century*, LXX
(September 23, 1953), p. 1069.

29 *Southern Presbyterian Journal*, XIII (September 1, 1954), p. 5.

30 Dornbusch and Irle, op. cit.

31 *Presbyterian Outlook*, CXXXVI (November 29, 1954), p. 3. For a list
of how the presbyteries voted see the *Atlantic Constitution*, May 1,
1955. The pro-unification forces rallied around the *Presbyterian Outlook*, which also supported desegregation.

32 James A. Cannon, Jr., "The Negro and Unification," *Christian Advocate*
(Nashville), LXXVIII (November 23, 1917), p. 10.

33 *Joint Commission on Unification of the Methodist Episcopal Church
and the Methodist Episcopal Church South*, II, pp. 113–14, 137, 122–30,
162, 233, 317. See also *Western Christian Advocate*, LXXXIV (January
23, 1918), p. 79; Philip M. Watters, "Unification to Date," *Christian
Advocate*, XCIII (March 28, 1918), p. 397; *Journal of the General Conference of the Methodist Episcopal Church*, 1916, p. 1307.

34 See the statement by southern Methodist John Moore in *Joint Commission*, II, p. 107.

35 *Southwestern Christian Advocate*, L (May 31, 1923), p. 6.

36 The total vote in the conferences among ministers was 10,855 to 721
for the plan and among laymen it was 7310 to 214 in favor of it. *Journal*

of the General Conference of the Methodist Episcopal Church, 1928, pp. 1847-9.

37 *Daily Christian Advocate* (South), XX (July 5, 1924), p. 37. Bishop Denny also warned that under unification Negroes might attempt to join southern white churches. Bishop Collins Denny, "Methodism Reorganized," *Christian Advocate* (Nashville), LXXXI (April 30, 1920), pp. 555-7.

38 *Daily Christian Advocate* (South), XX (July 5, 1924), p. 33. For a tabulation of the southern Methodist leadership's opinions, see the *Christian Advocate* (Nashville), LXXXVI (February 13, 1925), pp. 216-17.

39 *Christian Advocate,* C (December 31, 1925), pp. 1612-13; *Journal of the General Conference of the Methodist Episcopal Church, South,* 1926, pp. 316-17; Warren McElreath, *Methodist Union in the Courts* (Nashville: Abingdon Press, 1946), p. 104; Alfred Pierce, *Giant Against the Sky* (Nashville: Abingdon Press, 1948), chap. 14; Virginius Dabney, *Dry Messiah* (New York: Alfred Knopf, 1949), pp. 165-6.

40 See, for example, Bishop James Cannon, Jr., "Plan of Unification— Wise and Safe for Southern Methodism," *Christian Advocate* (Nashville), LXXXV (June 6, 1924), pp. 717-19; Bishop John Moore, "Fears and Facts About Unification," *ibid.* (July 4, 1924), pp. 839-41; George M. Traylor, "The Plan of Unification," *ibid.* (September 19, 1924), p. 1195; Frank Thomas, "The Status of the Negro," *Methodist Review* (South), LXVII (October 1918), pp. 65-9; *Southern Christian Advocate,* LXXXVIII (June 26, 1924), p. 2; *ibid.,* LXXXIX (April 30, 1925), p. 2.

41 Quoted in Trevor Bowen, *Divine White Right* (New York: Harper & Bros., 1934), p. 145.

42 For an excellent analysis of the unification issue and the Negro, see Paul Carter, "The Negro and Methodist Union," *Church History,* XXI (March 1952), pp. 55-70. See also John M. Moore, *The Long Road to Methodist Union* (Nashville: Abingdon Press, 1943); James Straughn, *Inside Methodist Union* (New York: Methodist Publishing House, 1958).

43 The defeated plan of 1924 had provided for a General Conference divided into two jurisdictions, one for each church. Negro annual conferences would have been in the jurisdictional conference of the former Methodist Episcopal Church. There was no separate jurisdictional conference for Negroes, but separate Negro annual conferences would have been maintained.

44 *Daily Christian Advocate,* XXIII (May 5, 1936), p. 87; Carter, "The Negro and Methodist Union," p. 63.

45 Daniel L. Ridout, "What the Negro Expects from the New Church,"

Zion's Herald, CXVII (April 26, 1939), p. 396. The Negro journal, the *Southwestern Christian Advocate*, opened its pages to Negro opinion but editorially supported the plan. *Southwestern Christian Advocate*, LVIII (March 19, 1936), pp. 179–80.

46 *Daily Christian Advocate*, XXIII (May 5, 1936), pp. 85–6, 92–3; *Zion's Herald*, CXIII (March 6, 1935), pp. 219–20; ibid., CXV (June 9, 1937), pp. 715–16; ibid. (October 6, 1937), pp. 1267, 1274; *Christian Advocate*, CXI (October 8, 1936), p. 964; Rev. Lloyd F. Worley, "The Next Step in Methodist Unification," ibid., CXII (April 29, 1937), p. 396.

47 *Zion's Herald*, CXIII (September 18, 1935), p. 893; ibid., CXIV (September 9, 1936), pp. 869, 877. The youth at the Berea College conference requested that the adult leaders of the conference express themselves, and the adults voted 97 to 20 against the plan.

48 *Christian Advocate*, CXI (September 24, 1936), p. 929. See also ibid. (October 8, 1936), p. 964; *Daily Christian Advocate*, XXIII (May 5, 1936), pp. 85–6, 89–90; *Epworth Herald*, XLVII (March 7, 1936), p. 144; *Christian Advocate* (Northwestern edition), LXXXIV (March 12, 1936), pp. 243–4.

49 *Journal of the General Conference of the Methodist Episcopal Church, South*, 1938, pp. 47, 251–2. A few churches in South Carolina refused to join the united Methodist Church, and Bishop Collins Denny also refused to join. McElreath, op. cit., pp. 46–51, 103–4.

50 *Daily Christian Advocate* (South), XXIII (April 30, 1938), pp. 7, 15–16; *Christian Advocate* (Nashville), XCVII (July 31, 1936), pp. 988–9; ibid., XCVIII (April 16, 1937), pp. 507–8; Bishop James Cannon, Jr., "The Only True Basis of Unification," *Zion's Herald*, CXV (September 22, 1937), p. 1211; *Southern Christian Advocate*, CII (March 10, 1938), p. 12.

51 *Christian Advocate* (Nashville), XCVIII (April 16, 1937), p. 509; Bishop John M. Moore, "The Plan of Methodist Union: An Interpretation," ibid. (June 4, 1937), pp. 713–15; *Southern Christian Advocate*, CII (October 20, 1938), p. 13; J. Emerson Ford, "Questions and Answers on the Methodist Church," ibid., CIII (June 15, 1939), p. 4.

52 *Christian Advocate* (Nashville), XCVIII (September 3, 1937), pp. 1125–6.

53 *Annual Report of the Woman's Missionary Council of the Methodist Episcopal Church, South*, 1935–36, p. 59; ibid., 1936–37, pp. 33, 62, 67, 142–3.

54 *Journal of the Uniting Conference of the Methodist Church*, 1939, p. 888.

55 *Journal of the Central Jurisdictional Conference of the Methodist Church*, 1944, p. 53; *Zion's Herald*, CXXI (September 15, 1943), p. 780; Chester A. Smith, "Fourteen Points," ibid., CXXII (April 12, 1944), p. 226; *Christian Advocate*, CXXIII (March 11, 1948), p. 334.

56 *Journal of the General Conference of the Methodist Church*, 1952, pp. 648–9.

57 Ibid., pp. 1169–70.

58 Ibid., 1956, pp. 1403–5.

59 *South Carolina Methodist Advocate*, CXX (May 17, 1956), p. 3; *Richmond Times–Dispatch*, May 21, 1956; address of Bishop Arthur Moore to the North Georgia Conference, reported in the *Atlanta Constitution*, June 22, 1956.

60 *Report to the 1960 General Conference of the Methodist Church by the Commission to Study and Recommend Action Concerning the Jurisdictional System*, January 6, 1960, p. 9.

61 *Journal of the General Conference of the Methodist Church*, 1956, pp. 280–90, 460, 475, 503.

62 *Report to the 1960 General Conference of the Methodist Church by the Commission to Study and Recommend Action Concerning the Jurisdictional System*, January 6, 1960, p. 9.

63 *Journal of the South Central Jurisdiction of the Methodist Church*, 1952, p. 83; *Journal of the Southeastern Jurisdiction of the Methodist Church*, 1952, pp. 109–10; ibid., 1956, pp. 154–6, 212–13.

64 *South Carolina Methodist Advocate*, CXVIII (November 4, 1954), pp. 4–5, 12; *Christian Advocate*, CXXX (July 7, 1955), pp. 854–5; ibid., CXXXI (March 15, 1956), pp. 330–32; *Zion's Herald*, CXXVIII (June 21, 1950), p. 598; ibid., CXXX (July 30, 1952), p. 727; ibid., CXXXII (September 29, 1954), p. 3; ibid., CXXXV (June 1957), p. 13; Culver, *Negro Segregation in the Methodist Church*, chaps. 1 and 3.

65 *Zion's Herald*, CXXXII (December 22, 1954), pp. 1, 5; ibid. (December 29, 1954), p. 1; ibid., CXXXIII (April 1955), p. 19.

66 Ibid., CXXXV (September 1957), p. 9; *Presbyterian Outlook*, CXL (November 3, 1958), p. 6; *Alabama Council on Human Relations Newsletter*, V (May 1959).

67 *Christian Advocate*, VIII (July 2, 1964), pp. 23–4; *Methodist Christian Advocate*, LXXXIV (August 11, 1964), p. 15.

68 *Journal of the Central Jurisdictional Conference of the Methodist Church*, 1952, pp. 144–5.

CHAPTER 7, PAGES 158–79

1 The Chicago Commission on Race Relations: *The Negro in Chicago — A Study of Race Relations and a Race Riot* (Chicago: University of Chicago Press, 1922), p. 325.

2 George Haynes, "Are Christians Finding Interracial Fellowship Within

the Church?," *Federal Council Bulletin*, XIII (October 1930), pp. 11, 26.

3 Frank Loescher, *The Protestant Church and the Negro* (New York: Association Press, 1948), pp. 77, 144–6. These findings are in general agreement with a survey done in January 1945 by the American Missionary Association of the Congregational Christian Church. L. Maynard Catchings, "The Participation of Racial and Nationality Minority Peoples in Congregational Christian Churches," *Journal of Negro Education*, XV (Fall 1946), pp. 681–9. Loescher's project did not include the Methodists, but Dwight Culver, estimating about the same time, speculated that approximately 640 Negroes attended "white" Methodist churches. Most of these churches were in New England and the Middle Atlantic states. Culver, *Negro Segregation in the Methodist Church*, pp. 143–50.

4 Loescher, op. cit., pp. 78–9.

5 Ibid., p. 15.

6 *New York Times*, July 5, 1959. There were approximately 100,000 churches in the South at that time. For the extent of Negro participation in predominantly white Unitarian congregations in the South, see *Christian Register*, CXXXV (September 1956), pp. 12–13.

7 *Interracial News Service* (March 1943), p. 1.

8 *Living Church*, CXIX (October 16, 1949), pp. 32–3; ibid. (November 20, 1949), p. 7; *Churchman*, CLXIII (September 1, 1949), pp. 22–3.

9 *Interracial News Service* (November-December 1935), p. 4; ibid. (November 1938), p. 1; Homer Jack, "The Emergence of the Interracial Church," *Social Action*, XIII (January 15, 1947), pp. 32–3.

10 The fellowship churches of Philadelphia and Baltimore were connected to community center programs. S. Gary Oniki, "Interracial Churches in American Protestantism," ibid., XVI (January 15, 1950), pp. 8–11.

11 Howard Thurman, *Footprints of a Dream* (New York: Harper & Bros., 1959), pp. 29–31.

12 Ibid., p. 31.

13 Ibid., pp. 46–50.

14 Ibid., chap. 3.

15 Ibid., p. 109.

16 Ibid., pp. 56–8.

17 *Advance*, CXXXVI (January 1944), p. 37; Buell Gallagher, "The Church Without Walls," ibid., CXXXVII (February 1945), pp. 12–13; John Hanna, "Community Church, Berkeley, California," ibid. (October 1945), p. 20.

18 Oniki, op. cit., pp. 7–8, 19–21.

19 *Christian Century*, LXI (June 7, 1944), pp. 705–6; ibid., LXII (July 11, 1945), p. 816; ibid., LXIII (July 31, 1946), p. 949.

20 Thorp McClusky, "Melting-Pot Parish," *Presbyterian Life*, III (March 4, 1950), pp. 24–6; Ross M. Sanderson, *The Church Serves the Changing City* (New York: Harper & Bros., 1955), pp. 191–206.

21 "South Congregational Church Study, April 1947" (Unpublished study: Department of Research and Survey of Chicago Theological Seminary, 1947), pp. 8–10, 33–4; Frank Dorey, "The Church and Segregation in Washington, D.C., and Chicago, Illinois" (Unpublished Ph.D. dissertation, University of Chicago, 1950), pp. 89–92.

22 Ibid., p. 101.

23 Ibid., pp. 101–9; William Lovell, "Changing Community — Changing Church," *Social Progress*, XXXIX (March 1949), pp. 4–8.

24 Jane M. Kristof, "Integration of First Presbyterian Church," *Counterpoint* (Fall 1957), pp. 9–11; Harold L. Bowman, "The First Presbyterian Church, Chicago, Illinois," *Social Progress*, XLVII (January 1957), pp. 5–7.

25 Kristof, op. cit., pp. 11–12; interview with Charles Leber and Ulysses Blakeley, June 10, 1959.

26 *Presbyterian Life*, V (June 7, 1952), p. 21; *Christian Century*, LXXI (April 14, 1954), p. 477; Virgil P. Moccia, "Bidwell Presbyterian Church," *Social Progress*, XLV (January 1955), pp. 26–7.

27 *Christian Century*, LXXIV (January 23, 1957), pp. 114–15; Martin E. Marty, "Inclusive Church — Inclusive Theology," ibid. (February 27, 1957), pp. 256–9; ibid., LXIX (May 21, 1952), p. 604; ibid., LXXIV (September 11, 1957), p. 1085; *Living Church*, CXXXII (January 15, 1956), p. 12.

28 James W. Hoffman, "Everyone Welcome," *Presbyterian Life*, VI (February 7, 1953), pp. 18–21; Maurice F. McCrackin, "West Cincinnati - St. Barnabas Church," *Social Progress*, XLV (January 1955), pp. 18–26; Sanderson, op. cit., pp. 127–44.

29 *Zion's Herald*, CXXIX (January 10, 1951), p. 31; *Interracial News Service* (September–October 1955), p. 3; ibid. (May–June 1956), pp. 4–6; ibid. (January–February 1957), p. 5; *Christian Century*, LXXIV (September 11, 1957), p. 1085.

30 *Zion's Herald*, CXXX (June 4, 1952), p. 23; ibid., CXXXIII (January 12, 1955), p. 4. For willingness on the part of Episcopal churches in the Diocese of New York to accept Negro ministers, see *Journal of the Convention of the Diocese of New York*, 1963, pp. 169–71.

31 Stephen C. Rose, "Student Interracial Ministry: A Break in the Wall," *Christian Century*, LXXIX (March 14, 1962), pp. 327–8; Robert Seymour, "Interracial Ministry in North Carolina," ibid., LXXX (January 23, 1963), pp. 109–11.

32 As quoted in ibid., LXII (August 8, 1945), p. 916.

33 Ibid., LXIV (June 25, 1947), p. 800; interview with Charles M. Jones, January 30, 1960.

34 *Presbyterian Outlook*, CXXXV (July 27, 1953), p. 3; ibid. (May 11, 1953), p. 8; Paul Hastings, "The Chapel Hill Story," *Southern Presbyterian Journal*, XI (April 15, 1953), pp. 6–9; *Minutes of the General Assembly of the Presbyterian Church in the U.S.*, 1953, pp. 65–6.

35 *Christian Century*, LXXIX (January 24, 1962), pp. 116–17.

36 A study by Alfred Kramer revealed that 83 per cent of the racially inclusive churches involved less than five Negroes. Alfred Kramer, "Patterns of Racial Inclusion Among Selected Congregations of Three Protestant Denominations" (Unpublished Ph.D. dissertation, New York University, 1955), pp. 52–3. A survey done by the Congregational Christians in 1956–1957 revealed that 84 per cent of the cases of racially inclusive churches involved less than ten Negroes. Herman H. Long, "Fellowship for Whom?," pamphlet (New York: Board of Home Missions of the Congregational Christian Church, 1958), pp. 18–19. For similar results among northern Presbyterians, United Lutherans, and Methodists, see Culver, "Negro Segregation in the Contemporary Methodist Church," pp. 175–6; H. B. Sissel, "Are We Segregated on Sunday?," *Presbyterian Life*, XI (June 1, 1958), p. 16; *Minutes of the Convention of the United Lutheran Church in America*, 1950, p. 622.

37 Long, op. cit., pp. 19–20; Loescher, op. cit., p. 77; Culver, *Negro Segregation in the Methodist Church*, pp. 144–6.

38 Long, op. cit., pp. 18, 36. For the Presbyterians, for example, see *Social Progress*, XLIX (September 1958), pp. 33–5.

39 Galen Weaver, "Racial Practices in Congregational Christian Churches," *Social Action*, XXV (January 1959) p. 9; *Social Progress*, XLIX (September 1958), p. 32; H. Robert Gremmer, "How Racially Inclusive Are Cleveland Churches?," pamphlet (Cleveland: Cleveland Church Federation, 1958), pp. 4–5.

40 Long, op. cit., p. 36.

41 Ibid., p. 20; Gibson Winter, *The Suburban Captivity of the Churches* (Garden City: Doubleday & Co., 1961), pp. 44–6.

42 For a discussion of the general socio-economic structure of Protestantism, see Liston Pope, "Religion and Class Structure," *Annals of the American Academy of Political and Social Science*, CCLVI (March 1948), pp. 84–91. For data dealing with how much ministers are paid, see F. Ernest Johnson and J. Emory Ackerman, *The Church as Employer, Money Raiser, and Investor* (New York: Harper & Bros., 1959), pp. 3, 9–13. See also "Christianity and the Economic Order," *Information Service*, XXVII (May 15, 1948).

43 Dorey, op. cit., pp. 170–74. For an interesting discussion of the dif-

ferences between Negro and white Protestants, see Gerhard Lenski, *The Religious Factor* (Garden City: Doubleday & Co., 1961).

44 Kramer, op. cit., pp. 248, 257–8.

45 Long, op. cit., pp. 23–4; Alfred Kramer, "Patterns of Racial Inclusion Among the Churches of Three Protestant Denominations," *Phylon,* XVI (September 1955), p. 291.

46 Long, op. cit., p. 17. The earlier, less detailed study covered urban and rural churches. Racial inclusiveness probably occurred more often in metropolitan areas, a fact that accounted for some of the increased percentage of racial inclusiveness revealed in the second study. Nevertheless, there was a trend toward more interracial churches among Congregational Christians during the twelve years between the two studies. See Galen Weaver, op. cit., p. 9.

47 Long, op. cit., pp. 20–27.

48 Sissel, op. cit., p. 16.

49 Ibid., pp. 14–15; Long, op. cit., p. 20.

50 *Social Progress,* XLIX (September 1958), pp. 33–5.

51 Sissel, op. cit., pp. 15–16. Sissel labeled these 228 churches as "integrated." Those with at least two Negro members and/or six Negroes in attendance were termed "inclusive." Although the precise definitions differ somewhat from those given in the Congregational Christians' study, the results are still similar.

52 Ervin E. Krebs, *The Lutheran Church and the American Negro* (Columbus: Board of American Missions of the American Lutheran Church, 1950), pp. 19–53.

53 *Minutes of the Convention of the United Lutheran Church,* 1950, p. 622; Kramer, "Patterns of Racial Inclusiveness Among Selected Congregations of Three Protestant Denominations," pp. 25–6.

54 For a comparison of the data obtained by Culver and Loescher in the mid-1940's, see Culver, "Negro Segregation in the Contemporary Methodist Church," pp. 173–6; and Loescher, op. cit., pp. 144–6.

55 It was similar at the time of Loescher's study. Ibid.

56 *New York Times,* November 4, 1963.

57 *Minutes of the General Assembly of the Presbyterian Church in the U.S.,* 1963, pp. 154–5.

CONCLUSION, PAGES 180–89

1 William E. B. Du Bois, "Will the Church Remove the Color Line?," *Christian Century,* XLVIII (December 9, 1931), p. 1556.

2 Pope, *The Kingdom Beyond Caste,* p. 105.

A Selected Bibliography

The main sources for the book are indicated in the notes. The church press was indispensable not only for its expressions of opinion but also for the information it contains about important events within Protestantism. In addition, the proceedings of local and national church conventions and the church year books were extremely valuable. The reports of various religious agencies touching upon race relations were also useful; the many pamphlets and studies published by these agencies contain important data. The books, letters, pamphlets, and autobiographies written by such leading churchmen as Atticus Haygood, Gilbert Haven, Liston Pope, and others were also important sources. The significant ones are cited in the footnotes.

Several church and secular groups allowed the author to consult their files. They were the Bi-Racial Sub-Committee on Negro Work of the Protestant Episcopal Church, the Department of Racial and Cultural Relations and the Church Women's Committee on Race Relations of the National Council of the Churches of Christ in America, the Commission on Interracial Cooperation, the Southern Regional Council, the Southern School News Reporting Service, and the Woman's Division of Christian Service of the Methodist Church.

For American church history the reader might begin with James W. Smith and A. Leland Jamison (eds.), *Religion in Amer-*

ican Life, 4 vols. (Princeton: Princeton University Press, 1961–63). Volume 4 of this excellent work contains a useful bibliography. Anson Phelps Stokes, *Church and State in the United States,* 3 vols. (New York: Harper & Bros., 1950) is valuable, as are the writings of William Warren Sweet on American religious history. William McLoughlin, Jr., *Modern Revivalism* (New York: Ronald Press Co., 1959) is excellent. H. Richard Niebuhr, *The Social Sources of Denominationalism* (New York: Meridian Books, 1959) and his *The Kingdom of God in America* (New York: Harper & Bros., 1959) are filled with insights. A recent, brief popular account of American Protestantism is Winthrop S. Hudson, *American Protestantism* (Chicago: University of Chicago Press, 1961). The historical quarterlies devoted to church history should also be consulted, especially *Church History.*

For denominational history, the "American Church History Series," published in the 1890's by the Christian Literature Company and later by Charles Scribner's Sons, is still useful. Among denominational studies that can be consulted with profit are Emory S. Bucke (ed.), *The History of American Methodism,* 3 vols. (Nashville: Abingdon Press, 1964); Clifford Drury, *Presbyterian Panorama* (New York: Board of Christian Education of the Presbyterian Church in the U.S.A., 1952); William W. Manroos, *A History of the American Episcopal Church* (New York: Morehouse, Graham Co., 1959); and Abdel R. Wentz, *A Basic History of Lutheranism in America* (Philadelphia: Muhlenberg Press, 1955).

Three interesting books dealing with contemporary Protestantism are Gerhard Lenski, *The Religious Factor* (Garden City: Doubleday & Co., 1961); Ross Sanderson, *The Church Serves the Changing City* (New York: Harper & Bros., 1955); and Gibson Winter, *The Suburban Captivity of the Churches* (Garden City: Doubleday & Co., 1961). Also provocative is Will Herberg, *Protestant-Catholic-Jew* (Garden City: Doubleday & Co., 1955).

Some of the works dealing with Protestantism and social issues contain material on white Protestantism and the Negro. For the nineteenth century Timothy Smith, *Revivalism and Social Reform in Mid-Nineteenth Century America* (Nashville: Abingdon Press, 1957) is excellent. Also covering this period are John Bodo, *The Protestant Clergy and Public Issues, 1812–1848* (Princeton: Princeton University Press, 1954) and Charles Cole, *The Social Ideas of the Northern Evangelists, 1826–1860* (New York: Columbia University Press, 1954). Standard works on the social gospel movement are Paul A. Carter, *The Decline and Revival of the Social Gospel* (Ithaca: Cornell University Press, 1956) and Charles H. Hopkins, *The Rise of the Social Gospel in American Protestantism, 1865–1915* (New Haven: Yale University Press, 1940). For the Civil War period see Chester F. Dunham, *The Attitude of the Northern Clergy Toward the South, 1860–1865* (Toledo: Gray Company, 1942); James Silver, *Confederate Morale and Church Propaganda* (Tuscaloosa: Confederate Publishing Co., 1957); and Lewis G. Vander Velde, *The Presbyterian Churches and the Federal Union, 1861–1869* (Cambridge: Harvard University Press, 1932). A good study of northern Methodism during Reconstruction is Ralph Morrow, *Northern Methodism and Reconstruction* (East Lansing: Michigan State University Press, 1956). Southern Methodists in the post-Civil War decades are treated in Hunter Farish, *The Circuit Rider Dismounts* (Richmond: Dietz Press, 1938).

A number of books deal directly with the churches and race relations. Among the more useful are Augustus F. Beard, *A Crusade of Brotherhood* (Boston: Pilgrim Press, 1909); Trevor Bowen, *Divine White Right* (New York: Harper & Bros., 1934); Ernest Q. Campbell and Thomas F. Pettigrew, *Christians in Racial Crisis* (Washington: Public Affairs Press, 1959); Dwight Culver, *Negro Segregation in the Methodist Church* (New Haven: Yale University Press, 1953); Thomas E. Drake, *Quakers and Slavery in America* (New Haven: Yale University Press, 1950); Leonard L. Haynes, Jr., *The Negro Community within American Protestantism, 1619–1844* (Boston: Christopher Publishing House, 1953); Frank S. Loescher, *The Protestant Church and the Negro* (New York: Association Press, 1948); and Willis D.

Weatherford, *American Churches and the Negro* (Boston: Christopher Publishing House, 1957).

For Negro history the basic work is John Hope Franklin's *From Slavery to Freedom* (New York: Alfred Knopf, 1947). Also valuable are E. Franklin Frazier, *The Negro in the United States* (New York: Macmillan, 1949); the classic, Gunnar Myrdal, *An American Dilemma: The Negro Problem and Modern Democracy* (New York: Harper & Bros., 1944); and C. Vann Woodward, *The Strange Career of Jim Crow* (New York: Oxford University Press, 1957).

Standard works on the Negro church are W. E. B. Du Bois, *The Negro Church* (Atlanta: Atlanta University Press, 1903); E. Franklin Frazier, *The Negro Church in America* (New York: Schocken Books, 1963); Benjamin Mays and Joseph Nicholson, *The Negro's Church* (New York: Institute of Social and Religious Research, 1933); and Carter G. Woodson, *The History of the Negro Church* (Washington: Associated Publishers, 1945). More specialized studies include Jesse Barber, *Climbing Jacob's Ladder* (New York: Board of National Missions of the Presbyterian Church in the U.S.A., 1952); George F. Bragg, *History of the Afro-American Group of the Episcopal Church* (Baltimore: Church Advocate Press, 1922); and Mason Crum, *The Negro in the Methodist Church* (New York: Board of Missions and Church Extension of the Methodist Church, 1951). *The Journal of Negro History* also contains much material on Negro religious history.

There are a growing number of unpublished studies dealing with various aspects of Protestantism and race relations. For the southern Baptists see Rufus B. Spain, "Attitudes and Reactions of Southern Baptists to Certain Problems of Society, 1865–1890" (Unpublished Ph.D. dissertation, Vanderbilt University, 1961) and Foy D. Valentine, "A Historical Study of Southern Baptists and Race Relations, 1917–1947" (Unpublished Th.D. dissertation, Southwestern Baptist Theological Seminary, 1949). Useful information on the Protestant Episcopal Church can be obtained from M. Moran Weston, "Social Policy of the Episcopal Church in the Twentieth Century" (Unpublished Ph.D. dissertation, Columbia University, 1954). An excellent dissertation dealing with the American Missionary Association is Richard B. Drake, "The American Missionary Association and the Southern Negroes, 1861–1880" (Unpublished Ph.D. dissertation, Emory University, 1957). Two excellent studies dealing with local church segregation are Frank Dorey, "The Church and Segregation in Washington, D.C., and Chicago, Illinois" (Unpublished Ph.D. dissertation, University of Chicago, 1950) and Alfred Kramer, "Patterns of Racial Inclusion Among Selected Congregations of Three Protestant Denominations" (Unpublished Ph.D. dissertation, New York University, 1955). "The Reminiscences of Will W. Alexander" (Oral History Project, Columbia University) is useful, as are Edward Burrows, "The Commission on Interracial Cooperation, 1919–1944" (Unpublished Ph.D. dissertation, University of Wisconsin, 1954); Oliver S. Heckman, "Northern Church Penetration of the South, 1860–1880" (Unpublished Ph.D. dissertation, Duke University, 1939); and Guy and Guion Johnson, "The Church and the Race Problem in the United States" (Unpublished monograph for the Myrdal study, Schomburg Collection, New York, 1940).

Index

DATE DUE